KING

The Bullitts of Seattle and
Their Communications Empire

KING

The Bullitts of Seattle and Their Communications Empire

O. CASEY CORR

University of Washington Press
Seattle and London

Copyright © 1996 by O. Casey Corr
Printed in the United States of America

All rights reserved. No portion of this publication may be reproduced
or transmitted in any form or by any means, electronic or mechanical,
including photocopying, recording, or any information storage or re-
trieval system, without permission in writing from the publisher.

Designed by Susan E. Kelly, Marquand Books, Inc., Seattle

Library of Congress Cataloguing in Publication Data

ISBN 0-295-97557-1.—ISBN 0-295-97584-9 (paper)

The paper used in this publication meets the minimum requirements
of American National Standard for Information Sciences—Permanence
of Paper for Printed Library Materials, ANSI Z39.48-1984

To Eugene and Kathleen Forhan Corr

Virtus in Arduis

Contents

The story of a communications company can be told in many ways. I have not attempted to chronicle in detail the many events and careers of King Broadcasting's forty-four years of Bullitt family control. Instead, I have tried to trace the origin, growth, and dissipation of the public spirit that made the company unique. The idea here has been to focus on a small number of people and examine whether their sense of values made a difference in King Broadcasting's singular involvement with Seattle, the largest city of the Northwest. To understand the idealism that drove both the company and the Bullitts, it seemed useful to portray key family members before the company began in 1947.

With the exception of Patsy Bullitt Collins, with whom I met briefly, the children of founder Dorothy Stimson Bullitt declined my requests for interviews and declined to provide access to corporate archives. Nonetheless, I have made every effort to represent their views fairly.

King Broadcasting's flagship station is identified here by its capitalized call letters, KING, to distinguish it from references to King, the company.

KING

The Bullitts of Seattle and
Their Communications Empire

S he was easy to overlook. She worked hard at that. Others did the talking while she listened and considered their motives. She dressed simply, avoided attention, hated speechmaking, and had the appearance of somebody's rather formal grandmother. In fact, the eighty-one-year-old woman was a great-grandmother. From her seat on the speakers' platform, she gazed out on the hundreds of anniversary celebrants gathered at Seattle Center that night in November 1973. A color guard entered the courtyard of the Pacific Science Center, carrying the flags of Canada, the United States, and Washington state. Her eyes, framed by heavy lids, looked sleepy. Skin hung heavy on a face sparingly adorned with makeup; her lips formed the hint of a smile. She wore a blue dress, a double strand of pearls, and a corsage that was a little too big. Nothing about her image suggested who she was: one of the wealthiest people in America, a shrewd and subtle boardroom player, and the controlling shareholder of a Seattle-based communications empire that spread south to San Francisco and west from the Rockies to Hawaii. She had staked everything on that company. Nothing would threaten its success. Not friends, not longtime loyalists, not even her own children. Many felt close to her, but she kept an unbreachable zone of privacy about herself. People knew not to ask about certain topics. She was often kind and generous, but when pressed, she could be ruthless. And the result was power. She wielded a degree of influence that was uncommon for anyone, especially for a woman of her era. For decades, Dorothy Bullitt had been a largely unseen presence in Northwest politics. Her King Broadcasting Company cheered for the liberal cause, civil

3

rights, protection of wildlife, civility in public life, fine music, decency in elected office, responsible journalism and, most important, for the Northwest. Her company helped give that neglected corner of America a sense of itself and an appealing image to the world: Salmon in the bay! An office just minutes from the ski slopes! A place of unspoiled nature and unsullied ideals. Nothing better represented the city's promotional zeal than this spot near the city's downtown, where Seattle had leapt into national consciousness as host to the 1962 World's Fair.

On that night in November 1973, few residents so aptly symbolized the radical changes that had taken place in her city, which now dared to think itself sophisticated because of a sprinkling of new office towers, a decent French restaurant or two, and a professional basketball team known as the Seattle Supersonics. Dorothy Bullitt's millionaire father, C. D. Stimson, had arrived in Seattle in 1889, nine months before Washington became a state. She was born three years later. Eventually, the city paved its mud streets and grew, its burgeoning workforce lured by the Alaskan Gold Rush and by jobs in timber, shipbuilding, fishing, and later, the Boeing Airplane Company. New industries elbowed their way, among them television, which began in Seattle in 1948. That TV station, the first in the Northwest, was soon bought by Dorothy Bullitt's King Broadcasting Company, and renamed KING-TV in the first TV-license transfer approved by the Federal Communications Commission. King Broadcasting later acquired or built other stations, both in radio and in television, and diversified into communication services: a magazine, cable-TV systems, and feature films. The Bullitt family, along with much of the city's economy, had shifted from sawing trees to selling services. And the city had become in some ways a counterpart of the Bullitt family: liberal, Democratic, progressive, incorruptible, and idealistic to a point that at times seemed foolish.

The 1973 party marked the twenty-fifth anniversary of that first broadcast. Governor Daniel Evans had proclaimed "King Television Month" and hailed the November anniversary as a milestone in broadcast history and "man's quest for progress." Praising prominent local businesses is standard fare for politicians, but Evans had special reasons to bless Dorothy Bullitt and her communications company. King Broadcasting had the means to praise or slam Evans, attack his rivals, support or condemn his issues, and rally the public to its own views. Fortunately for the governor, Evans was the sort of politician Dorothy Bullitt liked. An outdoorsman who himself came from early settlers of Washington, he stood for open government, protection of the environment, attention to the needy, and the expansion of government services. King Broadcasting showed its affection in many ways, including an admiring cover story in its *Seattle* magazine, with a photo of the young governor doing pushups at dawn. As the widow of a prominent Democrat, an ally of Franklin Roosevelt, Dorothy Bullitt tended to favor Democrats, but Evans was a new sort of Republican, a national leader of the party's liberal wing who had won a place on the cover of *Time* magazine.

Yet from the company's perspective, a far more important politician was on the dais that night. Though now stooped with arthritis and hard of hearing, sixty-eight-year-old United States Senator Warren G. Magnuson was still a forceful presence as he waited his turn to heap praise on King Broadcasting and his longtime friend, Dorothy Bullitt. Magnuson had entered Congress in 1937 and soon became one of the most powerful men in Washington, D.C. As longtime chairman of the Commerce Committee, he had controlled regulation of the broadcast industry. It was said that Dorothy Bullitt never asked Magnuson to intervene with the Federal Communications Commission (FCC), which decided who got and who kept the hugely lucrative pieces of public airwaves. But then again, with regulators knowing of Magnuson's friends and interests, perhaps she never needed to ask. She never had a serious problem with the FCC as her company grew, renewed its licenses, and sought other stations. Magnuson owed a personal debt to Dorothy Bullitt, but only a few in the audience knew that story.

Television had made her fortune, and this party was structured to serve the camera, not the woman. The party aired live on KING-TV, Channel 5. It started at 5:00 P.M. (following a commercial, of course), and its opening image was not Dorothy Bullitt but Seattle television's first couple, newscasters Jim Harriott and Jean Enersen. Harriott, with dark, pleasant features, was not quite handsome. His voice, deep and warm, had a soothing quality. Enersen's long blonde hair gleamed like a waterfall under the lights. With her radiant smile, intelligence, poise, and Nordic looks, she embodied two ideals: the pert suburban wife and the desirable girl next door. Nightly, for Seattle viewers, they retold the day's events like newlyweds at the dinner table. Harriott and Enersen were perfect for television news, a hybrid of show business and journalism. Neither was a reporter, at least in the traditional sense. They had other qualities critical to television, and there was the irony. Each became an anchor only after the newsroom traditionalists, the advocates of plainly delivered facts, had been pushed out. Harriott and Enersen had many impressive skills, but foremost, they were products of TV's deference to the power of image. They were KING-TV's showcase trophies.

On this night, Harriott wore a tuxedo with a ruffled shirt front. Enersen wore a simple dress that caught the light and broke it into a thousand sparkles. They greeted the TV viewers and the assembled audience and told them of the events ahead. KING's anniversary would be marked by a gift from NBC to the city—a full-size replica of the 1968 Apollo lunar module. Harriott explained that KING's "birthday" was being celebrated with this gift, which he called "an actual replica" of the module. An NBC official and an astronaut were on hand to comment, but no one explained the link between the anniversary of a local television station and a NASA moonwalk. Somehow both involved technology, the future, and a glamorous showcasing of public service. On a deeper level, though, King Broadcasting was suggesting that it had been a force for proper change in the region's history; that what was good about Seattle was partly owing to the goodness of King Broadcasting. Certainly the company saw itself as resisting the worst trends in television and promoting the best, and, with Dorothy Bullitt around, that would not change. Yet the company, like the city, had a tradition of overselling its virtues. KING, like all TV stations, had of necessity spent its years airing more cowboy shoot-em-ups, vulgar comedies, and endless commercials than high culture. But tonight's event was being played for the highbrows. The flags carried by the color guard represented the reach of KING-TV's signal across the border into Canada. A marching band played the two national anthems as a small clergyman, the Very Reverend John C. Leffler, worked his way to the podium.

"Let us pray," said the retired dean of St. Mark's Cathedral, Seattle headquarters of the Episcopal church. For decades Leffler had been minister and close friend to many of Seattle's wealthiest families. A liberal, he had spoken out against American involvement in the Vietnam War. Leffler had been particularly close to Dorothy Bullitt—for nineteen years, he had been nicknamed chaplain-in-residence of King Broadcasting, and upon his retirement from the church, he took an office next to hers. As much as anyone, Leffler knew the aspirations of Dorothy Bullitt and he attributed KING's success and quality to her stewardship. In effect, he sanctified the myth-making machinery surrounding KING's controlling shareholder.

"Oh, God," Leffler intoned. "On this happy occasion, we come not to celebrate the success of just another business enterprise but to reaffirm those ideals of service that we have tried to maintain for twenty-five years as the KING family. When we talk of competitors in this highly competitive field, we enjoy using adjectives: oldest, first, largest, finest, most popular—when the ratings justify it; sometimes when they don't. So God, forgive our occasional boasting and call us up to the standards of excellence which have always motivated our founder, Dorothy Bullitt." Dorothy Bullitt listened, the half smile unchanged, as Leffler spoke of King Broadcasting's deep sense of responsibility to the community. "Let these continue to be our goals, oh God, as we move on into an uncertain but exciting future. Amen."

The high point of the evening was Senator Magnuson's presentation of the lunar module to Seattle's Pacific Science Center. The old lion of the Senate was famous for his tangled syntax, but his message was clear: his roots ran deep with King Broadcasting, its employees, and its founder. Referring to the industry that he had alternatively nurtured, bullied, scolded, and joined (as a stockholder of KIRO in Seattle), he called television "the most exciting media that's ever occurred in the history of mankind. . . . TV has made history come alive. . . . All of us have our complaints but TV has made great progress in our country."

The lunar module was formally accepted by the Pacific Science Center; a brief film gave images of KING's twenty-five years; and Jim Harriott and Jean Enersen introduced Dorothy Bullitt.

"Now we have the woman who made broadcasting in Seattle possible and one of the most respected women in broadcasting today, Mrs. Dorothy Bullitt," said Jean Enersen. "I'm glad you can be with us, Mrs. Bullitt. Does it seem like twenty-five years?"

She replied in a husky voice, almost a baritone, a voice that sounded as if it had been filtered through alluvial till from the Cascade Mountains. It was that famous voice of Dorothy Bullitt, forever imitated by her admirers.

"No," she rasped. "Twenty-five years ago, I don't think I knew the difference between a decibel and a documentary." That sparked laughter from the audience. Those who didn't know her were surprised that an octogenarian would spring such quick quips, especially at her own expense. But that was part of Bullitt's style, charm, and strength: putting herself out of the picture, minimizing her role or knowledge. It disarmed people and gave her leverage, if needed. She was crafty, but never in a way that left people angry or exploited, just well matched. She said, "A lot happened in twenty-five years and I'm very glad for the opportunity to thank all the ones who made the station what it is: Fred Stimson, Henry Owen. I got pushed from behind quite a lot. I do want to thank all the ones who've done such good work."

She was always sparing with words, but it was interesting to note those names she did not mention. Several others had played huge roles in the company, much larger than that of her affable playboy cousin, Fred Stimson, the radio buff. Maybe she forgot their names. But she could not have forgotten one name: Stimson Bullitt, her son, the brilliant but oddball heir to the Bullitt political and business legacy, whose relationship with his two sisters and his mother was a tangle of love, disappointment, and perhaps bitterness. Stimson Bullitt had been replaced as the company's chief executive by Ancil Payne, whom a friend of both had called the Cardinal Richelieu of King Broadcasting. When Stimson left, most of the blame for KING's mistakes followed him, and most of the credit for the company's idealism and successes affixed to Dorothy Bullitt, the aging legend.

His ouster bore a disquieting resemblance to other schisms in Dorothy Bullitt's family.

L ate on a cold winter night in 1889, the steamer *Olympian* chugged into Elliott Bay, carrying a brash thirty-two-year-old millionaire named C. D. Stimson. Charles Douglas Stimson was shrewd, handsome, and tough. He had a square jaw, intense eyes that seemed to look through people, and a mustache that flared like the prongs of a Texas longhorn. He disguised the fact of his missing right arm with a false limb and a glove.

It was near midnight, but in the flickering lights of the city, Stimson could make out his new home. Over the hills that framed the city were some of the finest timberlands in the world. Drenched by rain, Douglas fir grew straight and big, their bases as wide as a grown man was tall. C. D. Stimson was there to harvest those trees. Most of the other men attracted to the boomtowns along Puget Sound came to work with their hands, but Stimson came to work with his money.

Stimson stepped off the boat with his wife, Harriet, and young son, Thomas. They passed Indian canoes, carved whole from cedar logs, that heaved in the foamy, dark water. The smell of seaweed, things left wet, and tossed garbage came up from the tideflats to the south. Stimson knew Seattle was not the most civilized place to raise a child. It was a frontier town, where a drizzly gloom blocked the sun and horses' hoofs sank in mud streets. Drunken lumberjacks bellowed in the town's Lava Bed (later called Skid Road), which rivaled San Francisco's Barbary Coast.

If Seattle had any national reputation, it was strongly colored by incidents of mob justice—Chinese residents who were forced out of town, or suspects who were dragged from jail and hanged. Crude and raw, Seattle had its problems. But apart from its stands of timber and its natural harbor, the city had other unrivaled assets—spirit, hustle, and a determination to make itself the commerce capital of the Northwest. It had grown at an astonishing pace, from 3,553 people in 1880 to more than 42,000 when Stimson arrived nine years later. With new rail lines linking the city to markets in the East, Seattle felt it owned the future. But what was that future? The town seemed split over a desire to make itself a righteous alternative to cities of the East, or a ribald "sin city" where everyone made a buck as the police looked the other way. The city had its politicians but no dominant voice. The city's newspapers were a diverse collection of shrill voices that spoke to small coteries of readers.

Stimson had chosen Seattle after four years of meticulous study financed by his father, Thomas Douglas Stimson, owner of a huge lumber and development company based in Chicago. Thomas Stimson had realized he was running out of trees in the Great Lakes area. So two of his sons, C. D. and Frederick, decided to establish a mill on Puget Sound, while two other sons established lumber yards in California.

C. D. Stimson was particularly suited to the challenge. As a boy in Michigan, he had been stocky, energetic, athletic, a leader, and a fledgling businessman skilled at swapping marbles for jackknives or other treasured goods. He stammered, but his parents insisted he could cure himself. They sent him down to the barn and told him to load his mouth with pebbles and practice speaking. The boy practiced for hours. After a time, his stammer disappeared, returning two generations later in one of Dorothy Bullitt's children.

At age twelve, disaster struck the boy. One day while swimming, Stimson scratched his right arm on rusty wire. The wound failed to heal, became infected, and worsened to the point where the arm had to be amputated halfway between the elbow and shoulder. C. D.'s stepmother, however, refused to give him special treatment, insisting that he dress himself and do the same chores as were required of his siblings. In time, he could play baseball, tennis, football, even golf, better than most of his friends. The left hand and arm became amazingly strong, the fingers nimble enough to tie shoes quickly.

C. D. Stimson arrived in Seattle on February 5, 1889, the year Washington became a state. With $500,000 of their father's money, he and his brother bought a waterfront mill in the nearby community of Ballard and set up an office in downtown Seattle. The Stimson Land Company eventually owned 40,000 acres of timberland in Washington and Oregon, not counting land bought by individual family members.

The mill purchase was more timely than anyone could have foreseen. One day in early June 1889, a cabinet maker in Seattle accidentally knocked over a pot of glue that was being heated on a stove. The hot glue hit the ground and ignited woodshavings damp from turpentine. The fire quickly spread through the wood building and within twenty minutes, an entire city block was aflame. By late afternoon, the business district was doomed. Smoke from the fire could be see as far away as Tacoma, thirty miles south. By sundown, the fire ran out of things to burn. Twenty-five blocks and every wharf, even the town's little telephone exchange, were gone. But Seattle wasn't dead. Merchants pitched tents on the ashes and resumed business. The downtown was rebuilt in brick this time, but floors, framework, and roofing were made of wood—much of it from the Stimson mill in Ballard. The Stimsons' first investment in Seattle was already paying off.

As part of a second wave of settlers who took the city to a new level, the Stimson family would continue to figure importantly in Seattle's development. C. D. Stimson could be a hard man. He shed no tears for the working masses. He did not want to uplift them. He wanted them to work without complaint in his mill. But he did have a vision of Seattle as more than a frontier town. He saw it as a place of elegance where men with clean shoes worked in modern office buildings. Over the next thirty years, he and his wife Harriet, a music lover and socialite, would help to build some of the city's finest buildings and social institutions.

Meanwhile, Seattle was growing at a gallop. Within a year of the Stimsons' arrival, the city added another 6,000 people. C. D. Stimson and his wife did their part. In 1892 a scrappy little girl was born.

Every day little Dorothy Frances Stimson watched her father mount a horse and ride north from their home on Queen Anne Hill down to the mill in Ballard. Her life followed a predictable, protected pattern, set by the traditions and expectations of her class. Her father taught her that a person with wealth could put people to work, make a building rise from the ground, and transform the landscape. Her mother taught her that a person with taste and connections could bring Mozart to the frontier. Together, they taught her to take risks, size up needs and possibilities, and to start things that would be good for the city.

Young Dorothy did not expect that she would ever work for a living or attend college. She had no particular career ambition. Like most girls of that time, she assumed that someday she would marry and have children. She became the neighborhood tomboy, scampering on sidewalks made from planks, hitching rides on streetcars, and dressing without regard for the seasons or her mother's commands. She was the only girl in the neighborhood who could hoist herself on a rope to a stable loft. She rarely played with her brother Thomas, who was eight years older than she.

The Stimson house stood close to the street, but the windows were covered by heavy drapes. Inside, life followed a measured pace. Servants made meals using fresh vegetables brought daily on a horse cart from the market at Second Avenue and Madison Street. When dinner ended, the men separated from the women and drank brandy and smoked cigars. The telephone came into common use, but the proper way to contact a friend was to send a letter. The women in the world of Dorothy's mother stayed home on certain days and received visitors who announced themselves with printed cards.

At ten, Dorothy got a pony, the first of many during her life. Once when a group of boys began teasing it, Dorothy picked up a buggy whip and drove them off. But that wasn't the only time she got the best of boys. One day her father discovered her examining the contents of a bag: dozens of agates won in marble-playing contests. Stimson was aghast to learn his little daughter was the local champion, the only neighborhood girl who played that game. He ordered her to stop playing with boys and to stop taking their marbles. Dorothy took the bag to a soda fountain, and she negotiated a trade with the store owner. For the marbles, she got a line of credit for ice cream sodas—plus the right to mix them herself. The last part was her own touch, the business genius she would display later in life.

Another gift for Dorothy astounded her playmates—a pair of bear cubs. When the cubs' mother was killed by a falling tree, a logger brought the cubs to Stimson at the mill. C. D. brought them home. The cubs were the sensation of the neighborhood, climbing telephone poles and staying there until coaxed down. Dorothy kept them until they grew so big they had to be given to Seattle's Woodland Park Zoo.

She loved to spend time with her father, no matter what he was doing. He often took her by carriage down to Green Lake, where they would sit by the still waters as he recited the deals of the day and taught her how to size up a business situation. When she was very young, he took her out in his seventy-five-foot yawl, the *Olympic,* and taught her to swim by tying her to the mast and throwing her into the Sound. She worshipped him. If he was too busy to talk to her, she just watched him do his work. Father, as she called him, was a magnificent man, but she knew his manners were not as polished as Mother's. Father could be tough in business and swift in dealing with threats, human or otherwise, as she found out. One day, a dog that belonged to the cook's friend suddenly leapt at Dorothy and bit her. A doctor came, placed Dorothy on her mother's lap, sedated her with chloroform, and stitched the wound. Stimson found the dog, and shot it.

By 1898 C. D. Stimson was president of what had become the largest shake mill in the world and one of the largest producers of lumber. With his expanding wealth, he built a 10,000-square-foot mansion on First Hill and then an even bigger home just north of Seattle in The Highlands, a wealthy enclave of which he was a founder. There he built a 21,000-square-foot mansion with a rooted old English name— "Norcliffe."

As C. D. Stimson rose in business circles, Harriet Stimson became a regal overseer of Seattle society. Somewhat detached and unassailable in demeanor, she had perfect penmanship and correct, if not starchy, manners. An invitation to her home was not so much a request as a command. She was said to be diligent, frugal, and sensible, with a strong sense of civic responsibility. And shrewd. Once during a dinner, a servant brought out a turkey and dropped it. "Mildred, take that back out to the kitchen and bring in the other turkey," Harriet said. It was a ruse: a coded instruction for the servant to go back, clean up the turkey, and present it as new. With other women, she helped found the Seattle Children's Home, the Children's Orthopedic Hospital, the Cornish School, and the Visiting Nurse Service. Music was her particular passion. She was a founder of the Seattle Symphony. Its first conductor had been her music teacher in New York. Young Dorothy sat with her parents during the symphony's first concert in 1908, as the musicians played in tuxedos loaned by husbands of symphony supporters. That concert was a major step in Seattle's cultural development. The lubberly town, so far from the New York concert halls of Harriet's youth, finally could lay claim to some sophistication. Harriet listened to the sound of Wagner's *Tannhauser* and tears began running down her cheeks. Her husband patted her hand. "That's all right, Hatty. Music is here," he said.

When Dorothy turned sixteen, she was sent East to a finishing school —Mrs. Dow's in Briarcliff Manor, New York, where the girls wanted to know: What was Seattle like? Dorothy's answer could have headlined a Chamber of Commerce poster:

"Like heaven," she replied.

After Briarcliff, Dorothy stayed in New York City to study music. She returned to Seattle in 1911, now a young woman, five-feet-two-inches tall with long, nearly black hair that she usually wore in braids wrapped around her head. She had a round face and kind eyes, but her mouth gave her a somewhat stern look until she broke into a smile, which came easily to her.

The frontier town of her father's arrival had become a major American city. Since 1900 Seattle's population had grown from some 80,000 to more than 237,000, as its boundaries spread north and south. Giant Denny Hill had been blasted by water cannons and sluiced and shoved onto the Duwamish tideflats. With four transcontinental railroads, Seattle had become a significant manufacturing center as well as a regional center for breweries, bakeries, and metalworks. Fishing vessels unloaded salmon at canneries along Seattle's harbor. In anticipation of expanding trade to the Northwest through the new Panama Canal, a system of locks and a canal were being built to open Lake Washington shipping to Puget Sound. Visitors found a city in transition, with signs of the future side by side with the past: cars rode on 221 miles of paved roads, sharing the streets with horse-drawn carriages. Native Americans sat on sidewalks, draped in blankets, selling cedar baskets. Lumber's share of the workplace, once the source of 80 percent of King County's manufacturing employment, had dropped to 40 percent. News came from several daily newspapers, each uncertain of its future and each battling for readers, advertisers, and influence over City Hall. Nothing more symbolized the rapid change in the city than the fact that timber heir William Boeing had taken an interest in airplanes. Within four years, he would cofound a company carrying his name.

Dorothy's father continued to be a major force in the city's development. From his position as president and largest stockholder of the Metropolitan Building Company, which held leases on prime downtown property, Stimson invested in many of the city's finest new office buildings: the Cobb, Stimson, Skinner, and White Henry Stuart buildings; and theaters: the Coliseum, the Music Box, and the magnificent, $1.5 million Fifth Avenue Theater, inspired by the Temple of Heavenly Peace in Beijing. Metropolitan also built one of the West's finest hotels, the Olympic, named after Stimson's yacht. Stimson invested in the Metropolitan National Bank and was an organizer and director of the General Insurance Company of America, later called Safeco.

With such a father, so much wealth, and her own engaging personality, it was no surprise that Dorothy Stimson attracted suitors. But why should she marry? For that to happen, she needed to find the man who would take her breath away.

Where was Scott Bullitt? Everybody was looking for him.

Dorothy Stimson had driven down from The Highlands to pick up friends gathered at the home of Dorothy Terry, granddaughter of Jacob Furth, the powerful president of Seattle National Bank. The occasion in 1917 was Dorothy Terry's wedding to Keith Bullitt of Louisville, Kentucky. Bullitt was the son of a distinguished East Coast family that traced its roots to Patrick Henry and beyond. The couple had met in Europe and were to be married in the chapel at The Highlands.

Dorothy arrived to take the group to the rehearsal. Keith's brother, Scott, was somewhere in the house but couldn't be found. Dorothy was anxious to meet him. She heard he was a lawyer who had caused a stir in Louisville. What was that all about? Finally, someone found him reading a book in a corner and brought him into the Terry's parlor. Dorothy looked up as Scott walked in. Their eyes met—and she gasped.

Fifteen years older than Dorothy Stimson, Scott Bullitt was a lean, rugged-looking man, who seemed taller than his five-feet-nine inches. He carried himself perfectly, his back and head straight, his eyes set deep beneath a forehead balanced by a sharply formed nose and a powerful jaw. He exuded strength, vision, and destiny. To some, he looked like a Roman emperor. To Dorothy Stimson, he looked like a Roman god. She had never seen a man so handsome or a smile so nice. She fell instantly in love. Dorothy was usually skilled at handling herself, at keeping her emotions hidden while watching and listening. But she couldn't take her eyes off the man from Louisville.

She had no idea, of course, how forty-year-old Scott Bullitt would change her life and outlook. He would sweep her into the political arena where she would be the first Stimson to play a direct, though small, public role in political campaigns. She would never enjoy speechmaking or the coarseness of politics, but Bullitt's passion for campaigns exposed her to a world she would otherwise have avoided, despised, and never understood. Scott Bullitt would show her that a campaign could be a noble cause, a means for good people to do good things. And that insight would enable her to tolerate, even to encourage, those who wanted to rally the people of Seattle and the Northwest.

Scott Bullitt's blood was about as blue as it gets in America. While the Stimsons were chopping logs in Michigan and sharing their home with unwashed mule drivers, the Bullitts were already established in the best social and political circles. Captain Thomas Bullitt had served with George Washington during the French and Indian War and was appointed to make the first survey of Ohio in 1773, laying out the plat of what became Louisville, Kentucky. Another Bullitt came to Kentucky from Virginia, presided over the state's second constitutional convention in 1800, and served as its first lieutenant governor. Scott Bullitt's mother was a great-niece of United States Chief Justice John Marshall, and his father, a prominent lawyer, was a great-nephew of colonial patriot Patrick Henry. Bullitt's eldest brother, William, was solicitor general of the United States.

An able student, Scott Bullitt studied under Woodrow Wilson at Princeton University, where he played football and won boxing bouts. After Princeton, he attended the University of Virginia Law School. He had everything—except money. Financially, the Bullitts of Louisville were no match for the Stimsons of Seattle. Scott Bullitt had nothing like Norcliffe to offer a bride. But he had a bright political future in Kentucky. An active Democrat, he had aligned himself with a reform movement led by Governor J. C. Beckham, who appointed him sheriff of Jefferson County in Louisville. As sheriff, Bullitt crusaded against gamblers, raided poolrooms, and stopped bookmaking at the race tracks. That angered much of the establishment but made Bullitt a hero to the Louisville *Courier-Journal*. His success propelled him into the office of county attorney in 1910.

After a brief courtship, Scott Bullitt and Dorothy Stimson married on May 16, 1918, at Norcliffe and moved to Louisville, where Bullitt set up a law practice and Dorothy Stimson Bullitt set up housekeeping in a rented apartment. A hired woman helped with the cooking. Dorothy didn't complain, but as a newcomer she was shy and completely unprepared for the role of housewife. Their furniture had not arrived, so visitors had to sit on apple crates. She missed Seattle terribly.

In 1919 the couple's first child, Charles Stimson Bullitt, was born. Scott Bullitt joined the U.S. Army just as the war in Europe was ending, serving two years as a major in the office of the Judge Advocate General in Washington, D.C. After the army, Bullitt joined C. D. Stimson's company and moved into a house on 4.7 acres in The Highlands, on property adjoining his father-in-law's land. Over the next several years, the Bullitts added a sunroom and other additions, built a children's playhouse on the property, and called the compound "Greenway." They spent more than $13,350 on improvements to the house, plus another $16,000 for furniture and decorations. No one sat on apple crates at Greenway.

Bullitt and Dorothy lived at center stage in Seattle society. They belonged to the best clubs, dined with the best families, and enjoyed their life. Bullitt was a rare Democrat among Seattle's fiercely Republican gentry, but he made friends easily.

The Highlands crowd chuckled over Bullitt's faithfulness to a 1916 Washington law, established four years before Prohibition, that banned liquor. While other homes continued to serve good whiskey, Bullitt insisted that no liquor be served at Greenway as long as it was illegal. He was too good-humored to be a prude, but his principles were inflexible.

"If you don't believe in the law, you change it. You don't break it," Bullitt would say. And there was another variation: "If you stand for it, do it."

Changing and making laws was what Bullitt wanted to do, much more than drafting real-estate contracts for his father-in-law. He was a public activist, unlike Dorothy. While his father-in-law wanted to build Seattle's economy, Bullitt wanted to restructure its political life and give power to the weak or the disenfranchised. He wanted to bring the vote to women and end exploitation of children in factories. In contrast, Dorothy worked incrementally through accepted institutions. She could solicit donations at a gathering of society women, who, between cups of tea, would agree on building a hospital, helping the symphony, or launching a program with goals that would never be challenged. Scott could denounce the established economic order, standing before men on sawdust and speaking to them as a true friend, a believer in their causes. He itched to get into politics. Dorothy, who did not like politics, reluctantly gave her husband permission to run for office.

In 1926, at age forty-nine, Scott Bullitt campaigned as a man set apart from typical politics, a principled man who represented all the people, not just the elite.

"He is a man of great ability, honesty and moral courage, coupled with a thorough understanding of public questions," declared the Scott Bullitt for Senator club in a letter to potential supporters that August. It may have been treasonous to his social class, but Bullitt didn't hide his affection for the labor movement that had shut down Seattle in 1919, the nation's first general strike. "He is in full sympathy with the desire of the producing masses of our people," the Bullitt campaign declared. For workers who wanted a beer after a sweaty day in a factory, Bullitt offered relief—a change in the Volstead Act. "Drinking an alcoholic beverage is not in itself a sin," he wrote in a letter to the Seattle *Times*.

Brave, but not winning words. Bullitt worked hard, crisscrossing the state for months, trying to paint incumbent Republican Senator Wesley Jones as a threat to the working man. But he lost, receiving 148,783 votes to Jones's 164,130.

Dorothy was relieved that the election was over. Her beloved Scott was home from the campaign trail. There would be fewer trips away from the children—now three, with Stimson, Priscilla ("Patsy"), born in 1920, and Harriet, born in 1924—no more late-night speeches before strangers, no more rude questions. As much as her husband loved it, she detested politics. Now they could relax and spend time together. One of their favorite pastimes was listening to the radio.

Radio was first licensed in Seattle in 1922. It quickly became popular, although barely profitable because of a proliferation of stations competing for advertising dollars. By 1926 eight radio stations offered uneven programs that often came weakly into the home, a sign of under-powered transmitters or faulty gear. Seattle radio was dominated by the

Fishers, who, like the Stimsons, had diversified from timber into real estate and who now owned KJR and KOMO. Radio was usually live—dance music from downtown hotels, dramas, concerts from studios, speeches, and even an occasional wedding. At the peak of his power in 1924, bootlegger Roy Olmstead owned radio station KFQX and allegedly used it to transmit coded messages to his fleet of powerboats. Supposedly, the code was worked into children's stories read over the air by Olmstead's wife.

The radio receiver was a handsome thing, designed to look rather like an elegant writing desk on four legs. It brought music, drama, and news from around the world. Scott and Dorothy Bullitt could listen to an orchestra on KOMO at 6:00 P.M., "sports and amusements" on KFOA at 6:25 P.M., or a stock-market report on KJR at 5:40 P.M. By day, KJR carried headline news from the *Post-Intelligencer,* including advice from Prudence Penny on what to prepare for dinner that night. In the evening, KJR's musical fare might include *The Mikado* or *La Bohème,* while KOMO offered a public-affairs program, *Town Topics,* that aired at 8:30 P.M.

Once, in the middle of the night, Scott and Dorothy sat on the couch wrapped in blankets and tuned in news of elections in England. On Sundays, if the weather was good, the couple would turn up the radio and go out into the garden. It was an intoxicating combination for a music lover like Dorothy. There she was, at home in Seattle, listening to a choir broadcast from Salt Lake City. Beautiful music, coming through the air from hundreds of miles away—for free. She was astonished. How did it get here? She wanted to know more about this invention. Thus began her lifelong interest in broadcasting as a means of both entertaining and informing the public.

But not everyone was happy at The Highlands. A schism was developing within the Stimson clan. Dorothy's brother Thomas seethed with resentment of his brother-in-law. It was bad enough that Scott Bullitt was inattentive to the family business, but it hurt to see C. D. Stimson so blatantly favor Bullitt over his only son.

Dorothy had long felt sorry for her brother. She saw him as shy around adults, troubled with self-doubts, and feeling unequal to the task of being a great man's son. He was technically president of the C. D. Stimson Company, but he felt like a functionary around his father, who lit up when Scott Bullitt entered the room. C. D. Stimson and Scott Bullitt laughed at each other's jokes and except for golf, which Bullitt disliked, they seemed to have everything in common. It pained Thomas to see Bullitt getting the love *he* wanted.

In December 1926, Thomas Stimson's resentments boiled over. At a meeting of the Stimson Company, Thomas announced his resignation as president and insisted it be accepted, despite the protests of the family. C. D. felt forced to choose between his son and his son-in-law, as a rift widened in the Stimson clan. It would not be the last time that a family conflict would threaten the family business. It would take a long time for the wounds to heal.

C. D. came up with a solution: Split the company. He listed all the assets and gave each a valuation based on his personal estimates. Two companies were formed: the Stimson Realty Company, owned by C. D. and the Bullitts: and the C. D. Stimson Company, owned by C. D. and the Thomas Stimsons. The split became official in June 1928. In business matters, Thomas was free from his brother-in-law's shadow.

Sadly, the struggle was over something Scott Bullitt had never wanted. He cared little for business. He had sworn off politics, but he couldn't honor his promise. Pressured by supporters to run, bored with private life, he couldn't stay out of the candidate's arena. By 1928 he was ready for another attempt, this time a run against incumbent Governor Roland Hartley, an abrasive, temperamental man who despised the working man and feuded with the press and legislators from his own party. Bullitt announced his candidacy in a statewide address over that medium he and Dorothy loved—radio. It looked like a good contest: the fiery, venomous, and seemingly vulnerable Hartley versus the charismatic, energetic Bullitt. "Exciting times are looked for," wrote a visiting reporter from the Chicago *Tribune*. "Leaders say perhaps 40 percent of Republicans have their axes out for Hartley, while as a campaigner on the liberal issue, Bullitt is described as 'a rootin', tootin' son of a gun.'"

Bullitt tried to make Hartley's personality the campaign issue. "He has no issues, no helpful policies, no new ideas for the public welfare," said Bullitt. "His hands are empty of all save political mud." Hartley campaigned as a populist in what was called his "cuspidor caravan."

He told audiences he alone stood between their wallets and lavish spending by legislators of both parties. As proof, he carried with him a $100 hand-tooled cuspidor ordered by some Olympia bureaucrat. He also carried a little black satchel that he would display before audiences, announcing it "contained enough stuff" to send many state officials to the penitentiary.

Late in the campaign Hartley forces worked a smear involving the University of Washington's ten-acre parcel in downtown Seattle. They put out the word that if Bullitt were elected, he would manipulate the University's Board of Regents to rewrite its lease on downtown property with the Metropolitan Building Company, led by C. D. Stimson. Bullitt replied that the governor, by state law, could not interfere in the lease, nor would he if he could. Bullitt ended his campaign at the Eagles Auditorium in Seattle with Dorothy at his side. More than 4,000 people jammed the hall. Dorothy hated public speaking, but she came straight to the point, calling herself "the handicap in Mr. Bullitt's campaign." It must have pained her to refer to the Hartley smear. "If it were not for me," said Dorothy, "Governor Hartley would have had nothing to complain about. The big [fault in] Mr. Bullitt seems to be that he married my father's daughter."

Hartley won big, with 281,991 votes to Bullitt's 214,334 votes.

Even after that, Scott Bullitt did not give up politics. He was elected national committeeman, worked with the King County Democrats, and became a leading force in the Municipal League, a reform group that issued studies of public utilities, port development, bond issues, taxes, and planning. Bullitt helped secure a job at the Municipal League for a young law school graduate named Warren Magnuson. Like Bullitt, Magnuson made friends easily and took quick advantage of his access to the city's leading politicians. Magnuson would never forget his debt to Bullitt for giving him a start in politics.

In August 1929, C. D. Stimson became seriously ill and died at age seventy-two. "I loved him," Bullitt told Dorothy, his tears a shock to his children, who had never seen an adult cry. C. D.'s death was a stunning blow to the family. It also came at a bad time financially, a few months before the October stock market crash that marked the start of the Great Depression. Stimson's assets were assessed for estate taxes at their highest value, and taxes had to be paid as tenants of Stimson Realty began skipping rent payments.

Dorothy's brother, Thomas, tried to fill his father's place in the weakening business empire. But he had little time to forge his own identity. In 1931 Thomas died in an airplane crash while piloting home a lamb intended to be a gift for his children. Investigators speculated that the lamb had wriggled forward in the small plane and jammed the controls, forcing the plane into a dive. KOMO broadcast the funeral, which was attended by more than 1,000 mourners.

Now Dorothy had to face the Depression without her brother or her father. She had Scott Bullitt and her children, but a financial crisis threatened the wealth and comforts she had known all her life. It was time for her husband, who previously had cared little about business or making money, to get serious about running the family business. But he couldn't change. Politics and public service remained his loves. The nation's economic crisis created an opportunity for the Democratic Party, and for him.

Chapter 5 | The Depression Hits Dorothy

B y 1932 it was all set. Scott and Dorothy Bullitt would be moving to Washington, D.C., once voters did the inevitable. The first step was that year's Democratic Convention in Chicago, where Scott Bullitt would stand before the delegates and nominate his friend, New York Governor Franklin Roosevelt, to be the party's candidate for the presidency of the United States.

Since his campaign loss in 1928, Bullitt had focused on building the Democratic Party in Washington state and preparing it for Roosevelt's run in 1932. The nation was ready to toss Republican Herbert Hoover and possibly primed to end the GOP's grip on Washington state. The Depression had hit Seattle especially hard. Few ships called on Seattle's docks. Mills closed. Thousands had no jobs. In the dumpy area south of Skid Road, hundreds of grim, unwashed men built a Hooverville. City government went bankrupt from the cost of relief programs. Thousands of Communists, Trotskyists, Socialists, Silver Shirts, Wobblies, Single-Taxers, and other political radicals roamed Hooverville and other parts of the city, offering theories and quick fixes to the tear in America's body politic.

Politics had a new face. Hungry men could still vote. The Unemployed Citizens League threw its support unofficially to three candidates running for city council. All three won. There was talk of filing an Unemployed Ticket to take over state government. In this time of radical ideas and radical change, Scott Bullitt was riding a sure horse in Franklin Roosevelt, with whom he had visited in 1931 to discuss nomination plans. Bullitt was scheduled to serve as chairman of the Democratic

National Committee and, after victory, to serve as Roosevelt's Secretary of the Navy. Dorothy and her husband would be heading East again. Scott's future as a national Democrat was bright. At least that was the plan.

In early February 1932, while attending a party meeting in Washington, D.C., Bullitt became ill with what the public heard was a flu. But after he checked into a hospital, doctors discovered cancer of the liver and gall bladder. No treatment would work. By April he was dead, at age fifty-five. He left behind three children—Stimson, twelve, Patsy, eleven, and Harriet, eight. After almost fourteen years of marriage, Dorothy was a widow at age forty. For her, the death was made more painful by the knowledge that Bullitt had died a frustrated man—he felt that he had accomplished none of his goals. But Scott Bullitt left a powerful imprint on his wife. He had put Dorothy Bullitt on a first-name basis with many of the state's leading politicians, as well as members of Roosevelt's inner circle and other national politicians. More important, he had exposed her to a kind of public service that was more dynamic and far-reaching than the social volunteerism of which her mother had been an outstanding example. For the rest of her life, Dorothy Bullitt would keep a hand in the arts and philanthropy. But because of Scott Bullitt, she would also maintain an involvement in politics and activism of a more modern sort. She would support a children's hospital but would also join groups that worked to employ the poor and improve race relations. By no means would she become the public progressive Democrat that her husband had been. Instead, she deflected attention from herself, working through others and through organizations. She never became the sort who would give a speech calling for dramatic change in social or government policy, such as an end to Prohibition. But she supported others who did. Much later, she would give those activists a new tool of communications to make those speeches. In time, she became more powerful than most politicians. Nothing better symbolized the beginning of her change than the fact that the Democratic Party in Washington state selected her to take Scott Bullitt's place in Chicago. There, amongst the sweat-stained Democratic throng, she read into the party's platform a call for strict child-labor laws.

At the beginning of this transformation, Dorothy Bullitt was not aware of her latent talents. She felt completely unprepared for carrying on without her husband. Dorothy had every reason to expect a man to take over the business left to her by Bullitt's death. Women rarely ran anything other than social clubs and the household staff in those days. So after Bullitt died, Dorothy walked over to the home of a cousin, Charles Willard "Cully" Stimson, expecting him to run the company. As president of the Stimson Timber Company who had organized sales of timber to Hawaii and South America, Cully Stimson seemed an obvious choice to relieve Dorothy of business worries.

"Well, you have another company to take care of now," Dorothy said to Cully.

"Oh, no," he replied, to her surprise. He told Dorothy it was time for her to go to work and run the business herself. Hurt and feeling betrayed, Dorothy went down to the Bullitt offices on Fourth Avenue and tried to familiarize herself with the company operations. But the room was full of her husband's possessions, each a reminder of her loss. It was his world, not hers. She and Bullitt's secretary began talking, and Dorothy learned that the secretary's fiancé had also just died. They sat at their desks, talked about their men, tried to console each other, and when the silences came, just cried.

Paralyzed with grief, doubt, and fear, Dorothy felt threatened for the first time in her life. She was a single parent, deprived of the men who had meant everything to her, and facing severe money trouble. The Depression was worsening. Even though she had learned much about business from her father, none of that was on her mind now. She had no experience or training. She did not have a lawyer to help her with leases fast becoming worthless. Going through company records, she discovered that profits from the Stimson Realty Company had dropped to less than $10,000 in 1932, and the outlook was for further decline. She told friends that she and other landlords were in a bottomless pit and no one knew how to get out.

Dorothy Bullitt owned four major assets: the Coliseum Theater, the new building at 1411 Fourth Avenue, the Firestone Building, and the Westlake Square Building. Weeks after Scott's death, she had yet to make a scheduled payment on the mortgage on the Fourth Avenue building. Its floors were still unfinished; tenants occupied just one-third of the building. Her income was shriveling: a tenant would simply announce he could no longer pay and would walk out, leaving the furniture. One major source of Dorothy's income was a monthly check for the ground lease on the Coliseum Theater. Not long after Bullitt died, the checks stopped without warning. The tenant, the Fox Company, said they were broke and left for California.

Dorothy was frantic to keep tenants. She decided to simply go door-to-door in the buildings, announcing that rents were being lowered and asking tenants to stay on, a strategy that took advantage of her ability to listen to people's problems and make them regard her as an ally. One tenant, Donald E. Frederick, co-founder of the Frederick & Nelson department store, insisted on paying in full. Some tenants offered advice, especially Bill Boeing of the airplane company, but saving the company was largely up to her. Of course, being a woman presented some problems. Some men refused to deal with her because they had to curb their negotiating style of shouting and pounding on the table. Then again, there were some with whom Dorothy refused to deal because they felt no inhibitions about shouting and pounding. And some went out of their way to help, in part because they did not see a woman as a competitor.

Then a break. A man called long-distance one day, saying he was with a Hollywood studio and wanted to see the Coliseum. Dorothy was anxious to rent the theater but was afraid a Hollywood slickster was coming to take advantage of her. Instead, Frank Newman turned out to be a very pleasant person who offered to give her lessons on managing a building. They became friends. He signed a lease that was fair to both of them, and Dorothy felt a deep sense of relief.

Saving the company consumed her. Before Scott Bullitt's death, Dorothy had often been away from her children, but now she seemed gone even when she was home. She turned the children over to a nanny and practically lived at the downtown office, even sleeping there some nights. Stim, Patsy, and Harriet saw more of the housekeeper, the cook, and the nanny than of their mother. When she came home to The Highlands, she was very tired and often took dinner in her room, leaving Stim reading in his room and the girls in the kitchen talking with the cook. The children could only guess at the depth of her troubles. Once, not long after their father's death, they saw her at her desk, in tears, searching through a directory of lawyers for a familiar name, for someone who could help her.

Though Dorothy was deeply interested in her children, she was not given to hugs or displays of affection. The children seemed to yearn for attention; their friends sensed a sadness about them. One friend watching Harriet Bullitt arrive at St. Nicholas School in a big car driven by a chauffeur was struck by how lonely she looked—sitting by herself in the car, she seemed so tiny and so distant from the man at the wheel. All of Dorothy's children felt isolated at The Highlands, which now had guarded gates because of fears of kidnapping. The children envied their friends who lived a more normal life in the city. Stim particularly bore a heavy burden. He hated The Highlands and hated being wealthy. He slumped down in the chauffeured car so people wouldn't see him.

This was a hard time for the children; they felt as if no one was helping them grieve for their father. Now, it seemed, their mother was removed as well. Other mothers baked cookies and talked about how to dress. Dorothy, who had learned from her father, wanted to discuss business with her children, but none of them cared. Harriet wanted to talk about stars and waterfalls. Stim was a boy suffering from a lack of confidence; he never felt he could win his mother's approval, a feeling that stayed with him for decades. She did not want her son to be spoiled, self-centered, or arrogant, so she praised him sparingly. (He perceived her comments as cold, controlled diatribes.) When the children were old enough, Dorothy sent them to boarding schools in the East: Stimson to Kent and Yale; Patsy to Ethel Walker and, though she didn't want a college education, Vassar; and Harriet to Chatham Hall and Bennington. The children loved their mother but also felt what one close family observer called "a glazed-over bitterness." Years later, that tangle of feelings would affect how they viewed their mother's business and whether they chose to continue her legacy.

Dorothy's social life dried up. She no longer had time to visit the Sunset Club, the elegant gathering place for the female elite of Seattle. Because people no longer saw her around town, she stopped getting invitations. People who had known her for years stopped calling. It didn't so much hurt Dorothy that the invitations had stopped, it hurt that her friends, when she ran into them on the street, had no idea what she was doing, what she was up against.

Gradually Dorothy, along with the rest of Seattle, began to pull out of the Depression. She kept an eye on each tenant, hustled for new ones, and watched every dime. By 1939, Dorothy's buildings were in good shape and financially she was strong. She was strong emotionally as well. Like millions of other Americans, she came out of the Depression forever cautious about debt, but she was never fearful about sticking to her instincts and taking on a difficult challenge. Many failed during the Depression; Dorothy Bullitt did not. She realized that she enjoyed business and excelled at it. She enjoyed talking over deals, analyzing the numbers, and thinking about cash flow.

In the years after Scott Bullitt's death, she was increasingly recruited to join civic and business groups. She became known as a person who arrived on time for meetings, had studied the issues, and had useful points to make. During the Depression, she served one day a week in Olympia as the only woman member of the State Emergency Relief Commission. As acting chairwoman of the commission, she signed the order starting work on the Grand Coulee Dam. She also served as chairwoman of the Cornish Council and was a member of the governing board of the Cornish School of the Arts. In addition, she chaired the Civilian War Commission's volunteer and placement section and served on the City Library Board as an appointee of Mayor Arthur Langlie, a Republican. As a library board member, she helped oversee construction of a new downtown library near City Hall. Later, she served on the mayor's Civic Unity Committee, the only public body concerned with race relations. She was also elected to the board of Pacific National Bank, a rare place to find a woman in those days.

World War II brought Seattle a flood of investment. Newcomers also poured in. The Boeing Airplane Company was a particular beneficiary. Its employment started at 4,000 in 1939, more than doubled by July 1941, reached 20,000 that September, and hit 30,000 when a re-armed United States entered the war. The city was as alive as when C. D. Stimson had arrived half a century earlier.

The war hit many American families, including Dorothy Bullitt's. Stimson Bullitt, a Navy lieutenant, went ashore with the first group at Leyte in the Philippines, got hit by shrapnel, and was awarded a Purple Heart. Not until the war was nearly over did Dorothy discover that Stim had never received many of the letters she had sent him. She wondered what he had thought about that. Did he think she hadn't cared to write? Such was the formality in their relationship that she apparently never asked, nor did he.

Not long after World War II began, cousin Frederick Stimson approached Dorothy Bullitt with an idea. Fred Stimson practically grew up in C. D. Stimson's house. His father, F. T. Stimson, had tried to interest his son in business and had placed him in various jobs, but work never appealed to the boy. Despite a tubercular hip, he lived a fast life. After his father's death in 1922, Fred Stimson inherited $500,000 and spent much of it on booze, women, and good times. Everybody had a story about him: he rode a motorcycle into the lobby of the Olympic Hotel; he tossed a large number of live turkeys into the back of his car and dropped them at friends' homes; he spent a night on a billboard; and he collected what the French called "Art Photographs." By middle age, he had little money and no regrets. Dorothy ignored the racy side to his life. She enjoyed having him around. He told good stories, was always in good humor, and liked to make people laugh.

"If you're going to be in business, why not pick something that's fun?" he asked Dorothy. Fred suggested radio. As a business, it involved a lot of lively people who not only enjoyed their work but who made a product that people wanted. It would be wonderful, because Dorothy liked people. Fred Stimson himself knew the technology; his radio engineer's license represented one of the few times he had stuck to a discipline. He offered to put up some money, though they both knew which of them had money to invest.

Dorothy was interested. Perhaps she saw radio as a potentially profitable business, though not in comparison with the fabulous profits of timber. Radio in the early 1940s remained a crowded industry. When the Fishers entered the business, they did everything first class, spending big money to buy the best equipment, bands, and announcers, which made their KJR and KOMO stations very popular. This drew advertisers.

Most other operators made little money because their audience share was so small.

But more than money was on her mind. Part of radio's appeal was that it might be a place, finally, where Fred could find himself. So she had a business and he had a job, on one condition—that he stop drinking. What later was celebrated as King Broadcasting's grand public-spiritedness began in part as an effort to dry out the rascal of the Stimson clan.

So, in 1941, the two unlikely partners started to explore the radio business. Getting an AM license in a city already crammed with stations seemed unlikely, so they looked at FM, a newer technology with the possibility of vastly improved sound quality but few listeners. Dorothy interviewed every expert she could find, including the inventor of FM, Edwin Howard Armstrong. Studying her notes, she decided that an FM station could be launched at reasonable cost. With an engineer, she and Fred drove around the Cascade foothills east of Seattle looking for an appropriate site for an FM transmitter. They found some land on Newcastle Mountain and bought it.

They also found a lawyer in Washington, D.C., with outstanding connections—Andrew Haley had researched the Federal Radio Act of 1927 for U.S. Senator C. C. Dill of Washington state and had helped to draft the Federal Communications Act of 1934. One of the smartest lawyers in D.C., Haley had befriended all the FCC commissioners and politicians with influence over radio regulators. Tremendously energetic, he could keep several secretaries busy at once, yell and throw things when angry, and roar with laughter when happy. He dressed as if he had slept in his clothes and he drank heavily, but he never let booze damage his work. Dorothy was lucky to get him, and for the rest of her life she rarely made a major move without seeking his advice. Andy, as she called him, submitted her application for the FM license in December 1941. Total expenses: $4,000, split equally between Dorothy and Fred Stimson. But the Federal Communications Commission shelved the paperwork for the duration of World War II.

When the war ended, Dorothy discussed her radio plans with two friends—Anna and John Boettiger. Anna was a daughter of Franklin Roosevelt, and John was publisher of Hearst's Seattle *Post-Intelligencer* and a leader of the Rainier Club, the elite downtown business club. The Boettigers wanted to try radio on the AM frequency, where the only possibility was a spot at 1540, which they felt was too high on the dial. (At that point, reception for stations below 600 or above 1200 was considered poor.) The Boettigers joined with Dorothy Bullitt and Fred Stimson for a while; then they gave up and moved to Phoenix, where they bought a newspaper. Fred Stimson and Dorothy pressed ahead for 1540 on the AM side and renewed work on getting the FM license as well. They bought land on Squak Mountain, fifteen miles southeast of Seattle, which was better than Newcastle for radio transmission, and decided to form a corporation and seek more investors. Dorothy's son Stimson, by then out of the navy, also helped.

In 1946, Stimson Bullitt visited Philip Padelford at his home in Broadmoor, a walled enclave in Seattle. He told them his mother was starting a radio station to bring quality music to Seattle and offered him the job of operating manager. A few years older than Stimson Bullitt, Padelford had also attended Yale. His father, Frederick Morgan Padelford, had been a prominent English professor and dean at the University of Washington. Padelford agreed to commit $25,000 to the new company, but turned down the job offer.

Dorothy found another candidate for manager, the husband of her close friend, Frances Owen, daughter of Stephen Penrose, the longtime president of Whitman College. Frances had been training director at Frederick & Nelson when she met Henry Owen, the company's vice president who handled personnel and other matters. Henry Owen was a suave Virginia native who worked a subtle charm on people. He never approached a problem directly. His skill was to strike up a conversation with people in his buttery accent and move them gently to the topic and to an agreement. Most felt charmed; a few felt manipulated.

Dorothy called Owen.

"I have in mind an investment in an area that I'm not very familiar with, but I'd like to find someone to help with starting a project," she told him.

"I'll be right down," Owen said. He hadn't even given Dorothy a chance to say what the "project" was. He arrived minutes later, heard Dorothy's ideas, and said he would get back to her after the weekend.

He then went down to the public library and checked out every book on radio he could find. That Monday, he called Dorothy.

"I'll take it," he said. "I found out it is a business like any other. You've got a product to sell." Henry Owen came in, the incorporation papers were signed from the FCC, and in 1946 Western Waves was in business. All it needed was permission to operate.

The FM application went through and a license was granted. There were problems, however, on the potentially more lucrative AM side. The 1540 spot was sought by stations in six other cities around the country. There were fears that the signals from one city would interfere with the others. Western Waves sought political help. Senator Hugh Mitchell, a Democrat appointed to fill the unexpired term of Mon Walgren, the new governor, wrote to the White House. The FCC told the White House that 235 cases were scheduled to be heard before the Western Waves case. It appeared that Dorothy would be without an AM signal for months or more, but then a solution emerged. One of her tenants in the 1411 Fourth Avenue building had a station to sell.

"It's silly to bring in another station," said Arch Talbot, owner of KEVR-AM and FM. "I have a station nobody listens to. Why not buy it?"

Western Waves bought the AM station at the dial position of 1090 for $190,000, a reasonable price. Two Centralia brothers, Elroy and Robert McCaw, delayed the license transfer by claiming partial ownership of KEVR. That was cleared up, and Western Waves took possession of the station May 1, 1947, hoping to reach many of the 653,015 homes in Washington state with a radio. Dorothy Bullitt and Henry Owen walked into the station offices on the twenty-first floor of the Smith Tower, Seattle's tallest office building. Owen sat at the manager's desk and began opening the mail. Out fell a check and a letter from the Hooper rating agency. "We've just made a survey of the Seattle situation, and we didn't find any audience listening to your station," read the letter. "Here's your money back."

In a field of eight Seattle AM stations, KEVR was last and losing money. It had no network affiliation and nothing compelling to attract listeners. The only thing going for the station financially was its strong advertising agency, the Joseph Weed Company. A good agency could hustle accounts and build interest in a weak station—but Weed dropped

KEVR. Dorothy and Owen canceled some programs, bought new ones and spent money on promotion—all of which caused losses to grow.

KEVR's problems seemed endless. Even its call letters were lousy. Some stations picked a sequence of letters that stood for a slogan. KEVR stood for nothing. Dorothy knew she had to change it. She went through a number of K combinations and settled on an obvious possibility: KING. It was catchy, referred to the surrounding King County, and suggested class and market dominance. But KING belonged to another radio operator, the freighter SS *Watertown*. Andy Haley worked his magic with the ship's owner and the Federal Maritime Commission, and KEVR changed its name to KING, which was followed by a corporate name change to King Broadcasting Company on June 6, 1947. The new name needed a corporate symbol, so Dorothy wrote to Walt Disney, asking if he would design an image for the company. His secretary responded brusquely that it was impossible for Mr. Disney to accede to all requests for commercial trademarks. That was that until Dorothy had a chance encounter with Frank Newman, the Hollywood businessman whose company rented the Coliseum Theater.

"Is there anything I can do for you?" Newman asked. "Maybe there is," Dorothy replied, asking if he knew Walt Disney. It turned out that Newman's company had been one of the first to show a Disney cartoon in its theaters, and the grateful Disney was eager to do a favor for Newman. Not long after Dorothy and Newman spoke, up in the mail came the sketch of an impish fellow with an oversized, boyish face and the head of a microphone. He wore a mink robe and had a floor microphone tossed casually over his right shoulder. His face was a grin, his hair fell loosely into his eyes, and his crown tilted at a jaunty angle—King. They called him "King Mike." Disney charged $75 for the drawing.

KING's programming was eclectic. It featured everything from band music to tips for housewives, songs of Scandinavia to Frank Sinatra. Montana Tom played Gene Autry records at noon. At night, Francis Armstrong played complete symphonies. John McCauley delivered the news as "King County Editor" five days a week. Children heard stories every Saturday morning, and on Saturday nights Norm Bobrow and Harry Jordan hosted KING's three-hour ballroom music program. The technical crew was led by Arthur Shultz, chief engineer, and Fred

Stimson worked as a studio engineer. The station was anything but a powerhouse of personalities, until KING 1090 began carrying the games of the Seattle Rainiers baseball team, announced by Leo Lassen. A gifted phrasemaker, Lassen became the city's first dominant broadcasting personality. On some nights, he held a third of Seattle's listening audience.

By 1949 KING had obtained permission to boost its signal from 10,000 watts to 50,000 watts, but not all of that power could be used. Because KING's AM signal could potentially interfere with stations in the southern United States, the FCC required that KING limit its transmission when broadcasting to the south. Nonetheless, the added power gave Dorothy Bullitt's station a reach into people's homes that often surpassed the circulation of Seattle's newspapers (each paper had fewer than 300,000 readers). The station owner had an unprecedented opportunity to influence public opinion—a message delivered by a voice into the privacy of a living room. In a promotional brochure, KING described radio as "the greatest single invention of the Twentieth Century," stating that "radios outnumber telephones by more than two to one . . . [and] are more universally used than toothbrushes." Dorothy Bullitt pledged to serve Puget Sound "with the best in radio entertainment, information and public service." At that point, her main goal was not to move minds but merely to give listeners what they already wanted, pleasant music and snippets from the news wire. No one at Dorothy Bullitt's company wanted to use KING's signal to lobby or persuade the public to a particular cause. Like other stations' newscasts, KING news offered a rewrite of newspaper stories, community notices, and government announcements. Nothing at King Broadcasting would offend—not till later, when the company employed people who didn't think they had done a good job unless someone got angry.

S eattle in 1948 was a city full of itself. It had emerged from World War II transformed. New neighborhoods sprang from land annexed by the city, which had grown during the war from 368,000 people to 480,000. Big B-47s rolled out of Boeing; the company was fat with $300 million in back orders. The Washington State Ferry System's ultramodern *Kalakala* crossed the bay like a low-flying Buck Rogers spaceship. Seattle's deep-water harbor no longer looked south to the lumber-hungry market of California but instead faced west to the markets of Asia. Business leaders hoped China's millions would soon be buying goods from the West, once the politics there settled down. A new international airport was being finished south of Seattle at Bow Lake. The University of Washington was gaining national prominence with its new health sciences center.

In politics, a freshman legislator from Spokane, Albert Canwell, staged hearings to root out suspected Communists in the UW faculty. The Democratic governor, Mon Wallgren, was ousted by the mayor of Seattle, Republican Arthur Langlie. And King County Commissioners appointed a new prosecutor, Charles O. Carroll, a Republican and a former All-American football player, to fill an unexpired term. In one of his first public statements as prosecutor, Carroll said he had heard rumors about illegal gambling in the region and, although the police chief and the sheriff had assured him the region was clean, he promised an investigation. Carroll would fast make himself the most powerful Republican in Washington.

The city seemed a worker's paradise. On weekends, dawn rose over Elliott Bay to show hundreds of dinghies full of anglers competing in union-sponsored salmon derbies. Seattle Police Department patrolmen made a starting salary of $2,700 a year, enough to buy a waterfront lot north of the city limits for $1,100. A beer-truck driver made $1.53 an hour, while a sheet metal worker made $2.21 an hour. Without saving too hard, a schoolteacher could afford a beach cabin on the San Juan Islands.

The single most powerful figure in town was Dave Beck, executive vice president of the Teamsters Union, who made the cover of *Time* in 1948. Beck had a special screened-off luncheon table at the Olympic Hotel, where his booming curses and cackling laugh filled the dining room. Writer Malcolm Cowley was amazed at the newness of the city and the apparent prosperity of its citizens: "Everyone seemed to be middle class and literate, no matter what his trade."

In Seattle and throughout postwar America, it was a perfect time for the public to experience television: a device to fill the leisure hours of workers and their families and to sell countless goods pouring from the factories—refrigerators, cars, furniture, clothing and more.

Americans had been reading about television for years. The Radio Corporation of America, owner of the National Broadcasting Company, opened its first experimental television station in 1930, using an antenna atop the Empire State Building. The first broadcast, Felix the Cat, was captured on receiver screens the size of playing cards. Columbia Broadcasting System launched its experimental station a year later. NBC displayed the technology at the New York World's Fair in 1939, featuring a telecast of a speech by President Franklin Roosevelt, and began regular telecasts that year. The first sponsored program aired two years later.

During World War II, the manufacture of television receivers was halted, leaving 10,000 sets and a shrinking number of stations. But after the war, the numbers grew. By 1948 there were close to one million receivers and almost forty stations, mostly in the East. No station existed north of Los Angeles and west of Minneapolis. TV networks began the fifteen-minute news broadcast that year with the CBS program "Douglas Edwards and the News," essentially a reading to the camera of the day's headlines. The National Broadcasting Company, the DuMont network, and the American Broadcasting Company soon launched similar programs. Network news generally ran at that length until 1963, when CBS debuted the first thirty-minute newscast.

The Fishers assumed that they would bring television to Seattle. In 1929 they tested a television system that sent a signal of a man's face to an experimental receiver at Mary Lawrence's house. The one-inch-square screen displayed only a hazy likeness. KOMO's chief engineer, Francis Brott, saw a big future in TV, with KOMO as an industry leaders. The Fishers were confident that, when the time and technology were right, KOMO would be ready with one of the finest TV studios in the nation.

But it wasn't the Fishers who brought television to Seattle. In 1947 a man named Palmer K. Leberman owned Seattle's KRSC-AM and FM and a license for an unbuilt TV station. Leberman believed television had a great future as a marketing and advertising tool. He also believed its greatest potential was in transforming the distribution of the newspaper, a product that required hundreds of people for its delivery. Someday, he believed, a television station would transmit an entire newspaper to people's homes, where a printer would reproduce the pages.

As with other business pioneers, Leberman's vision was ahead of the market. He had a serious problem finding cash. He needed $153,900 for TV equipment alone. Then there was the matter of what to broadcast. What could hold an audience for hour after hour? Could he possibly fill an entire day? Then another day? He guessed he could run some movies, something filmed in Seattle, and maybe carry something from the four TV networks, assuming he could get film from them to Seattle.

Born in the Midwest, Leberman attended the United States Naval Academy. He married a wealthy woman and, for a time, lived on the shore of Lake Washington and ran the Kelvinator Radio Sales Corporation (hence, KRSC) at Fifth and University in downtown Seattle. He started KRSC as a tiny, 50-watt AM station that struggled to stay afloat during the 1930s. After the war, he started Seattle's first FM station, although few homes had sets that picked up the static-free benefits of frequency modulation.

Leberman then moved to New York for a job as an executive with *Family Circle*, a magazine distributed exclusively in supermarkets and financed by Charles Merrill, founder of a stock brokerage company and of Safeway Stores. Merrill wasn't happy that his lieutenant was being distracted by weekend trips to Seattle, where TV problems kept mounting. In early 1948, Leberman flew out to Seattle and asked his employees for a blunt assessment: Was Seattle ready for television?

Philco, RCA, Westinghouse, and other TV makers, amazingly, had already sold some 6,000 sets in Seattle. A cheap TV in a steel cabinet went for $192. An RCA Victor set with a polished mahogany cabinet, 52-square-inch screen, and an "Eye Witness Picture Synchronizer" cost $339. The dealers promised a huge leap from the experience of radio— a chance to see boy meets girl, to see the play called back by the referee, to see news as it happens or cowboys trotting on ponies "right into your own living room!"

Leberman was feeling pressure from the FCC to build his TV station or lose his license. But TV was far more expensive than radio, and the extent of these costs was unknown. Television hardware was unreliable and it broke easily. Costly tubes lasted only weeks. Merrill was helping Leberman with the expenses, but the decision to go forward was not easy. Television was going to cost heavily, without any certainty of profit.

But Leberman had a vital asset—a twenty-two-year-old dynamo named Lee Schulman, one of the few people in broadcasting who had actually worked in television. In New York, Schulman had worked on experimental TV stations for the DuMont network and for NBC. TV had already advanced enormously. Ten years earlier, actors' faces had to be painted orange with purple and brown accents to keep from washing out in a broadcast. Schulman not only knew the technology but had endless ideas for new applications. He never seemed to tire. He was passionate about television, had a flair for finding the theatrical, and was a pain to everyone who knew him. He dominated conversations, bristled around authority figures, and seemed to view himself as a Hollywood director. When he first came to Seattle, he brought big-city driving manners. While most Seattleites patiently waited for green lights and then accelerated at a moderate rate, Schulman was quick on the horn, anxious to get past other cars. He was always in a hurry. He wanted everyone to jump when he barked. Most did.

But even though he could be exasperating, no one doubted his smarts or instincts. He would push engineers to do the impossible because his gut told him it could be done; and usually he was right. It was other people's money that started television in Seattle, but Schulman pushed it onto the airwaves. He was a true pioneer of television in Seattle but would get little public recognition of his achievement.

Schulman and the KRSC engineers spent most of 1948 trying to get their TV signal working, pushing back that first broadcast. The technical problems were enormous. The hardware was delicate and intimidating to any television engineer—but there was no such thing as a television engineer in Seattle, only radio people trying to make do. RCA sent one of its people to explain the operation of its $25,000 transmitter. When asked how long it took to become a qualified TV engineer, the RCA man answered: "I don't know. There aren't any yet."

Things got under control in late November. The transmitter tower was completed at a site across from Queen Anne High School just days ahead of a perfect candidate for Seattle's first live broadcast: a Thanksgiving Day football championship game between West Seattle and Wenatchee. KRSC had no studio, so it needed a well-lighted event. On Thanksgiving, most people would be off work and would have had time to find a television set. And, equally important, KRSC could broadcast the game for free.

On a cold, sunny day, the engineers set up their cameras on the north side of Seattle's Memorial Stadium, crowded with nearly 13,000 fans. The field was muddy. Sunlight reflected off pools of water, causing a distortion on camera lenses. The RCA cameras had another problem. They had to be kept moving or the image would burn into the screen temporarily, creating a ghosting effect. The football players had their problems, too. They slipped and tripped in the goo, dropped passes, and fumbled balls. Wenatchee, ridiculed in Seattle as a team that would rank last in the big-city league, scored early in the first period. Halfway through the game, rain began to fall.

Palmer Leberman had flown out to Seattle for the historic event and he made an appearance on camera. He even made a little speech, but nobody heard what he said. A sound cable lying in a puddle had shorted out, killing the audio. Jack Shawcroft and Tom Priebe operated the two cameras, each with four lenses that pivoted on turrets, following cues from Schulman. The images were microwaved with occasional interruptions to the Queen Anne antenna, about a half-mile away. Ted Bell, KRSC radio announcer, called the game for TV, AM, and FM—a triplecast. Water soaking into wires caused loud hums, but images and sound were going out over the airwaves. It was a ragged miracle of technology, but Seattle had television.

A lot of people in Seattle were excited about the broadcast. Several hotels set up TV sets for the public. Dorothy Bullitt watched a tiny screen at home. She had been keenly interested in television since 1939, when she saw it demonstrated in a department store in New York. She had watched that broadcast from a curtained area, the primitive camera needing so many lights that the heat scorched furniture. But she was hooked. From then on, she read everything she could find about TV, visited labs where TV was being improved, and kept asking questions. She particularly followed the finances of the early East Coast stations. How much money did they bring in? What did it cost to run a station? Dorothy never let emotion loosen her purse, but she admired Leberman's pioneering spirit. She sent him flowers on the day of his first broadcast.

As the football game progressed, Dorothy found it hard to follow the blurring shapes on screen. She never saw the ball and had to trust Ted Bell when he announced that West Seattle had tied the game, which ended 6-6.

After the broadcast, the manager of KIRO radio, Loren Stone, left the Washington Press Club, where he had watched the game, and walked back to his studio at the Cobb Building. Stone had been keenly interested in TV, but he now felt comfortable that radio would remain dominant.

"It's kinda interesting," he told his friend, Jerry Hoeck, owner of an advertising agency. "It's cute, but I don't think it'll ever amount to much."

The KRSC engineers did not conclude their day with a celebration. They still had work to do that night. The first television broadcast in Northwest history continued as follows: *Lucky Pup* at 5:15 P.M.; *Devil Horse*, Chapter 1, 5:30 P.M.; a Romeo Monk cartoon, 5:50 P.M.; *News Digest*,

6:45 P.M.; Weather, 6:55 P.M.; *Face the Music*, 7:00 P.M.; *Paris Fashions*, 7:15 P.M.; *To the Queen's Taste*, 7:30 P.M.; *People's Platform*, 8:00 P.M.; *Air Power Is Peace Power*, 8:30 P.M.; *Street Scene*, starring Betty Field, 9:00 P.M.; and signoff at 10:00 P.M. The following day started with a test pattern at 10:00 A.M., then a *Lucky Pup* program at 5:15 P.M. Various films ensued and, again, signoff at 10:00. No programs were announced for Monday or Tuesday, but Wednesday night featured a sure draw—the University of Washington versus Notre Dame.

KRSC had made history, all right, but not money. Nor would it for a long time. The station was losing $10,000 a month. Merrill refused to put up any more cash. *Family Circle* had a future, but not television in Seattle, he figured. Desperate for cash, Leberman and his station manager and minor partner, Robert Priebe, went to a bank and made their plea. All he needed was $50,000, Leberman told the banker. That would pay the bills for the short time before advertising dollars started flowing in. The banker replied that television had no future, so it was not reasonable to expect a loan. Leberman soon realized his situation was hopeless. He may have launched television, but he couldn't stay in it. He was about to make television history again, this time as the first person in America to sell a TV station. A grandmother was about to bail him out, but first she had to out-hustle a Chicago man with far more money.

I n early 1949, Dorothy Bullitt's telephone rang.

"I'm coming out to sell my station," said Palmer Leberman, calling from New York. "Are you interested?"

Dorothy had yet to make a dime in broadcasting. Many of her friends thought her crazy for throwing away her father's money. Why buy another loser? It was a natural question. Leberman had gone around to the city's other radio station owners to see if they wanted to try television. Dorothy Bullitt represented the last chance for a Seattle resident to buy KRSC.

The Fishers of radio station KOMO certainly had the money. Making money was a family talent. O. W. Fisher had made a fortune in Midwestern lumbering and milling. His family settled in Seattle in 1906, set up a logging operation, built a big flour mill on Harbor Island, and then went into land development. O. W.'s sons, led by O. D. Fisher, invested in one another's businesses and had powerful friends all over town. They spent heavily to make KOMO the best radio station in town. And that was why they didn't want KRSC. To them, it was a shabby operation. With their powerful connections and reputation, they would get their own license and build the finest television operation on the West Coast. By June 1948, they had a construction permit to build a television transmitter. All they needed was final approval on their license application from the Federal Communications Commission. They assumed it would happen soon. But the FCC, facing multiple applications for limited channels and worried that new stations were creating havoc in the airwaves, would soon impose a freeze on new station construction until standards for color broadcasting and a system of license distribution could be developed. The freeze would keep all but the owner of KRSC out of television in Seattle until 1952.

Broadcasters knew a freeze was coming, but many accepted the FCC's prediction that it would end within a few months. Dorothy, however, surmised that government engineers could not be rushed as they analyzed technical problems. She figured the freeze would last a long time. A late entrant into radio, she did not want to pass up a chance to get Seattle's only operating TV station. She wanted a head start in what she believed would become a big industry. She told Leberman that she was very interested but didn't know how she could get the money. He wanted the deal done quickly.

"OK," said Leberman. "Marshall Field wants it, and they have the money. . . . I will talk with the both of you or anybody else who comes along. It's going to be sold."

With Leberman on his way to Seattle, Dorothy wanted Andy Haley by her side. He was on business in Los Angeles when she called.

"Did you get me out of the shower to tell me this?" Haley boomed. "Are you out of your mind? Your radio station is running in the red and there are no receiving [TV] sets in the area." To Haley, 6,000 sets were few enough to be zero.

"I need you to get me out of this mess," she replied. But they both knew that was a pretext. She wanted the station, but on her terms. He promised to take the next plane to Seattle.

Dorothy had to work fast. Leberman was scheduled to see the Marshall Field representatives—an accountant, an engineer, some other aides, and the head of Field's broadcasting group—the following morning. He had already had some conversations with them, so she knew there had been progress in the negotiations. She also knew that they had been nickel-and-diming him over small issues. Leberman wanted $500,000 for the license, the station's TV equipment, and its property— a hefty price for a money-loser. But who knew what a TV station was worth? Dorothy figured she couldn't pay that much, and she knew Marshall Field would have no trouble paying it.

Leberman had an appointment with Dorothy at her office at 2:00 P.M. Shortly before the meeting, Haley called to say he had missed the plane but would be in Seattle by 6:00 P.M. Dorothy wanted to push back the Leberman appointment but feared he might start talking to the Field people again. So she met with him at 2:00 P.M. and set about delaying things, doing whatever she could to stall Leberman.

"Look, you're asking questions that I've answered at least ten times," Leberman said finally. "Are you interested or aren't you? We've been all over this."

"I really am," Dorothy replied. "Would you come to the house in the evening? Andy will be there and we can take some kind of action."

Leberman was irritated, but he agreed to come to Dorothy's new residence on Capitol Hill. "I'll come at six if you make me an offer," Leberman said. He didn't insist on a full-price offer, so Dorothy figured she had wiggle room.

Finally, Haley showed up, as did her station manager Henry Owen. Leberman came with John Ryan, a lawyer and Highlands resident who was a friend of Dorothy's. She was displeased, however, by the presence of a broker brought by Leberman.

After dinner, they met in the living room. "You've agreed to make an offer. You know my price," said Leberman, his impatience clear.

Haley started talking. Dorothy just listened. Then she and Haley went into another room to decide what she could really afford to pay. When they returned and Haley made an offer below that, the broker leapt to his feet.

"That's insulting!" shouted the broker.

"Shut up, you Arabian rug merchant!" snapped Haley. It was a line that just sprang into his head, he told Dorothy later. They went back and forth on the price and finally, near midnight, reached an agreement: $375,000 for the FM and TV stations, all the equipment, the tower and the brick building on Queen Anne Hill.

There was no deal, at least in a concrete sense, until money changed hands. Dorothy wanted Leberman to accept her money that night. He was to meet with the Marshall Field people at eight o'clock the next morning, and the Field people could easily pay the full $500,000. She had enough money in a safe at the 1411 Fourth Avenue building for a cash deposit. They arranged to meet at 3:00 A.M. at John Ryan's office, Dorothy picked up the money on her way, and they sealed the deal. The next morning, Leberman met with a stunned group from Marshall Field. Wait, they said. We'll pay more than she did. "No," said Leberman. "It's a done deal. I've given my word to a lady." Field's broadcast representative went back to Chicago with the bad news.

Dorothy later went to the board of King Broadcasting to ratify the deal, a formality since she controlled an overwhelming majority of company stock. The board members were all close to her: in addition to herself, the group included Philip Padelford, Fred Stimson, Henry Owen, Stimson Bullitt, and Stimson's friend, lawyer Richard Riddell. But Dorothy was never one to display her power. She always asked the men of her board to suggest the right course. She often spoke last, saying which of the men she agreed with, as if the thought had occurred to her only then. Of course, she knew from the start of the meeting what she was going to do. There was no opposition to buying KRSC, for which Dorothy personally provided $500,000 for the purchase money and working capital. The sales contract with Leberman was signed on May 6, 1949.

When King Broadcasting submitted paperwork to the FCC requesting the transfer of Channel 5, they had to prove that the potential owner had the financial strength to sustain the station. The papers showed that Dorothy Bullitt had emerged from the Depression and World War II with substantial financial resources: stock in Stimson Realty worth $1.3 million; Pacific National Bank stock worth $12,157; Northwest Airlines stock worth $5,123: King Broadcasting Company stock worth $315,400; Weyerhaeuser Timber Company stock worth $3,650; American Mail Lines stock worth $1,977; residences worth $117,532; and cash amounting to $52,239, plus other items—total assets of $1.8 million and debts of only $300,301. But that did not fully state her worth. Stock held by Stimson Realty in the General America Corporation had a book value of $154,500 but was worth at least $450,000. Stimson Realty paid $115,000 in dividends in 1948. A certified accountant said the Stimson Realty's buildings, mainly high-grade modern office buildings in an appreciating market, were worth $1.9 million.

On August 20, 1949, Dorothy Bullitt formally gained control of KRSC-TV and FM. (She relinquished the FM operation she had begun in 1946.) Almost immediately, she met with the employees and told them that they were one of the reasons she had bought the station. It was a smart and timely move. As the only ones who knew how to operate KRSC's equipment, she needed them. Already, they were getting offers to move to Los Angeles to help launch new stations and earn bigger salaries.

Without them, Dorothy was in trouble. But doubtless, her prime motivation was to convey a sense of appreciation, to show that she realized the company got by only on the talents of its employees. Her speech had a powerful effect on the group, most of whom were in their twenties and all of whom were believers in television's future. The employees felt an emerging sense of loyalty to her. Program Director Lee Schulman decided to stay at what was renamed KING-TV. Dorothy Bullitt's commitment appealed to Schulman. He felt she had integrity, and he shared her idealistic vision that television was a tool to serve the community. Public service was required of all broadcast licensees, but Dorothy Bullitt really believed it, as did Schulman. Dorothy said nothing about finances when she met the crew. She urged them to think about ways KING-TV could serve Seattle. Los Angeles was an entertainment center, a vastly bigger market than Seattle, but that first meeting killed any thoughts Schulman and others may have had of moving. That moment marked the beginning of KING-TV's singular esprit, its passionate commitment to serving the region, a commitment that future employees would redefine and expand, sometimes with a faulty understanding of what Mrs. Bullitt wanted.

Public service was a lofty ideal at that point. KRSC-TV was a daily miracle that triumphed over balky equipment and poor conditions. The station essentially put on whatever it could get. Everything was done in a hurry and things often went wrong. Many programs were old movies, or films of wrestling matches, celebrations of United States military strength, or educational materials and an expanding set of offerings from four networks: the National Broadcasting Company; Columbia Broadcasting System; American Broadcasting Company, and the DuMont Television Network, the feeble offshoot of DuMont Laboratories, which specialized in low-budget variety and sports shows. KRSC's locally produced commercials were clumsy—a camera was aimed at an easel that held cardboard slides. As an announcer spoke, the slides were quickly yanked to reveal type or an illustration; sometimes the slides got lost or were placed out of order. (Or, in one instance, were devoured by a visiting tiger cub.) For months, KING each day produced no more than eight hours of programs. Some days, the station was lucky to fill three hours. Rats scrambled around the studio, a converted grocery next to the transmitter on Queen Anne Hill. The facilities were hardly impressive and breakdowns were frequent—water-cooled transmitting tubes got hot, popped, and shut down the broadcast signal. KRSC's achievement was simply getting on and staying on the air. The loose assemblage of technicians, announcers, and ad salesmen had kept things rolling. Dorothy Bullitt would bring in professional management and— something the little company desperately needed—cash.

Henry Owen became president of the reorganized King Broadcasting Company and Dorothy took the title of vice president (in 1951 they switched titles). After the purchase of KEVR, Dorothy and Henry Owen had brought in a professional broadcaster, Hugh Feltis, a gruff personality who lived in the wealthy Broadmoor neighborhood, often wore a homburg hat, and had worked for the Fishers. Feltis joined KING Broadcasting's Board of Directors, which was expanded to include the spouses of Dorothy's children: Stimson Bullitt's wife, Carolyn Kizer Bullitt; Harriet's husband, William Brewster, who was a physician with the army in Germany; and Patsy's husband, Josiah "Joe" Collins. Feltis lacked the charm and finesse of Dorothy and Henry Owen, but he was strong-minded, the right person to deliver orders and get things organized. He achieved an important step—he convinced the skilled Blair Agency of New York to represent King Broadcasting in national advertising markets. Despite his gruffness, many people liked Feltis. They felt there was no politics behind what he said. In contrast, some saw Henry Owen's agenda as always veiled.

KING sent its advertising salesmen to knock on doors. Selling air time wasn't an easy task. Many business owners had no idea how TV even looked. They might have heard about it, and a few might have seen a TV broadcast, but in 1948, the whole concept of advertising on TV was new. KING's salesmen tried to sell the idea that TV did much more than radio

or print. With TV, a viewer could see somebody actually opening a re-
frigerator, driving a car, or drinking a can of pop, could sense the actor's
enthusiasm and catch the excitement of buying the product. To show
TV's effects, KING's representatives went out with a "portable" TV—
actually a big, heavy receiver with straps attached—to carry into the
offices of skeptical ad-buyers.

As the demonstration TV flickered or its picture rolled uncontrolla-
bly, business owners always wanted to know: How many people actually
watch TV? That's when the men from KING started a verbal tap dance.
Thousands, they replied, hoping to avoid specifics or demands for proof.
But, in truth, any number was a guess, based partly on what TV dealers
were reporting and the informal count of TV antennae by station employees. Anything that made the numbers look greater was used. Bob
Priebe, KING's operations manager, told salesmen that the region might
have 20,000 TV sets, but everyone knew it had to be half that or less, and
some of that count included sets in warehouses. If anyone saw an antenna in Mount Vernon or Tacoma, a mark was put on a map, and potential advertisers were shown the station's vast coverage area. In fact,
KING's signal did go far, into Canada and Portland. The initial rate for
ads on KING-TV was $32 a minute. Since businesses had no films of
themselves, Lee Schulman would use the cardboard slides or a still photograph—anything that would work. The city's prestigious department
store, Frederick & Nelson, was among the first to buy advertising time—
to sell its TVs.

Ads aired in a chaotic fashion. Feltis wanted to back up the salesman,
no matter the cost to the program schedule. If an ad was promised as a
lead into a 9:00 P.M. program, the program started a little later and
bumped the rest of that night's schedule. If more ads were sold, the
schedule was bumped again. This enraged Lee Schulman, whose schedule became meaningless. A 10:00 A.M. show might not begin till 10:30 P.M.

By 1951 KING was using a studio at the foot of Queen Anne and
making plans to move to a permanent home in a converted furniture
store on Aurora Avenue. Everyone at KING-TV was feeling confident
that TV was a success in Seattle. The flow of advertising dollars was
accelerating to the point where Dorothy had a serious management
problem. One day Dorothy halted payment to the station's three ad

salesmen, Dan Starr, Jim Neidigh, and Al Hunter, who were each owed more than $8,500. The problem: they were making too much money. They had a deal written by Feltis whereby they were paid commissions based on the dollars they brought in. As ad sales rose, so did the percentage of their commission. As advertising volume grew, the salesmen started making good money—$2,500 each during one month. That had to be more than Henry Owen earned. Starr figured Owen made $500 a month.

Starr, who later became publisher of Hearst's Seattle *Post-Intelligencer*, was short and scrappy. He wasn't about to let Dorothy hold the money he was owed. Besides, Feltis said, the money was rightfully theirs. They had worked for it. A deal's a deal, Feltis said. Starr consulted a lawyer, who said he had a strong basis for a suit, but the lawyer also pointed out that KING was the only station in town if Starr wanted to stay in television.

Dorothy called a meeting with the salesmen, Henry Owen, and Hugh Feltis. Dorothy had tremendous skills of persuasion and an ability to make employees feel like family. She used those skills that day, for not only did she want to change the commission deal but she also wanted to keep her successful sales force, whom she genuinely liked and needed. She explained that a mistake had been made and, in the telling, gave the impression that the men certainly would not want to take advantage of her. She said she would like to rewrite the agreement and pay each of them $6,000 for their cooperation.

Jim Neidigh, who had worked for KRSC radio, was the first to cave in for the sweet lady who owned the station. Six thousand sounded fine. "That's great, Mrs. Bullitt," said Neidigh. That left Al Hunter and Dan Starr, who knew their negotiating leverage had just crumbled, to also agree, and the meeting ended. Outside her office, they poked Neidigh in the arm. "You damn fool!" Starr said. "We could have gotten a lot more money."

The salesmen got a new contract, and Starr was still upset because it allowed the company to revise the contract at any time. And sure enough, a few months later, Dorothy wanted to change it again. Starr quit and wouldn't let Dorothy talk him out of it. "I made a mistake once and I'm not going to make it again. Every time this ball game gets in my behalf, you change the rules on me." Neidigh and Hunter stayed, but Feltis, too, was on his way out.

Feltis had confided to a young radio salesman, Roger Rice, that he had a good deal with Dorothy: a percentage of KING's AM, FM, and TV gross revenues went into his pocket. Feltis told Rice that Dorothy had wanted to renegotiate his contract, and he had refused. Rice noticed that, not long after that, flaws started being found in Feltis's management and he was soon gone. Whatever the reasons for Feltis's departure, it reminded people that Dorothy Bullitt could be tight with money and tough when her interests were threatened. It wasn't her style to confront anyone; she used others for that. But she was always the boss, no matter how kindly she seemed. Hugh Feltis would not be the last at KING to see his career abruptly ended.

Otto Brandt was young, ramrod straight, and handsome in an all-American way—like Jimmy Stewart, some thought. He was a rising star in the ABC organization, already a vice president in the Chicago office, one of the youngest ever at ABC, where he ran three major divisions: station relations, owned-operated stations, and national-spot sales. Dorothy heard about Brandt from Andrew Haley, who knew all the important people in the industry. After Feltis left, Dorothy flew to Chicago to talk with Brandt. Finding that they shared the same ideas of community service and of KING's potential, she decided to make him vice president and put him in charge of all the company's broadcast operations, leaving Henry Owen to manage financial issues. Brandt walked her out to the street and, as he helped her get into a cab, made what he intended to be a kind remark.

"Well, this must be a relief to you," he told Dorothy with a smile. "Now you can go back to playing bridge and picking out hats."

Brandt, perhaps understandably for that era, assumed that Dorothy, a widow, had inherited the King Broadcasting Company and was anxious to get out of men's work. He meant nothing disrespectful by the remark, and Dorothy gave no indication that she took offense. She was good at concealing her emotions. Besides, why let her sense of hurt get in the way of hiring a useful executive? Later, they would come to understand each other, and Brandt would never forget who was boss of King Broadcasting.

Although Brandt and his wife had been anxious to get out of Chicago and find a better place to raise their kids, she was not happy about going to Seattle. She viewed the city as a backwater. It was a town with Native Americans and potlatch festivals. To an Easterner, it seemed a place remote and raw. Seattle was Out There, near Alaska, far from the things that she loved, such as the theater. As they drove west, Thelma Brandt thought about a future stranded in the Outback, and cried.

Her husband was perfect for King Broadcasting and for Dorothy's vision of the company as a significant presence in the industry and the community. Unlike Hugh Feltis, Otto Brandt had connections to both ABC and its earlier parent corporation, NBC. Unlike Feltis, he had charm and an impressive style. He would make an ideal representative of the company. Meticulous and highly organized, he got things done. When he met with a subordinate, he pulled out a legal pad and wrote his or her name at the top. Can you do this or that? Can you do it by Wednesday? OK, fine. He'd file the memo. And people knew that on Wednesday, Brandt would call to check. Some called him The Prussian, but that was harsh.

At KING, he promoted cheerfulness. When he walked down the hall, he said hello to anyone he passed. They got another hello if he passed them later. A hello for every encounter. He expected others to do the same. Brandt took that cheerfulness into the community, joining the Washington Athletic Club, the Rotary, and many other groups. He made it a point to know and be known. He was a perfect counterpart to Henry Owen. Where Owen was subtle and indirect, Brandt was straightforward. While Owen served Warren Magnuson and other Democratic politicians, drank and played cards in private rooms at the Rainier Club, and drove his car like a crazy man, Brandt obeyed speed limits and served the Republican viewpoint. Like Owen, Brandt saw his outside activities as helpful for the station. Owen's work helped maintain a friendly set of politicians, especially those with links to the FCC. Owen was about influence; Brandt, about civic campaigns of no controversy. Brandt generally supported the Chamber of Commerce view in politics and civic causes. To Brandt, building Seattle and building King Broadcasting were virtually the same thing. If Seattle grew, so would KING.

He wanted KING-TV to be the country's finest station. Like Dorothy, he wanted KING to be a model of public service.

Brandt arrived during the summer of 1951, when the city was gripped by the biggest sports event in its history: the Gold Cup boat race. He immediately saw the race as a huge promotional opportunity for KING-TV. Throughout the city, anyone near Lake Washington could hear the gut-shaking roar of the thunderboats, the loudest, most powerful speed boats on water. The World Series of powerboat racing, the Gold Cup had never been held west of Detroit since its founding in 1904. Now Seattle had it, and the city unified around the sport. Children tried to get a piece of the thrill by making miniature boats out of shingles and dragging them behind their bikes. Seattle had always been known for its trees, rain, and Boeing. Now, thanks to the boat design of a Seattle man, the city had suddenly acquired a reputation for brains, daring, and technology, a combination that would help define the city. Along with Boeing's gleaming airliners, hydroplanes helped Seattle present a modern image to the nation. KING's role was significant. KING shaped the image of boat racing, promoting the drivers as heroes and the races as a test of man and machine. It validated racing by giving it abundant airtime. More important, it brought the race into people's homes, thus demonstrating the power and importance of television and of KING's role as a viewing point for civic events.

The boat credited with bringing this excitement to Seattle was *Slo-mo-shun IV*, financed and driven by car dealer Stan Sayres, designed by Ted Jones, and built by Anchor Jensen. Unlike the Detroit boats driven by bandleader Guy Lombardo and others, *Slo-mo* did not plow through the water on its keel but essentially flew over the water—hence, a hydroplane. A year earlier, the *Slo-mo* had set a world speed record of 160 mph—more than eighteen mph faster than the record then held by Britain's Sir Malcolm Campbell. Then Sayres took the boat to Detroit, easily won the Gold Cup, and exercised the winner's right to bring the following year's race to his hometown.

KING-TV, always on the lookout for local events that would attract viewers, could not have invented something as excitingly visual as a hydroplane race. First, the events took place on bright summer days, so lighting was no problem. The boats were easily followed, even with primitive TV cameras, because their propellers cast a huge spray in their wake—a rooster tail. The boats were noisy, so viewers at home had no trouble getting a feel for the sound of engines revving as the boats made turns and accelerated to full power, driven by unflinching men who charmed the city.

Even the problems were exciting. The event presented huge technical challenges: using several cameras, coordinating crews separated by a half-mile or more, and dealing with uncontrollable variables such as weather, crowds, and race delays. Lee Schulman organized KING's coverage as if it were a D-Day landing. Everyone was pulled into the weeks of planning and the week-long coverage of the arrival of the boats, interviews with drivers, the heats, and then the final race. Live shots were microwaved to Sacred Heart Villa atop a hill in Laurelhurst and from there to the station, where they were sent to the transmitter on Queen Anne Hill.

For two more years, KING would have the hydroplanes to itself. When KOMO went on the air in 1953, a fierce competition developed. Photographers would jostle one another, sometimes off the dock and into the lake. KING would sue to overturn KOMO's exclusive rights to a race at Lake Chelan in eastern Washington. KING would claim the longest, most powerful lens—a 36-incher, compared with the network's biggest, a 20-incher made by RCA. When KING announced a 100-incher, KOMO developed a 110-incher.

For that first race, KING's cameras were there for every scrap of news, not the least of which was the gathering of an incredibly large crowd, some 250,000 along the shores of Lake Washington—the equivalent of half of Seattle's population. In the third heat of the race, disaster struck. On the southwest turn, *The Quicksilver* blew up and rapidly sank, pulling driver Orth Mathiot and mechanic Thompson Whitaker down with it to their deaths. All that came to the surface were a few scraps of wood and a single shoe. KING-TV sports announcer Bill O'Mara followed his instincts. He instantly fell to his knees, crossed himself, and on camera and into his microphone said the Lord's Prayer for the lost men. Lee Schulman reacted to the tragedy with a dramatic sense of ceremony. He directed KING's camera to make a slow, dirge-like pan along the Mercer Island floating bridge. Even as O'Mara was saying "Thy will be done," the camera turned skyward. O'Mara was praying as the camera pointed to God. Schulman later chastised the Roman Catholic O'Mara for losing his objectivity, but O'Mara got a call from Dorothy. "You did what you felt," she told him, "and I approve of that."

In September 1951, KING launched its evening newscast starring a young man not yet thirty who had thick, curly black hair. Charles Herring started in broadcasting while a student at Whitman College in Walla Walla, where he worked for a radio station for thirty five cents an hour. He moved to Seattle in 1946 and worked for KJR radio as a newscaster. Schulman had used Herring earlier as host of a KING studio program, *March On,* a musical variety show featuring talent from local military bases.

The news department consisted of Herring and a cameraman, Ed Racine, who used a wind-up Bell & Howell camera with no sound (a $600 sound camera was judged too expensive for KING, which would always be tight with spending on equipment). Sound was recorded on separate machines. Each day they scanned the newspapers, looking for something they could shoot or read to viewers at home. They would also look at whatever film had been shipped by the networks. Sometimes, the filmed event was weeks old, but Herring used it anyway. The newscast started at 6:45 P.M. and ran fifteen minutes. For many months, Alka-Seltzer sponsored the entire program for about $3,000, a deal that required Herring to read their ads.

Herring had a deep, sonorous voice and a sober face. He gave newscasting the presentation that everyone expected, the look and sound of Edward R. Murrow. Murrow, the great CBS newsman who had grown up in Washington state, covered World War II for radio, and always opened his nightly radio reports with his famous line: "This . . . is London." The pause was a Murrow trademark. When television came along, viewers finally saw a dapper man who always lowered his face on camera, looking up at the viewer, squinting as cigarette smoke curled past his eyes. Murrow was tough and elegant. That was the look Herring wanted. Schulman wanted an interesting visual effect when Herring read the news, so he had the newsman stand in front of his desk, leaning on it as he smoked a pipe. Herring didn't feel right, so he was moved behind the desk, where he stayed. Schulman hated using cue cards because they gave the newscast a stagy look, so Herring, who was fortunately a quick study, had to memorize about three-quarters of his script. To remind himself when to look at the camera, Herring typed those on-cue portions single-spaced and the rest double-spaced. Herring looked and sounded like a serious newsman. Overnight he became one of the city's best-known journalists, the man in people's living rooms. The audience for TV news in Seattle would rapidly grow over the next three decades as newspaper circulation stagnated.

Herring's first big story was a huge fire in the logging town of Forks, 100 miles west of Seattle on the Olympic Peninsula. Racine and Herring rushed to the scene, driven by Fred Stimson in his Cadillac, a level of comfort rare in Seattle journalism. Herring quickly interviewed people with a sound recorder. Then the three raced back to Seattle and delivered the spectacular footage to be processed. After local broadcast, KING shipped its film to New York, where one of the networks gave the nation a look at the fire, one of the first reports on the Northwest ever carried by a TV network. In its first year of Dorothy Bullitt's ownership, KING was contributing to the network report, giving the nation a connection to the Northwest.

Herring had been at KING only a month when Lee Schulman asked him if he wanted to go on a Pentagon-sponsored tour of its air bases in Europe. The offer was breathtaking: ten time zones in thirty days. KING hired a freelance photographer who had a sound camera, and persuaded the National Bank of Commerce to sponsor Herring's fifteen-minute reports. The reports were primitive, to put it charitably. Herring and the photographer often had no time to leave the confines of the air bases and would wind up interviewing whomever they could find, looking especially for anyone with roots in the Northwest. It was a slow day in Athens, for example, when Herring put the camera on his English-speaking taxi driver:

"How many children do you have?" asked Herring.

"Three, plus my wife," said the driver.

"That makes five," said Herring.

"Five, that's right," said the driver.

Herring then visited a U.S. Air Base in Ankara, Turkey, and found an airman from Seattle. The airman was a supply officer, rarely got off the base, gave short answers, and made for a dull interview. After the airman said the base handled one flight a day, Herring, desperate to move the conversation, replied: "It must be interesting work here."

It was not spectacular television, but it demonstrated KING's willingness to try something, to take risks, to put its cameras where they hadn't gone before. Very few Americans traveled to Europe in those days, so there was Herring, the familiar face, introducing them to the capitals of Europe and asking the very questions they might ask. This was something no Seattle newspaper could provide: the sounds and images of an interesting place. The program's lack of polish was an asset—a hometown report of neighbors far away. Equally important, it was an early signal that KING's news department had expansive goals and a sense of showmanship, as well as a determination to go wherever a good story might be found.

The biggest story that year, however, wasn't very far away.

In late 1951, a young, ambitious politician named Al Rosellini had found a way to capture the public's attention. Rosellini, forty-one, a state senator from Seattle, had convinced the legislative leadership to let him form a special committee to investigate rumors of organized crime in Washington state. His model was the committee run by U.S. Senator Estes Kefauver. Its crime hearings had transfixed the nation with televised testimony by mobsters with twitching hands. Rosellini announced that his committee would hold hearings in several Washington cities, starting with Vancouver, and would invite politicians, criminals, and others to testify. When the hearings came to Tacoma, Lee Schulman saw a potential for good television, but he wasn't sure he could get the signal up to Seattle. He asked Rosellini for permission to televise it live. Sure, said Rosellini, figuring the exposure would do him good as he continued to look at a possible run for mayor of Seattle.

The hearings were popular beyond anything that Rosellini had expected. A parade of colorful witnesses took turns during the all-day sessions, broadcast in full by KING-TV. A minister testified of the widespread corruption in Tacoma, a network of payoffs to policemen and rings of prostitution operating with the tacit approval of city commissioners, one of whom was said to be a regular patron who got too drunk to walk. A tearful widow testified that her husband had killed himself after running up gambling debts he couldn't repay. Police spoke of prostitutes hiding in closets during vice raids. A politician angrily denied reports that he had taken money.

The most memorable testimony came from Amanda Truelove, a beefy woman who operated a reputed brothel called the Union Hotel. She said she had talked about her monthly payoffs to police in the presence of both the city safety commissioner and the city police chief.

"It's a damn lie!" shouted the police chief from the audience. "That's right," agreed the safety commissioner.

A taxi driver testified that he drove the safety commissioner to a liquor store and then to the Union Hotel, where the official stayed for several hours.

Each day, the audience at the Tacoma Armory grew, and so did the television audience. People gathered at the homes of friends and at sets in bars and department stores to follow the action. KING's Schulman not only telecast the hearings but helped direct them, counseling Rosellini on how to schedule speakers to maximize the drama. Sensational witnesses were held over a day to bring the audience back. When the widow started to reveal how her husband had committed suicide, Schulman told Rosellini the time had come to adjourn for the day—the politician and the TV man mutually exploiting each other to hold an audience. It was an early and clear example of how television could take over a political event. If the takeover distorted the event, no one seemed to care. It made for good entertainment.

The hearings ran for five days from 10:00 A.M. till 3:00 P.M. On the last day, Rosellini went out to dinner. To his surprise, people started coming up to him at the restaurant, having recognized him from the broadcasts. They said he had been terrific. Rosellini was astonished. Except for television, these people would not have known much about him. They might only have read about him in the paper. But because of television, they saw him in action and felt comfortable to judge him. They liked what they saw. They didn't need an editorial writer to tell them that Rosellini was a comer. Several people suggested that he run for governor, a thought that hadn't occurred to him until that night. Running for governor seemed like a good idea.

Albert Rosellini was the first Washington state politician whose career was boosted by television. He would never forget that. He saw TV as a powerful tool in politics. He would use TV again, but never with the manipulative skill of the destructive politician who was about to walk into King Broadcasting.

Chapter 8   The Good Fight

Senator Joseph McCarthy was the most feared man in America when he strode into the studios of King Broadcasting in October of 1952. The foe of communism was in a bad mood. He wanted to get through his speech promoting his pal, Senator Harry Cain, and attacking Cain's liberal Democratic challenger, Henry Jackson. He wanted to move on to Chicago. There, he planned to unleash a fierce attack on the Democratic presidential candidate, Adlai Stevenson, as an "associate of Communist fronters."

First, he had to appear on KING, Seattle's only TV station. Joe McCarthy had no reason to expect trouble. Journalists had been friendly, cooperative, or intimidated into spreading his alarms. But here, in a far corner of America, in an outpost removed from national politics, he was about to have one of the biggest surprises of his life. That confrontation would make headlines around the nation, just as Dorothy Bullitt's liberal son, Stimson Bullitt, was making headlines in Seattle facing a local strain of McCarthyism. In the hothouse of that year's politics, both mother and son were defined by how they handled the confrontations.

It was an ugly time, particularly so for Democrats, who were fiercely attacked by GOP candidates fueled by McCarthy's success. Two years earlier, McCarthy had leapt from his obscure position as a Republican backbencher when he announced in a speech in Wheeling, West Virginia, that he had a list in his hand of 205 known Communists currently working in the State Department. That those names were never released or subjected to measures of proof was not what politicians noticed; they saw instead the effect on a public deeply fearful of cracks in the foundation of American society. The United States was far and away the most powerful nation on earth; yet the public worried about spies in government, about soft bureaucrats who had "lost" China to communism, and about disloyal scientists who could leak atom-bomb secrets to the Russians. Soviet leader Joseph Stalin and the People's Army in Korea were evidence that the threat to American values was real.

Fighting communism was the dominant theme of nearly every campaign for federal office that year. It was not enough to declare one's abhorrence; the contest had escalated over who was toughest on the topic. Any politician with moderation in his views or past sympathies to left-leaning organizations was vulnerable to McCarthy's style of attack, and the zealotry was not limited to Republicans. Both parties invoked "Commie-hating" rhetoric because it worked. The Democrats, however, were the most vulnerable. They had held the White House as the tide of communism rose—and as Harry Truman's popularity shriveled. Now they had some explaining to do. Liberal Adlai Stevenson headed their ticket, while the Republicans had General Dwight Eisenhower, an amiable war hero of unquestioned loyalty.

Washington state's Democrats were particularly vulnerable to red baiting because of their long flirtation with Socialists, Utopians, and others with radical ideas. Scott Bullitt, Dorothy's late husband, had reached out to those elements when he tried to build the party. He was no Communist, but he did favor many liberal reforms. After Bullitt's death and during the Depression, the radicals took charge completely. The state Democratic Convention in 1936 had been dominated by members of the Washington Commonwealth Federation, who rewrote the party platform to favor nationalizing banks, utilities, and natural resources. The platform took no position on the reelection of the party leader, President Franklin Roosevelt. After World War II, Young Democrats at the University of Washington struggled with Communists who wanted to take over the organization. One of the moderates was Stimson Bullitt, a student at the law school. Stim's friends saw him as a likely candidate for public office, to pick up the torch left by his father.

Stimson Bullitt had been viewed as a possible candidate since his father's death in 1932. As a boy, "Stimmie" had been too young to understand his father's ideas, but he did admire his father's charm in dealing with people. Stimson had felt inadequate in his father's presence, a feeling worsened by a stutter that he never completely conquered.

Yet Stimson Bullitt had become a fascinating man. He was introspective, bookish, and given to quoting great philosophers. He was meticulous, driven, and above all self-controlled. He could be gregarious, warm, charming, energetic, and witty. He could also be darkly moody, relentlessly self-critical, and set apart. Even to those who knew him well, he seemed inscrutable. Like his father, Stimson had deep, piercing eyes that locked on to people. Many women found him attractive, and it didn't hurt that he was rich. Some people, however, were put off by his formal style, his dark clothing and scholarly air, and his courtly manners that seemed to come from another age.

During his boyhood, instead of letting him attend school in Seattle, Dorothy had sent him to the Kent School, in Connecticut, which he hated. The Episcopal Order of the Holy Cross monks who ran the boarding school fed the boys a cold soup of heavy bookwork, daily chapel (twice on Sundays), and lights out by nine o'clock. The religious training did not set; Stim would remain skeptical of organized religion. Yet the experience toughened him. Teased by his Kent classmates, Stim picked up boxing. Later, at Yale, he won the middleweight boxing championship. He showed an early interest in good works, helping to distribute blankets to the poor in New Haven. But at Yale, as at Kent, Stim felt unhappy and saw himself as a social misfit. And he *was* different. How many wealthy Yalies went home by boxcar? Stim was perhaps the only heir to a Highlands fortune who traveled with hobos.

Stim lived at his mother's house while attending law school, the first step in what he expected would be a career in politics. During those years and after, he filled his résumé: precinct committeeman; member of the King County Central Committee; delegate to party state conventions; member of a commission writing a charter for King County; vice president of the Seattle Urban League; fund-raiser for the Red Cross and the Episcopal Church; and a trustee for his father's old civic group, the Municipal League. There was more: charter member of the Americans for Democratic Action, a group of moderate liberals; regional vice president of the American Association for United Nations; and member of the Independent Veterans Committee for the Hoover Report. He kept in touch with others on their way up. He wrote to Henry Jackson in 1946, offering political help for the congressman from Everett, including an open invitation to his home whenever the congressman was staying overnight in Seattle. Jackson's notes quickly progressed from "Dear Stimson" to "Dear Stim," but Stim's letters remained "Dear Henry." Evidently the ever-formal Stim couldn't bear to address a congressman by his childhood nickname, Scoop, even though everyone else did. Stim was clearly determined to make connections and move up in the world, working hard as his father had when he moved to Seattle from Kentucky. Was he trying to follow his father? Finish the unfinished? Some of his friends thought so. Part of it, some thought, was to satisfy his mother, for though she hated personal involvement in politics, she was intensely ambitious for herself and her son. She expected greatness from him, perhaps a seat in the Senate. As for his own feelings, the task may have seemed more duty than pleasure. He was driven to do the noble thing.

In November 1946, he made his first appearance in the Seattle *Times* political columns in an article about King County Democrats looking for respectable young alternatives to leftists. The columnist singled out Stimson Bullitt, calling him an attractive new face, a moderate, a decorated veteran, and the son of a respected party leader. The party, said the article, was struggling "to rid itself of the taint of communism."

Stimson appeared again in the *Times* in 1948, with the announcement of his engagement to Carolyn Kizer of Spokane. She was the daughter of Benjamin Kizer, an attorney with national connections. A close associate of Harry Truman, Kizer had served as head of the United Nations relief operations in China after the war. He held leadership positions with the National Lawyers Guild as well as the American Civil Liberties Union, a group Joe McCarthy tarred as a pinko front. Ben Kizer was a skinny man with fiery red hair who walked at a fast pace through Spokane's downtown, swinging a cane mainly for dramatic effect.

Like many liberals of that time, Carolyn Kizer was a member of the Young Democrats. But none was quite like her. Most women arrived at the meetings in casual outfits, wearing bobby sox. Kizer made movie-star entrances. She came to those late-night policy discussions in drop-dead outfits purchased at the tony John Doyle Bishop shop. "Here I am, overdressed as usual," she'd say, while discussion of Spain and Franco came to a halt. She was a striking blonde with an overt sexuality—plus, she had brains. A graduate of Sarah Lawrence and a former fellow in Chinese government at Columbia University, she was now a teaching fellow at the University of Washington and also a writer and poet showing considerable promise.

Friends thought Stimson Bullitt and Carolyn Kizer shared nothing in common. She was gregarious to a fault; he was awkward in social settings. He hated making appearances; she loved center stage. Carolyn's mother was just glad that her daughter was finally settling down, a backhanded endorsement of their engagement. They were married in January 1948. Afterward, Ben Kizer bought stock in King Broadcasting, and Carolyn got a seat on King's governing board. It's possible that Dorothy Bullitt may have liked Carolyn Kizer at one time. To use as an engagement ring, she gave Stim, who had little money then, the diamond ring she had received from Scott. But Dorothy grew to dislike her daughter-in-law, and the feeling was reciprocated. Dorothy Bullitt could not abide Carolyn's blunt talk—Carolyn was famous for saying what she thought, often with witty, if stinging, results. Once, at a party, Carolyn showed up wearing a dress with a deep neckline. Henry Jackson, who was shy about women, couldn't help but take a peek. "Scoop, if you see anything down there, would you kill it?" she asked.

Stim tried to live frugally, never wore flashy clothes, and rode a bike to his small law office at the Fourth Avenue Building. Carolyn was a spender. Stim wanted them to live on acreage he had found on Squak Mountain, in a house designed by noted architect Paul Thiry. Carolyn refused. Somehow, they managed a life together. They quickly had Ashley, followed by Scott in 1949, and Jill in 1951. When Scott was born, a photo was sent to Henry Jackson. "One small Democrat wishes you luck!" said the note, signed by Stim and Carolyn Bullitt.

In June 1952, twenty years after the death of his father, Stimson Bullitt announced his candidacy for Congress. "His example made me a Democrat; my convictions have kept me one," Stim wrote in a letter to potential supporters. He offered ideas that blended liberalism with conservatism: economic security, interracial justice, and "better mileage for the public dollar." And, since this was Stimson Bullitt, there had to be a quotation from a historic thinker: "Clemenceau said that war was too important to be left to the generals. Congress has problems which are too important to be left to the Republicans."

His campaign slogan was: "You Can't Miss with Stimson Bullitt." The brochure showed a bull's-eye next to a photograph of Bullitt, steel-jawed, looking directly at the camera, a slight tightening of his lips at the edges, a semi-smile. Another photo showed him as a boxer, chin tucked down, gloves high. His literature made a bow to the fears of communism: "Overhead are dark and gloomy clouds. . . . We shall advance toward the goal shared by all Americans: Free Men in a Free World."

He was thirty-three years old, entering politics during a ground shift in the Democratic Party. After a period of maneuvering, Scoop Jackson emerged as the Democrat who would challenge Harry Cain, a former Tacoma mayor who had been caught up in a spectacularly embarrassing divorce, replete with his wife shrieking at him from the United States Senate visitors' gallery. Jackson had elbowed out Hugh B. Mitchell, one of few in the nation's history who served in the Senate and then in the House. Mitchell had been appointed to the Senate seat, was later defeated by Cain, and then was elected to the House. Mitchell wanted to try another run against Cain but instead decided to run for governor.

Campaigning for Mitchell's House seat, Stim was a terrible candidate. Awkward and uncomfortable with the easy greetings expected of a politician, he was also sensitive to brusque comments that came from shipyard workers and others he met on the campaign trail. In front of crowds, he spoke horribly, using archly formal cadences that sounded like Cicero in English. He sprinkled his talks with references to ancient Greece and Rome that went over most people's heads. He was running for the Roman Senate, not for Congress from Seattle. "My Children, hostages to Fortune" was a line from philosopher Francis Bacon that caused his own supporters to cringe. They tried to talk to him. Loosen up, they said. Speak to the people in ways they can understand. Appeal to their emotions. Irv Hoff, Senator Warren Magnuson's aide, told Stim's advisers that their candidate had to jerk a few tears. Cerebral Stim couldn't do it. He wanted to talk facts, marshal his arguments, and move people's minds. Magnuson, by contrast, moved hearts.

Stim had to get past J. Edmund Quigley in the primary. Quigley was a former chief deputy prosecutor and past president of the King County Young Men's Democratic Club, a group kept clean of leftists, he said. Quigley kept reminding people of Stim's membership in the Americans for Democratic Action (ADA)—"a gathering of Parlor Pinks," he said. He slammed Stimson Bullitt as "immature, inexperienced and absolutely inadequate to fill the position he seeks."

When Stim defeated Quigley, there was no traditional after-primary endorsement from his fellow Democrat. Quigley instead stayed rough, accusing Stim of having bought the election. That encouraged Quigley's supporters to vote for the Republican, a stuffy Chamber-of-Commerce type named Thomas Pelly, a friend of Patsy's husband, Joe Collins. (The Collinses handled their split loyalties by putting two bumperstickers on their car, one for Bullitt and one for Pelly.)

Pelly blistered Stim. His campaign kept trotting out the pink label, forcing Stim to defend his membership in the ADA. "Bullitt Asserts He's 'Proud' of Association with A.D.A.," said the *Times*. One night in Bremerton, a man in the audience finally had to know. He yelled out a question: Was Bullitt a Communist? It was a classic moment in politics, a moment when the audience turns its full attention to a candidate, who has one instant to define himself. Perhaps Scott Bullitt would have had a clever retort, used his wit as a foil, or charmed the questioner with his generous personality. Stim was not his father. He saw a principle, and he focused his answer on that. Stim replied that the question was a "disgrace and I am unwilling to submit to the humiliation of being asked whether I am a traitor to my country." The answer drew a burst of applause, even from Pelly, but it neither killed the issue nor turned it to Stim's advantage.

Irv Hoff, the Magnuson aide, was disappointed. The right thing to do would have been for Stim to step down and punch the guy, Hoff believed. Stim was a boxer. Why didn't he punch the guy?

Two days later, the *Times* noted that the Communist issue was still getting attention and quoted Stim making his defense to McCarthyism: "I am not now and never have been a Communist, and so I swore on oath according to law on becoming a candidate."

Then there was the labor problem. Stim angered union leaders by supporting a proposed King County charter that required job holders to pass a written examination. Stim had worked aggressively to woo labor leaders, but when he stubbornly refused to recant his support of the charter, they denied him the endorsement of the Washington State Federation of Labor.

Stim did have one advantage in this little war—a spy. Patsy Collins went with her husband to Pelly's meetings and later told Stim's campaign of the Republican's plans. Stim's campaign was often so quick to anticipate Pelly's moves that the Pelly crowd began to suspect a political double agent. Pelly refused to speak with Patsy again, which suited her fine. She had always thought him pompous.

Stim's masterstroke was a devastating TV ad that would ridicule Pelly and turn voters against him. The ad would run on the only station in town, KING. At that point, voters had seen little political advertising on television. Political ads usually ran in newspapers and radio, and especially in ethnic publications. The rare TV ads were somber, serious, and dull—a candidate sitting at a table speaking in a monotone to the camera, or taking dull questions and giving scripted, dull answers.

To date, the city's only memorable TV ad had been an unscheduled performance during a live interview with Hugh Mitchell in 1950. Mitchell's congressional campaign bought thirty minutes of time, which was a chore to fill because Mitchell was as stiff and awful on TV as Stim. One of Mitchell's advisers thought they could loosen up the candidate by surrounding him with family members, who also would be questioned. They made a perfect family: Mitchell, with his attractive and articulate wife, Kathryn; seven-year-old Bruce; and little four-year-old Lissa, who wore a fluffy dress with petticoats. The program went well until Lissa started telling something to her mother, who kept hushing her as Mitchell droned on about some issue. Naturally, the cameraman drew back to take in the action and showed Lissa squirming and scratching, her voice getting louder. Ancil Payne, Mitchell's congressional aide, was watching the scene at a tavern near KING's studio, feeling sick because he felt he was witnessing a disaster. Everyone in the bar had turned from their drinks to watch Lissa Mitchell's distress. Finally, Lissa got very loud: "Mommy, my bite itches!" and she flipped her petticoat up to scratch her fanny. The next day, everyone who saw Mitchell had the same smiling question: "How's Lissa's itch?" It was a campaign advertiser's dream. Viewers remembered Mitchell, and that counted at the polls. Mitchell won.

In 1952 Stim's campaign came up with an entirely new kind of television ad for Seattle. Jerry Hoeck's ad agency produced a withering short film, starring a puppet named Pom Telly, based on sketches secretly made of Pelly when he was riding the ferry. The commercial painted Pelly as just a puppet of the Chamber of Commerce. It was an excellent ad: memorable, biting, and funny. Nothing like it had ever been shown in Seattle.

The ads ran briefly on KING but were halted abruptly—killed, Hoeck was told, by Dorothy Bullitt herself. He never got the full story. The word went through KING that Mrs. Bullitt had found them too rough, at least for a member of her family. She didn't like that sort of politics, the nasty attack-style that had bruised her husband in his campaigns.

Of course, Senator Joseph McCarthy had no such standards. He was the roughest politician in America. He played for keeps. He destroyed reputations and careers. He was ruthless. A heavy drinker, he ate a cube of butter daily to soothe an ulcer burn.

On the day he arrived in Seattle in October 1952, McCarthy was near the zenith of his powers. Eisenhower wouldn't touch him, for fear of becoming a target. Nor would Truman.

Delayed by fog, McCarthy arrived hours late in Seattle for an after-dinner speech to the Washington State Press Club. Six hundred people were at the Press Club banquet, liquored and loud, not in the mood for a serious speech. Unbeknownst to McCarthy, the event was a political roast, aiming to spoof candidates, not to listen to them. Members acted in skits representing various politicians, including one described as "Ada Stimmie Bullitt" . . . "the simple barefoot little lass from The Highlands." Her opponent was "Tomasina Pelly," a prim young thing, frightened of left-wingers and pinks.

A debate was scheduled between Vic Meyers, a candidate for lieutenant governor, and McCarthy. Meyers, a political clown who had once campaigned for Seattle mayor dressed as Mahatma Gandhi leading a goat, told jokes. McCarthy tried to play it straight. He launched into his crusade but was interrupted by hecklers.

"Name a Commie, Joe!" someone yelled.

"Tell us about General Marshall, Joe!" yelled another, referring to George Marshall, whom McCarthy had attacked. "Pour it on, Joe!"

"I didn't come 2,300 miles to be a funnyman," McCarthy snapped.

Meyers shot back: "I didn't walk eight blocks to be serious."

McCarthy then left for KING, where he was scheduled to make a speech praising Cain and denouncing Henry Jackson. Senator Warren Magnuson would follow McCarthy to defend Jackson, an effort at balance that Dorothy Bullitt had required. The Cain campaign had paid $345 for fifteen minutes of prime time, a preemption of *The Sportsmen's Club*.

Dick Riddell, KING's lawyer and Stimson Bullitt's friend, was at home mixing a drink when the telephone rang.

"Dick, you better get down to the studio," said Henry Owen, president of King Broadcasting. "I smell trouble." Riddell hurriedly put on his jacket and walked out of the house in his slippers. He got there just before McCarthy.

McCarthy arrived ten minutes before air time. With him were Cain, Senator Bob Bartlee of Alaska, and Al Canwell, the red baiting former legislator who had gone Communist-hunting at the University of Washington and was now a candidate for Congress. When McCarthy walked in, he was told by Cain campaign aides that King Broadcasting objected to his script. Riddell came over to explain that some phrases were potentially libelous and had to be substantiated, deleted, or changed. Someone gave McCarthy a copy of a slightly amended script, deleting a section that named two aides to columnist Drew Pearson as Communists. Riddell had hardly gotten through his explanation when McCarthy blurted out that he would not be censored, that his appearance was paid political time.

Riddell, at age thirty-five, had no affection for McCarthy, whom he viewed as vicious and despicable. Riddell believed that McCarthy had ruined good people's reputations and that the man didn't care if there were evidence to sustain his allegations. The allegations were all that counted. Riddell wasn't going to back down. He told McCarthy: Either the script is changed, or you don't go on the air.

The clock was moving to air time. Lee Schulman hastily prepared a back-up program in case the McCarthy appearance was canceled. McCarthy insisted that, as a candidate, he could say what he wanted. You're a candidate in Wisconsin; our signal doesn't go that far, Riddell replied. McCarthy picked up the amended script and started scribbling in changes. The changes, said Riddell, were just as bad as the original.

McCarthy, the man feared by presidents, leveled his eyes at the young lawyer and challenged him: Either you put me on, or I'm going to file a complaint with the FCC and get your license revoked. Riddell knew the threat was credible. The FCC did have the power to yank a station owner's license. Without a license, all the cameras, transmitters, studios, and the other hardware of broadcasting were so much junk. The license was everything. Dorothy Bullitt's business was at stake, but there was no time for Riddell to call her and confer. He just did what he believed was right. Riddell told McCarthy that if he tried to use the offending words, his sound would be cut off. His mouth would move, but there would be no audio.

About this time, Magnuson walked in and quickly sized up the situation. McCarthy and Magnuson, although poles apart politically, were social friends who went to the racetrack together. "Maggie," as friends called him, always had a charitable view of people, including McCarthy. "He's a guy off on the wrong foot, but you still gotta like the guy," he told people.

McCarthy admonished his friend to remember what they were seeing because they would all be witnesses later, but Magnuson stayed out of the tiff. The clock reached 8:45 P.M. A statement was read over the air that McCarthy would not appear. Meanwhile, at home watching TV, Dorothy Bullitt had fully anticipated something like this. When, instead of McCarthy, her station carried a musician singing "Nobody Knows the Trouble I've Seen," Dorothy Bullitt broke out laughing.

At KING, McCarthy wanted the nation's attention. "Where's a telephone? I'm going to call the press," McCarthy said. Somebody in Cain's group had already dialed the *Post-Intelligencer's* city desk. McCarthy picked up the phone and began talking about how he had been censored. Otto Brandt, KING's general manager, called the Associated Press, the United Press International, and the Seattle *Times* to tell them what had actually happened. McCarthy and KING officials then began to argue over whether the station or McCarthy had canceled his speech. Finally, McCarthy left.

The story made headlines around the nation. "TV BLACKOUT FOR McCARTHY" blared the Boston *Evening Globe* in three-inch-high headlines. Hearst's International News Service reported that the talk was canceled because McCarthy "refused to let the station censor his address."

George Kinnear, a leader of the Republican Party in King County, wrote a letter to the *P-I* calling the incident a "shocking abuse of power—typical of the present Democratic leadership. KING-TV is controlled by a prominent Democrat, financial supporter, and friend of a number of Democratic officeholders." Senator Cain issued a statement denouncing "one of the most outrageous examples of censorship" he had ever seen. Within forty-eight hours, KING received 150 letters, about equally split over what KING had done. More letters came in from all over the country. No doubt Brandt was particularly pleased by the letter from a Mrs. Forsyth of Seattle: "We have had our TV set about two months and think KING-TV is wonderful."

McCarthy went back to Washington and announced that his subcommittee of the Senate Committee on Government Operations would take a look at the Federal Communications Commission. He said he had received complaints from senators of waste and incompetence at the agency and of favoritism in granting licenses. He declined to name the senators. He filed a complaint with the FCC regarding KING but did not pursue it aggressively, perhaps out of deference to his buddy Magnuson, who would have been forced to testify in a case involving his own friend, Dorothy Bullitt. At any rate, the FCC dismissed the complaint without even a formal investigation. It was hard to argue that KING's signal reached Wisconsin and played any role in McCarthy's campaign.

Stimson Bullitt did not go to Washington, D.C. He was beaten by Tom Pelly, who got 121,926 votes to Stim's 114,617 votes. Stim prepared for a second try in 1954, but that could have meant facing Hugh Mitchell, who had lost the governor's race and now was being urged by union leaders to run for Congress. Mitchell didn't want to run. He advised Stim to make peace with labor leaders and support the Wagner Act, a union-organizing bill. Stim refused on principle. Figuring Stim would lose to Pelly again without strong union support, Mitchell agreed to run.

By 1954, Stim and Carolyn had already split in what became a bitter divorce. Stim wanted custody of the children and all of Carolyn's interest in King Broadcasting stock. He got the stock but shared custody. Carolyn's parents donated $50 to Mitchell's primary campaign, responding to an appeal that Stim would have virtually unlimited funds. Mitchell knocked Stim out of the primary but lost to Pelly in the general election.

In November 1954, five months after his divorce from Carolyn was final, Stim married an attractive Phi Beta Kappa Radcliffe graduate, Katharine "Kay" Squire Muller, who had worked as office manager for the campaign. The two had been introduced by a mutual friend, and their first date included an ADA meeting followed by dinner. Just as his father had made two bids for office and then quit, Stim decided it was time to return to the practice of law. He lowered his public profile.

His mother, however, was raising hers.

She had entered a battle of her own, one that in time would vastly expand her wealth and would make her a true power in the Northwest. To win, Dorothy Bullitt had to outfox one of the biggest corporations in America.

Dorothy Bullitt was seated in a hearing room in Washington, D.C., when a sense of alarm came over her. The attorneys from the other side were wheeling in boxes full of documents.

"What's that?" she asked.

"It's all Hearst," someone told her.

Dorothy knew her weak point had been exposed. She would have to defend her partnership with the controversial Hearst Corporation.

Dorothy Bullitt listened as an examiner for the FCC gathered testimony on applications for a new license to be awarded in Portland, Oregon's largest city. It was 1953 and Dorothy Bullitt was going for her second TV license. The FCC's four-year freeze on new licenses had ended a year earlier. An avalanche of new stations had dramatically scrambled the competitive landscape.

In Seattle, King Broadcasting's television monopoly was over.

The imminent arrival of new stations would hurt KING in two ways. KING could no longer take its pick of the offerings by all four networks (CBS, NBC, ABC, and DuMont), but only what was offered by those networks that stayed with KING. And KING lost its claim on every dollar spent on TV advertising. KING now had to hustle for those dollars. In the first year after the freeze, King Broadcasting's net profits would drop 71 percent to $86,850.

The second TV station in Seattle was KOMO, which the Fishers had expected to launch in 1948 or soon thereafter, only to see their application delayed by a legal challenge, the freeze, and other red tape. Some at KOMO wondered if Dorothy Bullitt had used political muscle to hold off the Fishers, but no one had proof. It was no surprise, then, that NBC announced it would jump to KOMO-TV as the station prepared for its first broadcast. The Fishers' long association with NBC, established in radio in 1926, had made that certain. CBS, the self-described "Tiffany Network" with an unmatched stable of stars, also left KING to join another station launched that year—KTNT-TV (later KSTW) of Tacoma, owned by the Tacoma *News Tribune*. King Broadcasting kept two network affiliations, but both were weak—DuMont, long hampered by its small base of affiliates; and ABC, a perennially distant third, characterized at the time as a shabby organization run by fast-talkers who seemed to try anything to attract an audience. The networks would go through a shakeout over the next several years. ABC merged with United Paramount Theaters in 1953 and got its first big hit, *Disneyland*, the following year. In addition, it gained revenue after the DuMont network collapsed in 1955. A third Seattle TV station, KIRO, went on the air in 1958 and squabbled in court with KTNT for the CBS affiliation. The two stations shared the affiliation until 1962, when KIRO got an exclusive and KTNT became an independent. (The University of Washington's affiliate, KCTS-TV, had gone on the air as Seattle's fourth station in December 1954, assisted by a gift of used cameras, projectors, a transmitter, and other equipment worth $180,000 from Dorothy Bullitt. Dorothy Bullitt was deservedly praised for her support of educational television. The gift served a business purpose as well: it kept a commercial station from getting Channel 9.)

KOMO came on strong from its first days of operation in December 1953, helped by the Fishers' willingness to spend heavily. Its engineers had been preparing themselves for years, taking technical courses at the University of Washington and practicing closed-circuit telecasting, using windows at department stores as studios. The Fishers hired a talented newsman from the Seattle *Times,* Herb Robinson, to launch their news department. W. W. "Bill" Warren, the general manager of the station, told Robinson he wanted KOMO-TV news to be absolutely fair, without taking sides. He pointed to a radio in his office.

"People look at one of those and respect it as a device to transmit information and fact," said Warren, a descendant of the Fishers who had settled in Seattle in 1906. "We've tried hard to get people to trust what they hear from KOMO. We want them to feel the same way about KOMO television."

Within five years, the listener base for KOMO's main newscast caught up with KING and, with some exceptions, the two stations would slug it out for decades for first place in the ratings. KOMO always provided a solid, respectable newscast, but the two stations reflected the styles of their owners. People in politics and culture talked about KING; they rarely talked about KOMO. KOMO was colorless and sober, uninterested in changing the world. KING was eccentric, self-conscious, and exciting. Both stations found their audiences and made a pile of money for their owners.

By 1954, television had become a significant presence in Seattle. More than 250,000 homes in the Seattle metropolitan area had a TV set, a figure that closely rivaled the circulation of either the *P-I* or the *Times*. Nationally, the public spent more time watching TV than doing anything else except sleeping or working.

In Seattle, viewers could buy a Westinghouse mahogany TV equipped with a "5-stage electronic clarifyer" for $160 and take their pick from Channels 4, 5, and 11. Operating from the former furniture store on Aurora Avenue, KING-TV broadcast a test pattern from 9:10 A.M. until 9:30 A.M., followed by an assortment of movies and variety shows, including *King's Queen* (tips for homemakers), a fifteen-minute local newscast, the *Lone Ranger* at 7:00 P.M., and a variety of other evening programs, such as *Liberace, Four Star Playhouse,* a 10:00 P.M. newscast of fifteen-minutes, and another movie.

Television was quickly eclipsing radio, but the newspapers still carried detailed radio program listings that took up as much space as the daily TV listings. In a few years, radio listings would shrink as TV listings expanded.

Television had become an impressive industry, but Dorothy Bullitt worried that broadcasting remained volatile. Having suffered through the Depression, she feared that she alone did not have the money to carry KING, which had yet to show a significant profit. In the early years, after buying KRSC, she had steadily sold much of her real estate holdings, even jewelry, to keep her broadcast company afloat. The station drew on a $500,000 line of credit she had established. The engineers always wanted something new—a camera, parts for the transmitter, a truck.

At the end of 1950, the company turned its first profit, $72,000, and the next year would show even bigger profits, but Dorothy's loans to the company totaled $360,000 and she remained fearful that a sudden turn could wipe her out. When the station needed a new tower and transmitter—huge costs—she went to Saul Haas and the Fishers, whom she knew wanted to get into TV, offering each a 25 percent share in the station. She couldn't have chosen greater opposites as potential partners. The Fishers were sober, righteous people, while Haas was a heavy drinker who made wobbly entrances into business meetings. A former reporter and Democratic Party activist, Haas became owner of powerful KIRO radio with the help of his close friend, Warren Magnuson, whom he later rewarded with stock in his company that owned the station. Haas hated the outdoors but still managed to go fishing regularly with his pal, Supreme Court Justice William O. Douglas. Booze never kept Haas from making smart moves. "Saul Haas is smarter drunk than most people sober," said prominent real-estate developer Henry Broderick.

Years earlier, Dorothy had sought Haas and the Fishers as partners to help her buy KRSC. Once again, they turned her down. They would wait and get their TV licenses from the government. Dorothy considered selling, either the AM station or the TV station. She got some offers, but they were all too low. Then, in December of 1950, a big-money player came calling. Representatives of Hearst's radio division arrived with an offer to buy her out.

Dorothy recoiled at the idea of dealing with Hearst. She had grown up believing that William Randolph Hearst was a terrible person, a devil, really—a child's view from hearing her parents' Republican friends denounce Hearst as a reckless rouser of the working class. She found the idea of doing business with his company distasteful.

But Tom Brooks, the negotiator sent by the Hearst Corporation, was a charmer. In later interviews, Dorothy would only refer to him as Mr. Brooks, as a sign of respect, but she was fond of him. He was easy to talk to, he knew broadcasting, and Dorothy was a station owner in trouble. She found herself talking more than she had expected and she offered to sell a minority interest. No, said Hearst, which had a policy of buying all, never a piece, of a company. They had a rule against partial ownership, said the Hearst negotiator. He nonetheless invited her to New York to meet with other Hearst people, who looked over her books. Nothing happened, and Dorothy went home. Then Brooks called.

"I think they're going to break their rule," he said.

Hearst sent a team to Seattle to study King Broadcasting. They struck a deal in June of 1951 in which Dorothy sold Hearst 25 percent of King Broadcasting's stock for $375,000. Brooks and Dorothy talked about how Hearst could help KING by promoting the station through its Seattle *Post-Intelligencer* and by helping to sell advertising in New York. Hearst placed two people on King Broadcasting's board: Paul Ashley, the *P-I's* lawyer and a friend of Dorothy's; and a representative from Hearst headquarters. (It upset the *P-I* publisher that he didn't get one of the seats.) As part of the deal, KING launched some shows with *P-I* talent. The popular sportswriter Royal Brougham did an interview show with athletes. Brougham was a lovable personality but an awful TV host. He was always disorganized. He tried to overcome this by telling the athletes in advance what their answers should be. Before air time, Brougham would dash nervously around the studio. The director told camera operators to follow him. Wherever he was at air time was where the show began.

When the FCC ended the freeze on new licenses in 1952, Hearst encouraged Dorothy to go for one of the new licenses in Portland. Having changed his mind on the wisdom of television, Andy Haley especially urged her. There's little to lose and much to win, he argued. Dorothy didn't always take his advice, but this time she did.

One of her first steps after applying for the TV license was to buy KGW radio from the *Oregonian* newspaper, reportedly for $500,000. KGW was one of the nation's oldest radio stations, home of the famed *Hoot Owls* variety show. Owning KGW established King Broadcasting as a local presence for the TV application process. Dorothy thought it would also be a good idea to include local partners in both the radio purchase and the TV application, not for their money but for their prestige and history of civic involvement. That might strengthen King Broadcasting's case with the FCC, which tended to favor applicants with local ties and a commitment to public service.

Using the help of a friend who ran the Merrill Lynch office in Seattle, Dorothy got some names of prominent business people in Portland. She met there with five men—Prescott Cookingham, an attorney with Cookingham and Hanley; Henry Kuckenberg, owner of Kuckenberg Construction Company; Calder McCall, president of McCall Oil Company; Paul Murphy, president of Gas Heat, Oregon Iron and Steel, and other companies; and Gordon Orput, Oregon state general agent of New England Mutual Life Insurance Company.

The five agreed to join the partnership on one condition: if Dorothy Bullitt ever sold, they would get the same share price as she did. Dorothy knew that controlling shareholders typically got a premium, but she agreed, if they would meet a condition of hers: that if she decided to sell, they must sell, too. She explained that if she ever wanted to sell, it would be more attractive to a buyer if 100 percent of the company were available.

The five men balked. They weren't sure about that provision.

"OK. I'll go back to Seattle," she said. It may have been a bluff. But they quickly agreed and became 25-percent stockholders in North Pacific Television, Inc., which would be controlled by King Broadcasting Company.

The FCC required an astonishing amount of paperwork for the license application: multiple copies, financial disclosures, statements of programming philosophy, services that would be provided. It went on and on. Dorothy worked nights and weekends on the paperwork. Andy Haley's son and daughter collated and stacked copies of statements by people interviewed on behalf of King Broadcasting's application.

King Broadcasting faced three competitors: two Portland groups who had no broadcast TV experience; and Westinghouse, a large, diversified corporation with a famous name, a group of TV stations, and political clout.

When Dorothy Bullitt entered the hearing room in Washington, D.C., an almost audible sigh of relief arose from her rivals. She didn't look like much trouble and was accompanied by her close friend Gloria

Chandler, who was wearing a hat that looked like a flowerpot about to fall off. One of the Portland applicants, Tom Kerr, turned to a friend and said: "If we can't win out over those old ladies, we might as well get out of the business."

Westinghouse was considered the front runner, and Dorothy was pleased that it led off the presentations. That gave Andy Haley a chance to take notes and prepare a strategy for dealing with Westinghouse's arguments. Early on, it was clear that Westinghouse had made one blunder. Its lead lawyer was an aggressive criminal-defense specialist from a big New York law firm whose style was too coarse and hostile for the less formal process run by a hearing examiner. When a witness said something he wanted to challenge, he made exaggerated faces of doubt. Dorothy assumed the examiner was turned off by the lawyer's personality, since even his own colleagues shunned him during breaks. More important, he didn't seem to know the FCC rules, and it showed.

Another mistake was to put an uncoached Westinghouse executive on the stand to testify. Why does Westinghouse want to be in broadcasting? he was asked. The proper answer, even if insincere, would have been: to offer public service and public education. Broadcasting was a source of potentially huge profits, but the airwaves were public property, and license applicants had to bow to FCC sensitivities.

The executive gave exactly the wrong answer: Westinghouse saw broadcasting as a means of promoting sales of its toasters, iceboxes, and other products. He said nothing about promoting the community and covering news. Score one for King Broadcasting. The executive also spoke at length regarding Westinghouse's contributions to the war effort, but that was irrelevant to the issue of how he would operate the station. He was also asked what Westinghouse had done to acquaint itself with the needs of the Portland community. He replied that they had assembled various leaders of institutions at a luncheon and had promised to serve them.

Haley loved that answer. By contrast, on his initiative, King Broadcasting had formally interviewed business leaders, mayors, farmers, residents of small towns, and many others to get specifics on the problems they faced. Farmers spoke at length of flooding problems, for example. King Broadcasting had a plan for comprehensive coverage of those issues.

Dorothy was impressed by one thing Westinghouse had done. All of its papers were handsomely bound in individual volumes. To save money, King Broadcasting had used a cheap print shop. When its documents arrived and the boxes were opened, out came a nauseating ammonia smell that filled the room. Dorothy was horrified, but she could do nothing about it. FCC rules would not allow an applicant to change paperwork once the process had started. Dorothy asked the examiner if King Broadcasting could reimburse the FCC for reprinting. Not necessary, said the examiner. If the windows are opened, we can deal with bigger issues.

Dorothy's Portland partners had been given briefing books on what they should know and say in Washington, D.C. When partner Paul Murphy was put on the stand, however, he was hit by a zinger from the Westinghouse lawyer, who said disarmingly to Murphy: "You must be a capable businessman, given your successes and many assets."

"Yes," clucked Murphy.

"As a capable businessman, you must have read and understood many contracts in your career."

"Yes," said Murphy, but with a little less enthusiasm as he sensed a trap being set.

"As a businessman, you must have read your contract with King Broadcasting, then. Right?"

"Yes," said Murphy, sensing trouble.

"Then you realize that if you are to get the same price as Mrs. Bullitt would be paid in a sale, you also realize she could sell the whole thing to her son for thirty-five cents a share and that's all you get," said the lawyer. "You realize that?"

Murphy took only a moment to digest the question. Then his face went red. The Westinghouse lawyer was right. Dorothy Bullitt was in a position to make him the biggest fool in the Rose City, not that she had even conceived of that, as she told him later. But Paul Murphy felt humiliated. In his view, Dorothy had been slick with him. He and the other partners never felt the same about her after that. It was unfriendly from then on.

But the issue of Dorothy's contracts with her Portland partners was a sideshow, a lawyer having sport with a businessman. The real trouble with Westinghouse was contained in those boxes wheeled into the hearing room. Hearst? It didn't take long to figure out Westinghouse's aim. Hearst's reputation had shifted from populism to something less desirable. It was clear Westinghouse would try to pin Hearst's sins on King Broadcasting. Dorothy talked it over with Stimson, and she decided to see if Hearst would allow King Broadcasting to buy back its stock.

She called Hearst headquarters in New York.

"There's a whole stack of files on Hearst operations," she said. "I think it's going to hurt one or both of us. Would you consider selling back to us?"

Yes, said Hearst, to her relief.

Dorothy and Stim took the train to New York. Hearst agreed to sell for $450,000—a $75,000 profit, a reasonable amount, although no one took time to do a valuation of the company. Dorothy spent about half an hour doing the deal at Hearst headquarters. Negotiations went quickly, partly because Hearst had an application of its own in another bigger city. It couldn't afford a problem with the Portland application damaging its chances in a more lucrative market. Hearst's exit from King Broadcasting took less than three days.

Now King Broadcasting had a new problem. Changing the ownership group in the middle of an application was a risky step, one that might lead to KING's being disqualified as an applicant. Andy Haley knew the risk.

"She may tell you to take your application and go home," Haley said of the hearing examiner.

On a Friday, following lunch, Andy made the announcement.

The Westinghouse lawyer nearly choked with indignation. "This is outrageous," he sputtered. "This changes the whole situation of the case."

The examiner wouldn't decide quickly. She would think it over during the weekend. On Monday, she announced that King Broadcasting, minus Hearst, was still in the running. Westinghouse took its "Hearst" boxes away.

Dorothy got her license. The little old ladies had clobbered the opposition. "Dorothy Bullitt shoved our head into a pencil sharpener and ground it to a point," one of the defeated applicants later told a friend at KING.

Dorothy and Henry Owen practically lived in Portland for the next six months, making sure the TV operation got off smoothly. Several managers and engineers from KING were moved down to KGW, which went on the air in 1956. Because of sizeable start-up costs, the station did not realize a profit until 1965.

In 1957 another station practically fell into Dorothy's lap. Louis Wasmer, who owned KREM-TV, FM and AM in Spokane, Washington, the state's second largest city, wanted to sell. Like many broadcast pioneers, Wasmer was a character. He collected Cadillacs and Lincolns but drove around in a modest car—a VW bug at one point. He acted like a small-town tycoon and sprinkled his conversations with coarse references. Somehow, he saw Dorothy Bullitt as a friend and came to her with an offer to sell his stations in Spokane. She bought him out for $2 million. KREM did not make a profit until after 1969.

Dorothy Bullitt now had a three-station company. Despite this achievement, some still dismissed her position as the result of inherited money and luck. But her next move ended that perception forever, establishing the hallmarks of a business style built on shrewdness and warm personal relations.

Dorothy Bullitt had made no secret of her unhappiness at having lost NBC. Its emphasis on integrity, its commitment to news and technical excellence, and its strong base of affiliates had long made it her favorite network. The oldest network, NBC, ran second to CBS in the ratings but was usually more innovative, with such programs as *Meet the Press* (1947), *Today* (1952), and network specials, then called "spectaculars." Dorothy wanted NBC back. Helped by Otto Brandt's contact with NBC, she went to work on "the General," David Sarnoff, head of RCA, owner of NBC, to try to drive a wedge between him and the Fishers. The Fishers were well aware of the trouble Dorothy Bullitt could cause. In 1949 she had tried to lure ABC away from the Fishers' KJR radio to her AM station. ABC told her that KING's AM signal was too weak.

For this run at NBC, nobody at King Broadcasting worked as hard as Dorothy Bullitt, then approaching age sixty-five. She did her homework. To prepare herself for every meeting with an NBC official, she compiled a set of index cards on Sarnoff and his top aides, listing their personal and professional interests, including their favorite drinks. She made many tiring trips to New York City, NBC's headquarters, and reworked her schedule elsewhere so she could bump into NBC officials at industry meetings. When she heard Sarnoff was taking a train trip from Washington, D.C., to New York City, she booked a seat where she would have a "chance" encounter and an opportunity to talk with him for hours. When she heard that Sarnoff was visiting the Cascade Mountains and was not being hosted by his old friend, O. D. Fisher, she arranged a dinner for the General in her home. Her pitch: that KING would promote NBC in Seattle more aggressively than KOMO did. To sweeten the deal, she offered NBC affiliations with Seattle and Portland, the Northwest's two largest cities—a deal the Fishers couldn't touch. (She hadn't yet bought KREM in Spokane.) Looking for allies, she enlisted Senator Magnuson to gather news on the talk about her inside NBC.

The result made headlines: In October 1958, Don Mercer, NBC's head of affiliate relations, flew out to Seattle and met with Bill Warren of KOMO. The people at KING heard that Mercer spoke briefly with Warren at the airport, gave him the news, and took the next flight back to New York. An announcement went out from NBC headquarters: NBC was dropping KOMO and switching to KING. It also switched its Portland affiliation to King Broadcasting's KGW. Warren, who rarely spoke to the press, decided to talk. His rage, embarrassment, and shock came through clearly. The Fishers had abruptly lost the network they had carried for decades, beginning in radio.

"NBC's announcement that it will change its affiliation in Seattle came as a complete surprise to us," he said. Then he referred to the Fisher-NBC relationship that had begun in radio's early days: "We do not know what political, economic or ulterior motives were brought to bear on NBC to destroy thirty-two years of successful partnership."

What was Warren hinting at by his reference to "political" motives? Was he suggesting that Senator Magnuson had pressured NBC to switch to the station owned by Scott Bullitt's widow? Had Andy Haley pulled a string in Washington, D.C.? Warren would not elaborate. Part of Dorothy Bullitt's achievement was in leaving no public evidence of what she had done. Years later, Dorothy insisted it had been very simple. "KOMO had been careless," she said. When problems arose in NBC's mind, the Fishers didn't take care of them. "So we walked in."

Leonard Goldenson, ABC's president, later said it helped Dorothy Bullitt that Otto Brandt was close to Robert Kintner, a former ABC executive who went to NBC. Kintner had a score to settle because he had been fired from ABC, said Goldenson.

The Fishers had definite rules about how business should be conducted and, in their minds, Dorothy Bullitt didn't measure up. Maybe some of it had to do with the fact that she was a woman, and a businesswoman who could play hardball, but they never forgave her for that public humiliation. Bill Warren would walk right by King Broadcasting executives at affiliate meetings. Other KOMO people would say hello to KING station counterparts, but not Warren. If he met a King Broadcasting person at a party, he was brusque; KING remained the enemy.

After that, few would continue to view Dorothy Bullitt as that harmless lady in hat and gloves. She was a tough competitor, who grabbed business from others when it suited her interests. She moved against whomever she viewed as a threat or troublesome. When a *P-I* reporter wrote articles she didn't like, she went straight to Hearst in New York and asked that he be reassigned. Inside King Broadcasting, she typically had Henry Owen handle the messy business of firing people. Nobody had absolute job security. Even cousin Logan Bullitt was expendable. When he failed to measure up, his supervisor told him he was out. By working through others and keeping herself out of confrontations, she protected both her image and her company.

In only two years, Dorothy Bullitt had evolved from a single operator to owner of three growing broadcast operations in the three largest cities in the Northwest—five radio stations and three TV stations, marketed under the name Crown Stations. By December 1958, she had made important strategic moves and had dramatically transformed herself into the leading broadcaster in the Northwest. Hers was the only media organization whose signal gave it influence in the three principal Northwest states. (Spokane's station carried into Idaho.) She was a regional force, and uniquely so because she was a woman. She had no idea how powerful television was about to become, with its phenomenal ability to focus public attention on issues and personalities, to swing elections, to intimidate politicians, and to sway people at a deep emotional level.

More than 87 percent of American households owned a television, watching an average of five hours per day. Overnight, TV could create villains and heroes for a national audience. It could also enlighten and uplift people as no other invention in history. With her own Northwest broadcast network, Dorothy Bullitt effectively had that power during a period of political, cultural, and economic transformation of the region. Seattle was about to make a major leap. In the next fifteen years, there would be new shopping malls and freeways, a world's fair to attract presidents and world leaders, explosive growth at the University of Washington, and a budding sense that Seattle, a little less anxious to prove itself to outsiders, had something precious to protect. Seattle, in its hubris, was about to start thinking of itself as better than the rest of the nation.

Dorothy Bullitt, as empress of a Northwest media empire, had the instrument to put her stamp on a burgeoning city and region. Now what would she do with it?

By law, the holder of a broadcast license must "serve the public interest." Dorothy Bullitt took that obligation seriously. As King Broadcasting's controlling shareholder, she did not issue detailed instructions as to what should be put on the air but knew its choices were important. Otherwise, a station was just a conduit for network programs. She saw that there were certain areas where KING could make a difference: in children's programs, public affairs, and news. She hired spirited people and encouraged them to do something useful. KING could be a force for encouraging the better elements in society. She stood as a role model, serving on the boards of hospitals, a university, and other institutions. She told people she wanted King Broadcasting to be more like the New York *Times* than the sensationalist New York *Mirror.* That may have been her greatest ambition for King Broadcasting.

In its early days, television was not the sort of thing that the "right people" watched, or at least admitted to. Not many at the University of Washington would speak approvingly of television, even of Dorothy Bullitt's station. It was something for the masses, not for the learned or the serious. When KING newsman Charles Herring interviewed Boeing Chairman William Allen in the early 1950s, Allen had no interest in when the report would be broadcast. "I don't have a television," Allen said, looking down at Herring over a long, thin nose, not even trying to conceal his disdain for the new medium.

Allen saw no need for television. Had he been decades younger, he might have thought otherwise. Television was an immediate hit with children. KING gave Seattle's children something to do on a rainy day

—to watch an afternoon show called *Sheriff Tex and Safety Junction* featuring puppets, rope tricks, old movies, and advice from Tex (in real life, Jim Lewis). Sheriff Tex told kids to keep their rooms clean and not to play with matches. The program was live, so not all the skits or commercials went smoothly. "I can't drink that stuff. It makes me sick," said a boy when offered a sponsor's apple juice. (Lewis jumped to Elroy McCaw's Channel 13 in 1957, triggering a flap with KING over who owned the Sheriff Tex name.)

Then came Pepita the Flea, a little piece of metal wiggled around by a hidden magnet on *KING's Clubhouse,* Stan Boreson's popular show for children. Did mothers and children know the mayor's name? Could they name the head of Boeing? Hardly, but they knew Pepita, and hundreds of kids sent in tiny clothing and furniture for Pepita to use. The biggest star, of course, was No Mo, a basset hound with long ears, mournful eyes, and an unchanging personality. He never moved (hence, "No Motion"), no matter the chaos on stage. Boreson dressed No Mo in all sorts of costumes. He even put him on a miniature hydro and dragged him around the lake. Kids roared, the word spread, and kids demanded that parents buy TV sets.

With Lee Schulman's guidance, *KING's Clubhouse* debuted in 1955, the same year *The Mickey Mouse Club* started on ABC and *Captain Kangaroo* on CBS. The opening theme song was "Zerodachus mucho crockus hullabalooza bub! That's the secret password that we use down at the club." Boreson aired cartoons, played piano, aired *Our Gang* comedies, hosted appearances by Tarzan and Howdy Doody, and brought on Girl Scouts to promote their cookie sale. Boreson's original No Mo was hit by a car and died soon after the show started, despite the efforts of a heart surgeon who had volunteered to save the dog. A skinny No Mo look-alike was brought in and quickly fattened up as Boreson kept the camera away by telling kids the dog was sleepy.

Among the more remarkable characters were those created by Doug Setterberg, who had lost his vocal chords to cancer and whose Foghorn Peterson communicated in a growly buzz, generated by an artificial larynx. Setterberg also created Phineas the Frog, who spoke through a burping technique that Setterberg mastered. Five days a week, Setterberg and Boreson showed up at 3:00 P.M. to plan the skits they would ad-lib live at 5:00 P.M., such as No Mo going to a costume ball (imagine a shot of No Mo's droopy ears in hair curlers). The fact that kids were the secret weapon of TV sales coincided with Dorothy Bullitt's passion for children's programming, in which she wanted KING to be a national leader. In New York, she found Gloria Chandler, an expert in the field who did a children's radio program there for the Junior League. Chandler was brought out and given special status at KING, initially in radio, where she created a children's storytelling hour. Raised in affluence, Gloria's family became nearly penniless after her father's death. Among KING employees, she became Dorothy Bullitt's closest friend. She liked good food and stiff drinks and was fun to be around. She makes me laugh, said Dorothy.

In 1949, Chandler approached Ruth Prins, a theater instructor at the University of Washington, and asked her to do an educational television program on reading, to be called *Televenture Tales*. Prins had appeared previously on KING's first studio show, *Charades,* but felt dubious about the artistry of television. A friend at KING, Tom Dargan, told her of the good money to be made. A director, Dargan was making $400 a month, he said, and the money was sure to get better. "This is going no place but up," he told Prins, who agreed. Parents, teachers, and librarians loved *Televenture Tales,* which won national honors and helped establish King Broadcasting as a prestige broadcaster.

Dorothy's commitment to children's programming was demonstrated in 1950 when Prins announced that she was leaving KING to move with her husband and two children to Montana. Dorothy was stunned that one of her stars was leaving.

"Can you cancel this?" she asked Prins of their intended move.

Dorothy wouldn't take no. She asked Prins and her husband, Bob, to come to her new residence on Galer Street in Seattle. Later, she turned to Bob Prins: "We've got to work this out. I can give you a good position at KING." But Bob Prins had accepted a teaching post at the University of Montana. So Dorothy asked Bob if she could pay his wife to fly to Seattle every week to do *Televenture Tales* and during the absence, Dorothy would pay for child care. Always thrifty, Dorothy proposed that

Ruth Prins stay at Galer Street, where Gloria Chandler also lived. So they agreed. *Televenture Tales* continued, and Ruth Prins got a rare outsider's look at Dorothy's private life.

Dorothy's house, Ruth Prins discovered, was largely run by a tough bird named Jean, the cook, who announced what she felt like serving that night at dinner and that was that, no changes. The living room was probably the only one in America where the molding was painted by a noted artist, Mark Tobey, because he noticed the existing shade "fought with his painting," as he put it. There were various house cleaners and other servants who did chores, were not introduced, and, in Ruth Prins's view, were ignored as if they were sticks of wood. There were dinners with Carolyn and Stim when they were married. Carolyn would talk animatedly; Stim would say little. Many dinners included guests from the broadcasting business. Patsy and Harriet rarely came, Prins said. During this time, Ruth Prins felt very close to Dorothy. She felt like a friend but not an equal. Prins liked to hug people but never hugged Dorothy, who was not the hugging type, Prins felt. After about a year, Otto Brandt convinced Bob Prins to take a job as KING's manager of public affairs, for triple his Montana pay, and the Prinses moved back to Seattle.

Gloria Chandler remained at the Galer Street house for the rest of her life. Gloria was one of the people closest to Dorothy, but even this relationship had limits. There were times that Gloria wanted to do something at KING, went directly to Dorothy, and got a no. To Ruth Prins, Gloria always seemed humiliated when she came back from Dorothy's office, a reminder that Chandler's past social status did not change the fact that she was an employee.

Ruth Prins's big show began in 1952. It represented the highbrow children's entertainment that Bullitt and Prins advocated. In *Wunda Wunda*, Prins played a sweet lady dressed in a harlequin outfit who came out, greeted children, sang songs, and introduced books and pleasant characters. The noon show never had great ratings, but it was a class act—strictly education, no cartoons.

Not all the entertainment was scripted, such as the time a supposedly tame lion was brought onto the show and children watched, live, as the brute closed its jaws on Prins's right arm and squeezed. Prins, dressed in a giant bow tie, harlequin pants, and a tall, pointy hat, kept talking as the jaws pinched harder. Eventually the lion let go and roamed around the studio until it was captured. Another time some cops, pursuing a burglar in a store adjoining KING's studio, burst onto the *Wunda* set during a show. *Wunda* fans got to watch two policemen escort a suspected burglar from the back to the front as Prins clung to a stuffed animal. In 1958 *Wunda Wunda* won a prestigious Peabody Award, the first non-network children's show to do so. The Peabody Award was the industry's highest honor and, as Andy Haley pointed out, FCC commissioners read about the winners in *Broadcasting* magazine.

There were many other shows, usually created by Lee Schulman. To fill morning time, KING launched a chat show, *Telescope*. Bea Donovan's cooking show, called *KING's Queen*, ran five days a week for half an hour. When it came to technical obstacles, Schulman rarely accepted excuses. To engineers who said no, no, no, it couldn't be done, Schulman would reply: Try it. Figure out a way. To the surprise of the engineers, they often did. KING's studio had a large support column that limited camera movements. So what? Work around it, Schulman said. You want snowfall inside a building? Dump cornflakes from the ceiling. On black-and-white cameras, it was the best snow ever seen in Seattle. When Florence Chadwick, the famed English Channel swimmer, tried to swim the straits from the San Juan Islands to Victoria, about eighty miles northwest of Seattle, KOMO placed its cameras on the shore; Lee Schulman rented a barge to tow the cameras alongside the swimmer.

Some athletics were not so heroic, or so spontaneous. KING carried professional wrestling live from the Eagles Auditorium, promoted by Bob Murray, owner of The Doghouse restaurant. No matter how fierce the contest, with two snarling men circling each other, threatening to break bones, when the clock approached 9:30 P.M., Murray raised his hand and, boom, somebody got pinned and the match was over.

Schulman was the Boss. On his shows, everything moved at his command. Everything.

"Cue the choir," Schulman said, while directing the start of a live Easter sunrise program at dawn in 1953. The choir started.

"Cue the minister," said Schulman. The reverend spoke the opening comments.

It was still a little too dark.

"Cue the sun," the cameramen heard Schulman say. They did not think he was joking. Schulman looked to the east and, sure enough, the heavens heard his call. One more story was added to the legends of Lee Schulman, master showman.

With time, Schulman got better tools to do his magic. The sets got better; the performers got smoother; things got slicker. A color signal was broadcast in 1954, the result of $100,000 in new equipment and research. But the most significant advance in programming was the invention of a machine that could tape video for editing or re-use.

In 1956 KING-TV director of engineering Jim Middlebrook was attending an industry conference when he saw a prototype of the new Ampex machine. He immediately saw its importance, ordered one of the $45,000 machines, and then sought permission for the expense. KING got the first model made for a non-network station. CBS and NBC got the three prototypes. "The industry has been waiting for something like this since the birth of TV," Middlebrook told the Seattle *Times*. "Now we don't have to hide behind the skirts of the motion-picture arts and sciences."

Till then, the only way of preserving a telecast was to film the projection on what was called a Kinescope, which had to be processed like any other motion-picture film. Before cables and microwaves were set up, Kinescopes of live programs were shipped out to KING from the networks, but broadcast quality was poor. A Kinescope needed at least an hour to be processed, while videotape could be reused immediately and had superior broadcast quality. The Ampex machine made it much easier to prerecord a group of programs and "stack" them in the schedule.

As KING gained new gadgets and added programs, station publicists pumped out a steady steam of announcements to keep the station in the newspaper columns. Probably the most spectacular promotion was *The Crown Stations' Treasure Hunt* launched by Otto Brandt in 1958. The idea was to stage events that would start a buzz about King Broadcasting's Crown Stations in the advertising circles in Chicago, San Francisco, and New York. Brandt got the idea from a party his wife had thrown for his fortieth birthday, but John Blair, whose company represented KING, warned him the idea was corny and would flop. They did it anyway.

In New York, they gathered 300 contestants at the Waldorf Astoria and formed them into five-person teams. The teams received instructions on where to find clues and were then sent off in a fleet of taxis. Clues included finding an athlete in a track suit at Penn Station, a clue in a personal column in the Seattle *Post-Intelligencer* (shipped to Times Square), a live cigar-store Indian, and a man walking a basset hound. The final goal was to find one of five crowns concealed in storage lockers at Grand Central Station and return with it to the Waldorf. Every participant won something. First-prize winners would get a $1,800 tape recorder.

In California, KING staged a promotional salmon derby, air-freighting live fish that were deposited in tanks at the Sportsmen's Lodge in the San Fernando Valley. The fish, all twenty- to thirty -pounders, had been kept alive in water pumped with oxygen, an effort supervised by Clarence Pautzke, assistant director of fisheries for the State of Washington. Cooks from the state's Swinomish tribe prepared the catch. Actor Walter Brennan served as master of ceremonies. Among the celebrity anglers were Frank Sinatra, Broderick Crawford, Jack Kelly, Roy Rogers, Lawrence Welk, Gene Autry, Betty White, George Reeves ("Superman"), and Walter Lantz, creator of Woody Woodpecker.

It was, said one ad executive, the most original sales promotion he'd ever seen. "The Crown Stations apparently haven't heard of such things as tight money," he said. "They go after money. And you may be sure they get it." It was true. Dorothy Bullitt spent heavily on the Treasure Hunts because they paid off handsomely. Till then, Seattle was viewed as a province somewhere on the road to Alaska, not as the twentieth largest city in the nation. Easterners didn't know Seattle was growing and had people with money to spend. KING worked up a slide show on the region, which employees called The Pitch, to brief ad executives on Seattle's natural, scenic, and economic wonders ("more boats per capita than anywhere else in the United States . . . largest manufacturer of men's ties . . . forty-five minutes from snow skiing). The Pitch and the Treasure Hunts helped identify Seattle in the minds of the East Coast media buyers. And as far as the ad executives were concerned, there was only one station in Seattle and one place to advertise, and that was KING.

KING's news matured, too.

At first, KING broadcast the election returns from its studios. Later, the broadcast was moved to the IBM building, where computers were used to crunch early poll returns on a statewide reporting system that Lee Schulman had set up. Schulman, always inventive, had persuaded school parent-teacher groups around the state to call in selected returns. KING's payment to them was just a small donation. He worked up the sampling with experts at the University of Washington. The system allowed KING to predict the outcome, a major advantage that TV news had over newspapers. Readers would have to wait till the next day to find out who won, but KING was telling viewers before they went to bed.

On election nights, a small closed-circuit TV placed next to news anchor Charles Herring fed him results or background information about a race or candidates. Viewers at home assumed the information was all in Herring's head. Periodically, Herring would summon an expert or politician before the cameras to give an analysis of the incoming returns, which sometimes made for surprising scenes.

"Go get me Maggie, will ya?" Herring one night asked production director Kit Spier. Spier went looking for the senior senator, Warren Magnuson, a two-fisted drinker. He approached Magnuson and asked if he would appear. "Sure," said Magnuson, who started to get to his feet and then collapsed back into his chair. He couldn't walk or stand. So Spier helped Magnuson to his feet, wrapped an arm around the senator to steady him, and guided him to the cameras. Magnuson was perfectly lucid and articulate during the interview, not a word slurred, except viewers never got the name of that friend standing so close to him. Spier's wife was astonished to see her husband on TV for the first time.

In 1954 KING added a helicopter to its news-gathering equipment, which soon helped the station provide the first on-the-scene footage of a spectacular bank robbery in the Greenwood neighborhood. KING eventually discontinued its use of the machine, the first use of a helicopter in Northwest TV news, decades before the start of Seattle's TV news "helicopter wars."

People recognized Herring all around town. He had no passion for advocacy journalism; that came later at KING. He was the showman of an increasingly smooth and ambitious newscast that skimmed through stories and once in a while actually influenced the news.

In 1957 KING sent Herring to Washington, D.C., as the only broadcast journalist covering the Senate committee hearings on allegations of corruption in the Teamsters Union. For two days in March and two in May, Herring sat in on morning press briefings by Robert Kennedy, the committee's counsel, who tipped reporters on the day's schedule. Some of the most aggressive questioning came from Senators John Kennedy and John McClellan, the latter as chairman of the racketeering committee.

The spotlight was on Seattle's own Dave Beck, who had risen to become president of the Teamsters Union as well as a regent of the University of Washington and a power in local politics. Beck, labeled the "portly president" in news stories, repeatedly refused to answer questions about $300,000 in union funds he had supposedly misused. He even refused to answer whether he knew his own son.

The hearings brought forth streams of stories on Beck's clout and lavish tastes. Testimony disclosed, for example, how beer maker Anheuser-Busch granted its largest distributorship to a company tied to Beck, whom brewery executives called "His Majesty, the Wheel." In return, Beck intervened to solve labor problems involving drivers of Anheuser-Busch beer trucks. One telegram by Beck to the brewery referred to then-Governor Mon Wallgren as a "100 percent" supporter of Beck's beer company. Later, Beck pressed for more territory and for a commission of five cents on every case of Budweiser sold in Alaska. Anheuser-Busch concluded there would be no end to Beck's demands.

Senator Kennedy pressed Anheuser-Busch's general counsel, Dwight David Ingamells. Why was Beck's company given more territory than any other company? "Was it because he was head of the Teamsters?" Kennedy asked.

"I'm just the company's lawyer, I don't know," Ingamells replied. "I certainly don't think that had something to do with it."

Wasn't Beck's conduct extortion? Kennedy asked.

"I don't believe I can answer that," Ingamells said.

For a local TV station, KING's commitment to covering the Beck story was exceptional. *Time* magazine described how King Broadcasting had arranged a string of six stations to carry Herring's reports. KING covered every witness, using borrowed cameras. Morning reports were carried live in Seattle. Afternoon sessions were filmed, with the footage air-shipped to Seattle. After one appearance, Herring asked Beck if he would consider resigning for the good of the union. Yes, said Beck. The Washington *Star* bannered the reaction: BECK WOULD QUIT FOR GOOD OF THE UNION. Herring was thrilled. Not many local TV reporters could claim a piece of a national story. It was exciting stuff. But Dorothy Bullitt wanted KING to do more than titillate viewers. She wanted the station to educate the community. On a trip to Boston, she spotted a commentator on a Boston station and hired him to be Seattle's first TV commentator. Many at KING regarded Geoffrey Harwood as erudite but so dull that his brief commentaries seemed to take hours. Harwood liked to practice that night's speech while walking the halls, twirling his Phi Beta Kappa key. Salesmen kidded him by calling him Jeff, which he didn't like. He supplied a bit of worldly class to the land of Seafair, Boeing, and hydros, but the studio floor crew, perhaps closer to viewer preferences, would roll their eyes when he began to speak.

Each night it was another obscure topic. Harwood only lasted a few years. "He gave us a nightly lecture on the Gulf of Acaba for three minutes. No one, nowhere, gave a shit," said Spier.

So Dorothy found someone who knew how to make people pay attention.

Chapter 11 "We Can Open Eyes"

Channel 5 had been on the air for just over ten years when, in 1959, a strip of tarred rope arrived at selected offices throughout Seattle. A shipping label attached to the rope read *"Lost Cargo, 8 P.M. Thurs. June 25, KING-TV Channel 5."* That was it—a clever gimmick designed to arouse people's curiosity, with no declaration that KING was about to launch a completely new era in Seattle's broadcast journalism.

Till that night, KING—along with virtually every other TV station in America—was known more for filling time than for moving minds. Local program managers nationwide had hours to book and had not been picky about what went on the air, as long as it held viewers, satisfied the FCC, and kept advertisers happy. Network journalism was a step higher, led by Edward R. Murrow's *See It Now* on CBS, beginning in late 1952. But, as many TV critics noticed, there was only one Ed Murrow, and in 1959 he was taking a year off from broadcasting.

In Seattle, this changed when Robert Schulman, the Pacific Northwest bureau chief for Time-Life, Inc., was told by headquarters that it was time for him to move to a new post. Schulman (no relation to Lee Schulman) had done an outstanding job in Seattle. Along with Ed Guthman of the *Times*, he was one of the few journalists in town who challenged and investigated Seattle's sleepy establishment. Seattle then was run by a small group of businessmen who kept a firm grip on the City Council, which in turn was largely a province of the Chamber of Commerce. Whenever anyone petitioned for new funding, the City Council would reply there was too little money, and that would be the end of the idea. Schulman saw himself as a reformer who used facts to move the public.

Schulman was a slight, balding man who wore bow ties. His somewhat professional air set him apart from most journalists, but he was intensely competitive and resourceful. He had written tough investigative pieces for Time-Life on such high-profile topics as Dave Beck and corruption in the Husky football program. Schulman saw Beck as "a conniving, power-wielding wretch" who should be exposed.

A native of New York, Schulman had sunk his roots into Seattle. He was active in local charities and served on the state board of the American Civil Liberties Union. He had a house in the Laurelhurst neighborhood and socialized with others who saw themselves as part of the thinking elite. Schulman didn't want to leave Seattle.

After getting the word from Time-Life, Schulman called Dorothy and met with her and Stimson Bullitt to explore possibilities at KING. Dorothy did most of the talking with Schulman. Stim said little and, to Schulman, seemed to have marginal interest in the discussion. Schulman admired Dorothy's toughness in having yanked NBC from the Fishers. More important, he felt she shared his belief in the potential of television, which Schulman called "the thousand-pound pencil."

In late 1958, KING put out a news release announcing that Schulman had been named director of special features for the King Broadcasting Company, quoting Dorothy as follows: "This move follows the company's concept of responsibility to the end that true reporting, researched, developed and objectively produced, will give the area a clearer understanding of vital issues. Mr. Schulman's activities will complement and augment our news service by adding depth, contributed by a trained specialist whose full-time employment is devoted to this purpose."

One phrase bore scrutiny: "a clearer understanding of vital issues." This was a little different from what Chuck Herring's understaffed news department was trying to give. Herring's group was struggling to cover the basics and to produce what could only be called a sketch of the day's news. Schulman's assignment was to bring a new dimension to Seattle journalism. First, a sense that certain issues were being overlooked by others (chiefly the political-reporting establishment, including the *Times* and the *P-I*), and that KING-TV was capable of covering those issues. Second, a view that TV could bring clarity; that alone was a statement of ambition, that TV could do something very well, maybe even better than the newspapers. KING was subtly, perhaps unconsciously, claiming a special status in Seattle journalism, a sense of mission that would take hold and last for decades. The pressure was on Schulman to produce something big.

Schulman had heard of problems at the Port of Seattle from John Haydon, editor-publisher of *The Marine Digest*. Haydon complained of business being lost to other ports, cronyism among the three port commissioners, inefficient dock equipment and theft by longshoremen. It was a mess. Haydon's was one of few voices publicly raising the cry over a deteriorating piece of Seattle's economy. Schulman immediately grasped the significance of the port story and its suitability for television. The camera could show dramatic evidence of ships and piers in decay and, with any luck, might even show thievery at the dock. Lee Schulman assigned production director Kit Spier to direct the program, which would run ninety minutes.

Ninety minutes? asked Spier. The idea was astounding. This was ten times longer than any single news segment KING had aired before. Ninety minutes was the length of a feature film. KING's documentary would require the structure of a three-act play, with individual scenes and varying tempos to hold an audience. They spent weeks on the project, traveling to different ports on the West Coast and interviewing critics, experts, and port commissioners. They surreptitiously filmed longshoremen who "accidentally" broke open crates of frozen chicken and Scotch and held dockside barbecues.

As the broadcast day of *Lost Cargo* approached, Robert Schulman wrote an internal memo assessing the documentary, characterizing the material as unprecedented in local television, and "the most candid and comprehensive report yet attempted by any medium of communication on the crisis along our waterfronts." He predicted the report would "galvanize a citizenry" to reform the Port of Seattle. KING aggressively promoted the upcoming show, getting plugs in local news columns and coverage in *TV Guide* and *Channel* magazine. In an early coup, they signed up the National Bank of Commerce as sole sponsor.

During the week preceding the broadcast, local newspaper columns were filled with the visit by Senator and Mrs. John Kennedy, Cold War headlines, the commitment of Louisiana Governor Earl Long to a mental hospital, and construction of a freeway through Seattle. The city had just broken ground for the Century 21 Exposition, a world's fair pushed by Eddie Carlson and other downtown visionaries despite claims of under-financing and poor planning. To prove that Seattle's futuristic visions hadn't killed the *Times*'s sense of community newspapering, the paper carried a photo and a story on Sister Joseph of Seattle, the former Patricia Snider, taking her perpetual vows as a member of the Mission Sisters Servants of the Holy Ghost.

The headlines were jarring: A nuclear attack on the United States would kill 48.9 million people; the nation was totally unprepared for an attack; Castro was tightening his grip on Cuba; Klaus Fuchs, "the atomic spy," was being sent to East Germany. Yet despite the reminders of nuclear terror, the pages of the *Times* were filled with ads for leisure equipment, cameras, and boats, while smiling beauties presented themselves in the Miss Washington contest. Seattle was gobbling up tidbits about Jackie Kennedy's views of the Kennedy clan and was reading of plans for the upcoming tenth Seafair festival, featuring appearances by Bob Hope and Bing Crosby. "We all enjoy Seafair," declared a *Times* editorial. "We all take pride in it. We should all support it."

The *Times* gave some passing mention to the upcoming *Lost Cargo* broadcast, but the cover of the TV program guide that week featured a picture of singer Pat Boone with his four daughters. Competing programs that night were *Bachelor Father* on Channel 4 and the *Zane Grey Theater* on Channel 7. For those who could receive the weak signal from Tacoma, a Rainiers baseball game ran on Channel 11. A movie, *The Little Minister*, ran on Channel 13. KING preceded *Lost Cargo* with *The Real McCoys*.

On the night of the broadcast, Otto Brandt invited Maxwell Carlson, president of National Bank of Commerce, others from the bank, and representatives of the ad agency Cole & Weber to attend a special reception preceding the show. They met at the Cloud Room of the Camlin Hotel, which rivaled the Harbor Club for the best view in town. They had cocktails and dinner and then gathered around a television to watch Schulman's show.

The program opened with the shrill sound of a ship's whistle, a shot of a cargo ship entering Puget Sound, and the strains of a maritime song. Then came Schulman's dramatic voice-over: One of every three Puget Sound dollars comes from waterborne commerce, "but the danger is near." Mood music shifted suddenly, underscoring Schulman's alarming words: shipments were off; the dockworkers' payroll down by $1 million; steamship companies were transferring to other ports. Then viewers saw a life-ring labeled "Seattle" bobbing in the water, as the heavy music swelled ominously.

The scene then switched from the melodramatic to the academic: a shot of bespectacled Schulman, in bow tie and looking in need of a shave, standing behind a table as he spoke. It was almost comic, the image of a high school science teacher reciting statistics. Seattle's spirit was in decline, Schulman said. The camera showed images of decaying piers, unsafe decking, and sheds too congested for easy movement of cargo or trucks. Schulman's voice recited improvements at Portland's port, thanks to its "heads up" commission. San Francisco and Portland were spending millions a year on new docks, larger cranes, and other equipment. By contrast, Seattle had written a plan of improvements in 1948, but nothing had happened.

The program interviewed shipping executives, longshoremen, and port commissioners in other cities. Not all of the footage or the interviews were stimulating, but each portion of the program established one more point in Schulman's arguments. The thoroughness was impressive, especially so for a TV news program. Schulman showed a Seattle port official claiming that his agency hustled for business, but then the camera showed a Yakima shipper who used Portland because Seattle never asked. As the program went on, the arguments piled up convincingly. Each time the camera returned to Schulman it seemed his five o'clock shadow had deepened. He was intense. The camera recorded from a slightly low angle so it looked up at his face, emphasizing the set of his jaw and underscoring a look of moral authority. His delivery was crisp and exacting.

The camera took viewers to the sleepy offices of the port commissioners and the feeble statements of their defense. Two commissioners were shown operating businesses that used port facilities. The message was clear: they were backwash bureaucrats, not the forward-looking types that Seattle needed. D. E. Skinner, owner of a shipping company and a Seattle blue blood, argued that a port was like a wife who had to be nurtured or she would run away. He warned that Alaskan shipping, 40 percent of Seattle's commerce, was being wooed to other ports. Near the end of the broadcast, Schulman said: "Toes are going to have to be stepped on if there is to be progress." Stepped on? Stomped seemed to be Schulman's preferred reaction. The last guest was Senator Warren Magnuson, Dorothy's friend, whose Senate committee oversaw maritime commerce. Bringing national political clout to endorse KING's findings, Magnuson said that urgent steps were needed to revive Seattle's harbor, which should be placed in a regional authority for coordination with other ports.

At the program's end, Schulman stood up from his desk, which had two chairs, and stepped away from his papers. His body language was telling viewers that they, too, should stand up and get going if they wanted to save Seattle. He closed with a ringing question, a call to action—"Will you let it be known that you care about the waterfront?"

After a commercial, KING returned to its usual program, airing *Colonel Flak,* then *Danger Is My Business* and KING's fifteen-minute late newscast, *The World Today.*

The next day's *Times* carried two paragraphs at the end of the TV column. "Schulman pulled no punches as he recited the woes of the waterfront," wrote critic C. J. Skreen. "Longshoremen, port officials, civic leaders, an apathetic public all got a share of the brickbats. A lot of time, money, talent and research went into a production that should qualify as local television's most ambitious undertaking to date. Whether its controversial observations and conclusions are accurate is beyond this department's province, but as television reporting it ranks with the most ambitious the TV medium has turned out."

Viewers reacted immediately. Calls and letters poured into KING as well as to the *Times* and the *P-I.* On the following Sunday, the *Times* devoted its entire editorial column to the waterfront, crediting KING for putting the topic in sharp focus. The *Argus,* a weekly for the city's elite that had long been a voice for reform of the waterfront, heaped praise on Dorothy Bullitt for showing a willingness to take on a controversial subject, and lauded the National Bank of Commerce for backing the program. KING put out a news release quoting from some of the letters, including a cocky dig at the local newspapers: "The program was fair, thorough, accurate and hard-hitting and very much needed in view of the disposition of the local daily press to avoid this kind of reporting."

At Schulman's suggestion, KING staged a town meeting at the Moore Theater, hosted by New Yorker George V. Denny, Jr., famous for his *American Town Meeting of the Air,* who was flown in to give the event added importance. Denny's arrival by itself generated press coverage. But the real event lay with the hundreds who gathered at the theater to question representatives of labor, shipping, and the port. One of Stimson Bullitt's friends, businessman Robert Block, set out to attend the meeting but fell and injured his arm. That didn't stop him. He arrived late, his arm in a sling, to put in his question. More news stories followed. One commissioner suggested that the entire commission should resign and be replaced by a larger, unsalaried board. The *Times* and the *P-I* took up the topic with front-page stories. "A great deal of hue and cry has been raised in the Seattle area by the presentation of *Lost Cargo,*" said *The Marine Digest.* "The public has been awakened." The furor sparked a $420-million bond proposal, a change in how commissioners were elected, and, in some people's minds, a general appreciation of the waterfront which led eventually to a wholesale modernization of the port.

Also important, Robert Schulman had shaped a legacy for every TV journalist in Seattle. For an entire generation, *Lost Cargo* would be cited as the first real impact documentary, proof that pictorial television could cover a topic in depth and with probing intelligence. It would be the standard against which all other local documentaries would be judged. It proved that TV in Seattle could be more than Uncle Miltie and pies in the face. TV could be a serious tool to inform and move the public. TV journalism was an awkward blending of entertainment and serious issues, but Schulman showed that a good documentary could be both entertaining and serious. For eight years, Seattle had seen Edward R. Murrow's *See It Now* cover national issues on CBS. Now the city saw what the same instrument could do with a local issue. Schulman had lived up to his promise.

In 1960, Schulman produced perhaps his finest documentary, *Bitter Harvest,* a stunning treatment of the abuses of migrant workers which ran a week before Murrow's *Harvest of Shame.* With its powerful footage by three teams of directors and photographers, *Bitter Harvest* was even more compelling than *Lost Cargo.* It opened with children "in dust and in filth," in crowded, airless shacks, as their parents, "who sometimes do not even own a cup," worked the fields from 4:00 A.M. till 10:00 P.M. The camera was unsparing. When Shulman spoke of the refuse strewn about the camps, the camera showed cans tossed everywhere. When he spoke of clogged toilets, the camera showed human excrement. Such conditions support the American harvest, Schulman reminded viewers. These people, paid less than $1,000 a year, "bring food to our white table-cloths." The camera went from Texas to Yakima, following families from job to job. Schulman's view was that the migrants' problem was society's problem. (He did not report dissension in the KING crew. Earl Thoms, who recorded sound for the program, shared Schulman's over-all sympathies but wondered why the migrants never picked up their own beer cans. Thoms argued with Schulman that it wasn't the farm owner who threw the cans around.) The evidence of neglect was over-whelming: families of seven were given one room to share, showers that didn't work, hot water heaters broken, one toilet for dozens of people to share. It was hard to accept the view of one farmer who blamed it all on the migrants, saying they didn't "have the ambition to keep it clean."

Schulman pressed for answers. Why did one state do a better job of protecting migrants? Who blocked reforms in the Legislature? Where were health inspectors? Schulman warned viewers that efforts were under way in Olympia to weaken the already inadequate health regula-tions for migrants. Letters "can be sent on that topic," he suggested.

A program to save Seattle's waterfront had stirred KING viewers' sense of a romantic past. There was no such romance with *Bitter Har-vest.* And migrants were not a cause to which the business community rallied. They were poor and did not own TVs. They did not buy wash-ing machines, refrigerators, pleasure boats, and half-price dresses at The Bon Marché in downtown Seattle. They were not the sorts of people coveted by banks or other advertisers in Seattle. No advertiser was interested in *Bitter Harvest*. Dorothy Bullitt decided to air the program anyway.

Dick Larsen, a young reporter then working in eastern Washington for the Wenatchee *World,* saw Schulman's report and was astonished. Although he thought the program had gone overboard in places, he was struck by how television, still a toy to most people, had been first among the news media to take up the cause of farmworkers. And the broadcast had impact. A number of reforms were begun in Olympia, led in part by one of Stimson Bullitt's friends, a rugged Okanogan legislator and liberal lawyer named John Goldmark.

In 1961 Schulman produced *The Volcano Named White,* a sympathetic treatment of a twenty-four-year-old black man convicted of killing two people. Schulman portrayed Don White as a strong case for the insanity defense: White had been an abused and neglected child. He grew up to become a man with a violent, uncontrollable tendency who couldn't get treatment. He was a volcano just waiting to explode, and thus, in this portrayal, society bore some responsibility for what had happened. "Fighting to me is like eating," White said.

Inspired by articles on White by Barry Farrell in the *P-I,* the program centered on White in extreme close-up speaking about his life, responding to questions from Farrell as wisps of cigarette smoke twisted up towards his cheeks and eyes. Cutaways brought in interviews with relatives, caseworkers, and others. White's last drunken hours before he exploded and killed were detailed with shots of where he walked, who he talked to, what he drank. All the while, sound effects built a sense of impending violence—What can we learn from this case? What can we do to prevent future cases? asked Schulman.

The program was painful to watch. A full hour on a killer's life, the camera so tight to White's face you could see blemishes on his cheeks and spittle glistening on his lips. Again, no local sponsor would back the program. Some of KING's managers suggested that it be toned down, but Dorothy Bullitt loved it, so it ran without commercials. To portray the life of a black man in Seattle in such depth was a stunner for KING's audience. Less than a month earlier, a visit by Martin Luther King, Jr., to Seattle had sparked threats on Dr. King's life, and racist material had appeared on the desks of black Boeing workers. Beyond that, to detail the violence of White's childhood and early adulthood in unsparing detail was too much for many viewers, who flooded KING with protest calls. Yet many watched it—49 percent of that night's TV audience saw *Volcano*, almost the combined total of the region's four other stations, a telling example of KING's ability to reach people and deliver a message.

Many disputed the wisdom of giving attention to a black person. Although the program justified itself as an examination of the juvenile- and criminal-justice systems, its main interest was White's life. Reflecting the liberalism of its time, the program implied that some government help for children like White would have made a difference. Society has judged Don White, but who will judge society? asked KING. Setting aside White's death penalty became a *cause célèbre* for many of Seattle's liberals, including Ken MacDonald, a friend of Stim and one of many lawyers who helped White. Programs like *Volcano* explained why liberals looked to KING for validation and inspiration. KING carried the good fight. Dorothy Bullitt made a point of personally telling Schulman she approved of what he had been trying to do.

Later, the program aired in New York City on WPIX to mixed reviews. The New York *Times* complained that KING had exploited a "wounded animal" for a dubious social purpose. The New York *Post* said KING should have asked more questions of social workers. The *Herald Tribune* wondered if the program's "horror and brutality" was justified. When KING and its sister stations won a prestigious Alfred duPont Award for its programming, *Newsweek* heaped praised on Dorothy Bullitt and called *Volcano* "unlike anything ever done in television" and typical of the company's courage and financial commitment to public service. Costs are so high that at least one Crown station each year loses money, the magazine reported. "With a smaller staff, buying films instead of making them ourselves, we could pay the stockholders," Dorothy Bullitt told *Newsweek*. "But our stockholders would rather have good programming."

Such statements made KING, and Dorothy Bullitt, the talk of the industry. Inside the company, some took her words as a commandment: Disregard money; enlighten the masses. Robert Schulman, especially, was a believer. In a speech to a Seattle business group, Schulman explained that TV had a special obligation to do something beneficial with "the most extensive audience ever corralled in the history of mankind. . . . I speak as a former newspaper and magazine writer when I suggest that the television documentary, at its best and most responsible, is contemporary society's best key to achieving provocation among many of the unconcerned while alerting the already concerned. On any given social issue, it is, if you will forgive the analogy, the Ph.D. thesis with sex appeal." To provoke the unconcerned—Schulman had a mission. With each new documentary, on such topics as urban growth and school financing, Schulman helped to define KING as different from the typical broadcast station.

In an ad in *Broadcasting,* Otto Brandt stated KING's mission: "Television, to us, is a tool with which we can open eyes to challenge, as well as brighten them with diversion. . . . We and our advertisers give new impact to an old phrase: crusading journalism." But the journalism had a special flavor; it was not simply reform-minded in the traditional way. It was liberal and activist, and aggressively so, in a manner that KOMO and KIRO would shun.

Dorothy Bullitt could support this because it flowed from her Victorian values of good citizenship and, equally important, it did not jeopardize the company. Liberalism and profits were not mutually exclusive. Activism gave a luster to KING's name that attracted audiences, who drew advertisers. King Broadcasting did spend more on documentaries and news, and did pay modest dividends to Dorothy Bullitt and other shareholders. Long term, it was a wise strategy. Dorothy Bullitt held as her example the New York *Times,* which became the most profitable of New York's newspapers. Quality, in the end, would win out.

Her son Stimson did not care about profits, many believed. He was not interested in being a good businessman. He wasn't practical. He was an idealist, an elitist, a thinker. He saw Seattle as a town that needed uplifting. He saw television, by contrast, as a polluting influence, and the people in it as coarse and unsophisticated. Yet he saw his duty: to follow his mother into the company, just as she had succeeded her father and husband.

In late 1961, Dorothy Bullitt decided to step out of daily management and turn King Broadcasting over to her son. Stim invited his close friend,

Bob Block, to join him for drinks at the Rainier Club. As they toasted Stim's assumption of power, Block thought it strange that Stim had picked the Rainier Club, the bastion of the downtown business boys who plotted the latest Chamber of Commerce campaigns. Stim despised the club's smugness, its symbolism of the Seattle establishment, yet he said nothing to explain his choice of locale. The question vanished from Block's mind as the two toasted Stim's good fortune.

It was the first of many occasions that left people guessing about Stimson Bullitt, who had largely disappeared from the news columns after his runs for Congress. Stim was known in legal circles as a capable lawyer and in the real-estate community as the developer, with Bagley Wright, of one of Seattle's first postwar office towers, the Logan Building. Stim returned to public attention when the *Times* identified him as the owner of a pet donkey that created a neighborhood fuss with its daily braying at 4:00 A.M. One neighbor said it sounded like a dog being murdered. Stim said he had no idea that gentle Francis had disturbed anyone.

The literary crowd knew of his 1959 book, *To Be a Politician,* a dry, academic treatise on politics that commented at length on great philosophers and trends in campaigning but gave few personal anecdotes. The book was praised in *The New Yorker* and the New York *Times.* Political scientists saw it as a contribution to their field and added it to class reading lists. A few reviewers quarreled with Stimson Bullitt's argument that an educated elite gravitates toward liberalism, while the lower class reverts to chronic conservatism. Those of personal worth, Stim argued, have nothing to lose from social change. The elite would show a disproportionate number of Jews, he argued. "Urban life under persecution made them the only recognizable group in the world that has been subjected to the process of natural selection on the basis of brains for enough generations for it to take effect." The ranks of smart gentiles were diluted through the ages, he wrote, by being killed on the battlefield or by joining the clergy and not having children.

That was the sort of social theorizing expected from a tenured professor, not from a Seattle businessman at the Rainier Club. Whether or not he was temperamentally right for the job, Stimson Bullitt, like a Prince of Wales, was ascending to Seattle's broadcasting throne and was becoming one of the city's most powerful people during a remarkable period of civic self-discovery. As Seattle acquired national clout through Senators Magnuson and Jackson, Stimson Bullitt, the failed politician, acquired a position of control in television—the most powerful tool in politics. Yet as much as he valued the opportunity to influence society, Stim despised the workaday particulars of the coarse instrument placed in his hands.

Things would soon change at his mother's company. Over the next decade, Stimson Bullitt would set out on a course full of contradictions. He would seek to make King Broadcasting and Seattle unique models to the rest of the nation. He saw KING as an Athens of the business world, a center of intellectual activity that would spark useful dialogue and fresh thinking in the city he loved. The effort would be wonderful, exciting, and ultimately damaging, both for the company and for his mother. He would become a very serious problem for Dorothy Bullitt.

Stimson Bullitt became president of King Broadcasting in 1961, a pivotal period in Seattle's history. He took his mother's office and she moved to a building next door. Stim was forty-two years old. A year later, Dave Beck would begin serving time in prison for tax fraud; the World's Fair would start; Elvis would visit; the Opera House would open; kids would ride the space-age Bubbleator; *Life* magazine would gush; and Seattle would feel like an awkward teenager at a debutante ball. The centerpiece of the Fair was the Space Needle, a graceful spire topped by a saucer-shaped restaurant that rotated 360 degrees every hour. Stim had declined a chance to join the group that built the Needle. He said the idea was crazy.

The Fair itself demonstrated who ran the city—a small group of downtown men whose chief advocate organization was the Central Association. A key powerbroker in that group was Ross Cunningham, the pipe-puffing editorial page editor of the Seattle *Times,* who had near-total authority from the Blethens, majority owners of the paper, to deliver strong backing to ideas launched by the Association. A former aide to Republican Governor Arthur Langlie, Cunningham favored heavily starched shirts and wore his pants hitched high on his waist. His lips always formed a faint, knowing smile. Cunningham used to boast that with a quick call or two, he could easily launch a civic movement. He championed a mild form of environmentalism, civil rights, and clean government; but mostly, he supported the Chamber of Commerce and the Republican Party. He showed fatigue with any group that challenged the collective wisdom of projects such as Seafair and the World's Fair.

He didn't challenge the system. He believed in the system. He *was* the system. He represented the opposite of Stim's approach to journalism.

Cunningham's favorite politician was his boating buddy, Republican King County Prosecutor Charles O. Carroll. The *Times* missed few opportunities to promote Carroll, noting his every flicker of interest in higher office, every birthday party, even his rescue of an injured pigeon. Despite evidence familiar to anyone who studied certain neighborhoods in Seattle, Carroll said the city was absolutely free of prostitution and defied anyone to find a brothel. "If you can find one, let me know and I'll wipe it out," he told a class of University of Washington journalism students. Carroll presented to Seattle the image it wanted to have—a clean city, blessed by its isolation from the rest of the nation. And so long as Cunningham ruled the *Times's* editorial pages, Carroll had reason to feel secure in office. Carroll in turn used his power to wield tremendous influence over political life in Seattle. By reputation, he ruled the King County Courthouse, where no judge crossed him. He had influence over who got judgeships, who was elected to city and county offices, and he could even boost careers in the police department. No Republican dared cross him. And few Democrats tried.

The World's Fair presented KING with a giant opportunity to strengthen its relationship with its viewers and with advertisers, network executives, and others. Otto Brandt had a studio set up at the Space Needle from which daily broadcasts were made. He invited executives from the East Coast to Seattle and organized his staff to entertain them from the time they stepped off the plane until they were airborne again. Brandt made sure that a guest's every moment would be fun and interesting. He hosted parties attended by staff members who were told to memorize the name, spouse, and other personal information of every guest.

The Fair reminded Seattle to look to its future, but the city's establishment was dominated by entrenched politicians and tired ideas. Stimson Bullitt deeply mourned the quality of Seattle's two major newspapers, both of which he saw as uninteresting and uninterested. A Seattle resident could pick up the paper, read it for a year, and have no idea who ruled the city and how. KING-TV could never topple the *Times* as the dominant media influence, but it could shed light on some new issues.

Bob Schulman had proved this could be done with documentaries. Soon after becoming president, Stim made some moves to improve KING's news department.

In August 1962, during the peak of world attention on Seattle, Stim invited a mustachioed New York *Times* writer and former NBC reporter named J. Herbert Altschull to visit Seattle and consider a job at KING. Stim didn't specify the job; he just invited Altschull to look around and see if anything interested him. Altschull agreed, but only because he wanted to see the Fair. Altschull had previously worked for the Associated Press in Germany and was considering a return to NBC.

Stim and Ancil Payne drove out to the airport to meet him. Since neither had ever met Altschull, and the airport would be crowded with tourists, Payne wondered how they would recognize him.

"Well, he's been a foreign correspondent and must look like one," Stim replied.

They took two positions and, sure enough, a guy in a trench coat approached. The man was balding, had a twitching mustache, and walked with his chin planted on his chest. Bingo: It was J. Herbert Altschull.

Later that day, Stim invited Altschull to his home. Altschull was amazed to hear a broadcaster put Mozart on the record player. Stim in turn was amazed that anyone in broadcast journalism could recognize Mozart. They both talked about how KING could be made a force for progressivism. Little was said specifically about what Altschull would do, though Altschull had in mind Edward P. Morgan, the distinguished radio newsman and analyst. After a meeting with Otto Brandt, Altschull was offered a job: whatever he wanted to do. Altschull, flabbergasted, accepted. Sometime later, after he had been at KING for a few weeks, he sent Stim a memo proposing a radio program he would host. He waited for what seemed like a long time and got no answer. Finally, he went in to see Stim. "What? You haven't started that yet?" Stim asked.

Altschull started doing radio commentaries. When TV news expanded from fifteen minutes to a half hour in 1963, Altschull began doing nightly commentaries of three minutes each. That was far more commentary than Geoffrey Harwood had done. Altschull was liberal and not shy about pushing his views on local topics. As a result, some at KING were nervous about audience reaction to Altschull who, because of his status as one of "Stim's Boys," never had to submit his scripts for advance review. No one had any oversight of what he would say. He was a rogue elephant, free to say what he wanted about anything, to point out social problems he felt the city ignored. Few in broadcast journalism had ever had such freedom, and at KIRO and KOMO, no staffer ever would.

From time to time, Altschull did political reports, including some from Olympia, where he generally supported the Democratic line but had good relations with a group of young Republican legislators, including Dan Evans, Slade Gorton, and Joel Pritchard. He also did reports from Europe, including a 1965 report on Vietnam done live with four cities linked by satellite, the first use of the new technology by an affiliate. When the civil rights movement took hold in Seattle, Altschull was an early proponent. He praised the work of activists such as Edwin Pratt, the charismatic head of the Urban League. Like Bob Schulman, Altschull was an effective liberal who used brains and facts to carry the cause. He stayed close to Stim, meeting him at the office or at home to talk about issues. And like Bob Schulman, Altschull showed up at the right parties. Around town, he was a player, not in the league with Ross Cunningham, certainly, but Altschull was in the political loop far more than most newspaper reporters. Altschull was there not as a creature of the governing class but as a member of a self-styled liberal elite seeking power and influence in the city.

In 1962 King Broadcasting and the Bullitts stood apart from Seattle's mainstream. The city was dominated by careful politics. Seattle had shed its image as a radical union town with Socialist leanings. It was a quiet town as far as race relations went, but the city and the region had an undercurrent of far-right politics, led by the John Birch Society and fed by genuine fears of the Soviet Union, which that year was installing missiles in Cuba. In addition, an obscure preacher named Richard Christensen was running with God to give Warren Magnuson a scare that hardly anyone expected.

Nothing alarmed Washington state's liberals more than the smearing of John Goldmark, one of Stimson Bullitt's closest friends and a state legislator who was defeated in that fall's Democratic primary. An anti-Communist publication in Goldmark's northeast Washington district suggested that Goldmark's membership in the American Civil Liberties

Union and his wife's membership in the Communist Party many years earlier raised doubts about his loyalty to the United States. Hinting that the Goldmarks were outsiders establishing a Communist cell, the Tonasket *Tribune* added that Goldmark's eldest son, Chuck, attended Reed College in Portland, "the only school in the Northwest where Gus Hall, secretary of the Communist Party, was invited to speak."

Almost immediately after Goldmark's defeat, Bob Schulman took a film crew to Okanogan County to cover what had happened. Schulman was outraged. If a good man could be smeared by false allegations, was the political process safe? Both he and Stim were active in the ACLU, and Schulman knew Stim and Goldmark were close, but Schulman decided to do the documentary without hearing from Stim. He didn't need the go-ahead. The issues were clear.

The result was *Suspect,* a powerful documentary that KING advertised as dealing with "this year's most significant election." KING alerted viewers, "This affects you. It happened in Okanogan County. It can happen here."

The documentary gave ample time for the *Tribune's* owner, Ashley Holden, to make his case. But for every allegation or innuendo, Schulman sought out the evidence that proved the opposite. When Holden insisted he had gotten information on Goldmark from FBI files, Schulman told viewers that FBI files are never released to unauthorized individuals.

The program did not give Goldmark himself much air time. He had rugged good looks, but producer-director Kit Spier thought Goldmark had a cool patrician style and New England accent that worked against his cowboy boots and plaid shirts. Instead most of the talk for the family came from his wife Sally, who had a warm, relaxed personality that worked well on camera. Before the camera rolled, Spier got right-wingers in Okanogan County to relax and open up by starting his interview with: "I can't stand liberal pink bastards." One Goldmark critic was so pleased with this remark that he took Spier into his basement to see his collection of Thompson submachine guns.

If Ashley Holden was the villain of *Suspect,* the hero of the show was George Wilson, the Democratic county chairman. Wilson said he had heard about the rumors and, taking the direct route to the truth, had confronted Goldmark: Are you a Communist? No, said Goldmark. Checking further, Wilson contacted Senator Jackson's office and, through it, got a letter from the U.S. Navy saying John Goldmark had been given security clearance—strong evidence of Goldmark's loyalty. Wilson spread the word of his findings and was told that that was the end of it, but the rumors stayed alive. Goldmark lost the primary. "I've been in Okanogan politics thirty years and I have never seen a campaign like this," Wilson said to the camera. "The tactics used are almost unspeakable and unthinkable."

Schulman ended the program by warning viewers: "In the struggle for liberty in the world, the nation loses each time this happens, each time we allow fear to come ahead of fact and to make a man a suspect."

After the documentary aired, Holden used another of his publications, the Spokane-based *Vigilante,* to lash at KING in the only way he knew—with a smear. He pointed out that Schulman and Stim were members of the ACLU, "a front with a rosy-red record and they have been organizing feverishly in the Tri-City area, home of the atomic works." Understanding why KING did *Suspect,* Holden wrote, was key to understanding "the entire Socialist structure in this state."

"We always suspected [Schulman] was hired for reasons other than his professional competence, and this latest production fans the flame of that smoldering suspicion," declared *The Vigilante.*

If anything, the sort of trash circulated by Ashley Holden illustrated how the news media could do harm. It underscored the need for quality journalism. Stim looked at KING's news department under Charles Herring and found it unimaginative. Stim wanted someone else running KING-TV news.

On paper, Samuel M. Sharkey, Jr., was an outstanding candidate to take KING news to a higher level. He was news editor and night news manager for NBC and he supervised content and style of news and documentary programs for TV and radio. He had run NBC's political convention coverage in 1956 and 1960. He had contacts with the FCC and the White House. He had worked for the New York *Times,* running its national news desk. He seemed perfect: a man who could bring the depth and intelligence of the New York *Times* to a local newscast.

Sharkey arrived in early 1963 and was put in charge of a restructured news department, combining radio and TV at the three stations, plus the activities of Altschull and Schulman. The job came with a grand title, managing director of news. Sharkey was now the boss of KING news.

Chuck Herring, who had built KING's news department, was livid. Sharkey got the job that Herring, and others at KING thought Herring deserved. Generally a congenial person, Herring thought Sharkey was a horse's ass. Sharkey thought Herring was stodgy and wanted to replace him. They did not get along. Instead of just talking to one another, Herring told people, they typed memos and had them routed the forty feet or so that separated their two offices. Herring was confused. KING news was killing KIRO and KOMO in the ratings, so why was Stim changing things? What was the problem? This was just one more mystery about Stimson Bullitt, who had perplexed Herring from the start.

Shortly after taking charge, Stim had called in Herring and the others, all of whom expected to be thanked for their long-term contributions to the company and told by a broadcast novice that he would welcome their help, as his mother had done when she bought KRSC. Instead, as Herring told the story, Stim told them they were all on notice that they had to work hard to keep their jobs. Herring was stunned by what he saw as foolish arrogance. Then, after Sharkey was put above him, there were problems every day.

Production director Kit Spier also saw Sharkey as a disastrous choice. Sharkey took a keen interest in the news writing and would lean over people's shoulders as they typed, demanding changes. Spier was appalled. A newsroom was tense enough as deadline approached, and now the KING reporters had to deal with Sharkey. But Sharkey only lasted eighteen months before taking a job with KIRO. He represented the first of many futile efforts by KING management to find someone who could control its independent news staff, at that time merely disorganized, but later disorganized and unruly. KING's talent was never easily led or controlled, but the effort to put a leash on the news department would outlast two successive presidents.

By 1965 Sharkey was gone, but that left a bruised Herring to wonder about his future. From time to time, he would see Stim in the cafeteria, but Herring never felt he could approach the company president. Stim would arrive with an apple and something to read, often something deep like Plato, and would take a seat in the cafeteria without speaking to anyone. People would whisper. Is he really reading Plato? If he's here to read, why bother to show up? To many of them, Stimson Bullitt was an odd duck. His mother was in the cafeteria all the time, sitting there with a smile, drinking coffee or eating a candy bar, listening to employees tell about their lives at home and at KING. People felt so good around her, they told her everything. Only a few noticed how little she volunteered about her own personal life, or her views about how KING was run. They only thought how nice she was. Everything good about KING was owing to her. Yet her son was not content to be the custodian of his mother's success. He wanted to give Seattle something it needed, yet it came at cost to his standing within KING and within his family.

Years before he became president of King Broadcasting, Stimson Bullitt dreamed of launching a serious publication that could serve as a rallying point for Seattle's intellectuals. But where and how to begin? What form should such a publication take? He didn't know. But one of his first goals as company president was launching that publication.

Stim had been exchanging ideas with Peter Bunzel, a dapper New Yorker serving as entertainment editor of *Life* magazine. The two knew each other through their mutual friend Bagley Wright. In their talks, Bunzel argued that if Stim wanted to have an impact on Seattle, King Broadcasting's new publication should be a magazine. Stim agreed. He appointed Bunzel as editor.

Among Stimson Bullitt's many efforts, the magazine most clearly revealed to the public his civic passions and quirky interests. Its development involved a host of various talents, especially those of Bunzel, whose own personality greatly colored the publication, but it was the one project that most closely held Stim's attention. Not for a moment would anyone assume that the magazine reflected his mother's values. And while television was a medium constrained by audience expectations, a magazine could reflect a singular vision and individual tastes. Moreover, because King Broadcasting was controlled by one person, the magazine could be given as much freedom as Dorothy Bullitt was willing to give her only son. For a time, that freedom was nearly total, no matter the financial and social costs. Hence, any problems with the magazine would reflect completely on Stimson and would contribute to tensions between mother and son, ultimately fueling Stim's ouster from King Broadcasting.

In May 1963 Stim presented to the King Broadcasting board his proposal for a magazine that would serve three purposes: to provide its readers with an understanding of the truth; to give its readers pleasure and to hold their attention long enough for them to absorb the truth; and to help the community fulfill and realize itself. Stim wanted no passions, no community chest-thumping: "Its purpose would not be love, revenge, sincerity, civic promotion, indoctrination of opinions, or providing faith in anything except reason," he wrote. It was especially noteworthy that Stim banned "civic promotion," another example of his standing apart from the city's ruling elite. Stim did not want a sexy publication for the masses. He wanted something literary, like a Harvard journal, or *The Economist* magazine. "I see this as basically appealing to our FM audience," Stim told Bunzel, who was horrified at such a limited goal.

Bunzel was a dynamic, interesting man who loved good writing and provocative story ideas. To those who appealed to him, he was fascinating, lively, even glamorous. He had an engaging laugh that "sounded like an automobile accident—loud and disruptive." To others, he seemed aloof and arrogant, a snob. At any rate, he may have been the worst choice for what Stim had in mind. Bunzel was an entertainment editor for a mass market publication. His section chronicled the comings and goings of Hollywood starlets, not the latest ideas for disarmament, world government, or urban planning.

Despite their incompatible goals, Bunzel took the job in Seattle because it was the one chance in his career to be staked to a new magazine. He immediately began nudging Stim into accepting what he himself wanted to do: that is, to put out a brash city magazine. Little if any thought was given to business considerations: What was the market for such a magazine? Who would buy it? Would anyone advertise in it? When would it make a profit? Perhaps anticipating the inevitable, Stim and Bunzel agreed that the magazine might never become a major profit center for the company. Instead Stim saw the magazine as helping to diversify King Broadcasting, to get it some experience in print as a hedge against the vagaries of broadcasting, and to offset the vacuity he saw in Seattle's dailies, with their "excessive emphasis on the verified but undigested and unexplained facts."

Before Bunzel trekked west, Stim wrote him a detailed letter. Stim was clearly excited about launching the magazine. He offered Bunzel pages of ideas for circulation campaigns, features, and even a logo styled after the *Manchester Guardian Weekly*. He liked the *Guardian*'s use of a single photograph on its cover, "its tranquil tone contrasting with the turbulence and tension of much of the matter which the articles discuss." He suggested business coverage in the magazine, since the topic was important, and since coverage in the daily press "tends to be venal and incompetent." To understand the Northwest, Stim suggested Bunzel read several books, in this order: *The Oregon Trail, The Canoe and the Saddle, Honey in the Horn, Winds of Morning,* and *Farthest Reach.*

He counseled Bunzel to restrain himself from having too much contact with the public, which would waste his time. Take risks, he said. To achieve our high goals, he wrote, perhaps you should follow Einstein's advice when asked what was necessary to make pioneering advances in thought: "Discard axioms," replied Einstein. Stim had a few ideas that were nonstarters for what Bunzel had in mind. Stim wanted a column on the problems caused by automation, and another on "how to keep the world from being blown up." Bunzel artfully deflected these suggestions.

It was perhaps a sign of the erratic management ahead that Bunzel arrived in Seattle only to find that Stim had already hired someone to plan the publication, a young Reed College graduate with no experience in magazines. The young man was very bright but had no desire for a career in journalism. Stim's first reporting hire was another rookie, a young woman just out of Radcliffe, Suzanne Braun.

The staff and Stim spent a lot of time trying to find the right name for the magazine. Stim wanted *The Navigator,* a name that suggested the goal of steering readers among the difficult shoals of contemporary life. Bunzel hated it; he thought it sounded like a boating mag or something pretentious. Bunzel spent hours trying for alternatives: *The Thorn, Cerebellum, Focus, Spectrum.*" Stim sent a note: "Would you be content with the name, *Seattle Star*? "No," retorted Bunzel. In the end, the desire for a format tailored to national advertising drove the choice. Several magazines at the time had formed an association that jointly solicited advertising. All were named after their cities. So there it was: *Seattle*. It was probably the only significant decision involving the magazine which bowed to business considerations.

Stim became aggressively involved in the production of the magazine, suggesting ideas for stories, even copyediting articles that Bunzel had already approved for publication. He might kill an edited article and leave Bunzel guessing as to why. At most publications, when an owner intervenes, it's generally to see writing toned down, softened, made less critical. When *Seattle* later wrote about Henry Jackson, who broke with liberals over Vietnam, Stim wanted the writing harsher and more searching. Bunzel loved the financial and philosophical support he got from Stim, but he found it aggravating that his boss would fuss over a single word. Yet Stim's appearances were not always solemn occasions.

"Miss," Stim announced one day to the young reporter from Radcliffe, loud enough for others to hear, "you are the apotheosis of femininity." What did that mean? Was it a come-on? To those who watched, the young reporter seemed offended. But Bunzel overheard the line and burst out laughing.

There were no formal controls on the magazine's budget, except for the rule that individual salaries be kept low. As the magazine was prepared for its launch, there was no budget. No one challenged Bunzel on the paper he wanted to use, the costs of color pages—anything. In those early years, no one required him to provide a financial statement of any sort. The magazine was Stim's project, and that was that.

In April 1964, *Seattle* made its debut—its cover, a silhouetted man on the move, holding an umbrella. An introductory note explained its purpose: "Facing the elements, he is undaunted—note the jaunty way he leans into the storm. Though he is anonymous in silhouette, his spectacles and fedora mark him as a man of flair and distinction. He intends to get where he's going, but not at the price of getting drenched. . . . His whole stance, conveying purpose as well as personality, implies more about this publication than any long-winded prospectus. May he make it home dry—and awaken to sunshine."

Bunzel was embarrassed by the first issue.

Certainly the magazine was off to a poor financial start. Not a single major advertiser graced its pages, especially none of the critical mainstays found in Seattle's dailies, such as Frederick and Nelson, the prestige advertiser ever since Dorothy's mother had done her shopping. Instead, *Seattle* magazine featured an odd collection of ads from flower shops, Mr. Emile's hair salons, Exercycle of Washington, Alaska-Arctic Furs, Bel Square furniture, and the Madison Park pharmacy.

Bunzel had expected a slow response from advertisers. It was the editorial content that depressed him. For openers, his lead story was a total misfire: a lengthy investigation of Dave Beck's life in prison. The story bombed with readers because, Bunzel believed, Seattle just wanted to forget its one time power broker. That may have been true, but the story had another problem. It was dull. What it revealed was a portrait of a cranky convict expecting special treatment. Other features included a poem by Theodore Roethke, a trashing of right-wingers ("Wacky World Way-Out Rightists"), a down-the-nose look at suburbia; a nostalgic look at the Wawona sailing ship; and a feature article on the gowns to be worn at the high-society Poncho auction (including a photograph of Mrs. Bagley Wright).

The magazine's last page carried a column that had been proposed by Herb Altschull, the TV commentator, who wanted to write a continuing series inspired by the *New Yorker*'s "Wayward Press." Initially, Stim had opposed the idea, not wanting a frontal attack on the dailies, but he grew to like the idea. Altschull's first column, called "The Press Club," examined a month of editorials in the *P-I* and *Times* and found them to be tigers on topics afar but lambs at home. He also pointed out flawed reasoning and contradictions. The *Times* endorsed the Boy Scouts, denounced litter, and praised the Junior Chamber of Commerce, but said nothing on a proposal to ban racial discrimination in housing. "The *Times* and *P-I* are rather like a couple of elderly, genteel ladies," he wrote.

Despite Bunzel's view of the magazine's debut, *Seattle* established itself as the most interesting voice in the city's journalism. To liberals at least, its writing was often deeper, smarter, and more surprising than anything seen in the dailies and fresher than the city's sober journal of analysis, *Argus*. Many readers loved the new voice. No other publication seemed so willing to plunge into untouchable topics—homosexuality, contraceptives, racism in the police department—and deal with them in such frank ways. The magazine not only touched new topics but visited old ones—such as traffic congestion or city politics—in bold ways. It pointed fingers, attacked tired ideas, identified knaves and fools. It brought a sharp eye to politics. While the dailies typically reported press conferences, *Seattle* examined the influence of lobbyists in Olympia. Written in large part by newcomers and for newcomers, the magazine rallied to save the environment from developments by "wrong-headed" native-born residents. It crusaded to stop freeways, to clean Lake Union, and to save the Public Market. For many of the educated elite who came to Puget Sound to work for the university, for Boeing, for the law firms, for the burgeoning service industries, *Seattle* was the first local publication that explained to them who ran the city, where to shop, what to see, how to think about local issues, who were the right people to know. As one writer happily put it, *Seattle* "was very discussed."

In one early issue, *Seattle* magazine crystallized the sentiment that the City Council needed new blood. The idea for the article came from Bunzel, based on League of Women Voters' research. It was entitled "Our Musty, Crusty City Council." The illustrations were typically irreverent and cutting: mug shots of the aging Council members superimposed over old etchings of British jurists in long gowns and powdered wigs. Neither of Seattle's dailies would have done that. Such an approach would have seemed to them mean-spirited, or at least unbalanced. But *Seattle* came to each topic with a point of view and a determination to turn over some rocks.

Describing what then was a weak mayoral form of government, the magazine declared: "Few Seattleites realize, in fact, the mayor's function is to be, for all practical purposes, little more than a glorified public relations agent for the city. The power that his counterparts wield in other cities resides here in the Council." It went on to detail how Council members had power, functioning as ten independent mayors, each defending turf, "dedicated to perpetuating the system's worst consequences." The members not only lacked "vision but courage as well."

That was certain to stir City Hall. Then, a few months later, Bunzel pronounced Seafair a snore, except for the hydros, a collection of events that were "humdrum at best and sheer Babbittry at worst." Much of Seafair, wrote the heretical Bunzel, "gives the impression that Seattle is a hick city." To replace Seafair, he suggested a highbrow arts festival.

If anyone got upset, the staff would just chuckle, certain that the complaints justified the criticism. When they launched a campaign against Washington's lousy wines, they were right. The wines *were* lousy, but the company's broadcasting division lost wine advertising from angered retailers. *Seattle* writers were blind or indifferent to these consequences. At times, their work had almost a sophomoric quality—smart, but foolish. They were insensitive to the community they covered, even contemptuous at times. If they found a good restaurant, it came out as a back-handed compliment to the city. They spoke of surprise at finding a decent eatery in Seattle—a not-so-subtle reminder that they were from somewhere else that was better.

"[Mayor] Dorm Braman is against us, and Frederick and Nelson insists we're too controversial, and professional Democrats don't think we're gutsy enough, and the newspapers *hate* our guts, and the only thing going for us is a steadily climbing circulation," Bunzel wrote in early 1965. Then, joking, he added: "No wonder I have a persecution complex."

Bunzel made little effort to join the city's Old Guard. To the surprise of advertising executives, he didn't play golf and therefore was never found on the greens of the exclusive Seattle Golf Club (founded by Dorothy Bullitt's father). Bunzel scorned all that. Instead he was part of a new elite, the educated class from distant schools who flooded the Seattle area after World War II and who joined the Municipal League, determined to save Seattle. He did live in the exclusive Washington Park neighborhood and belonged to the Seattle Tennis Club—not to join that crowd, he hastened to say, but only because his sons played tennis. Like Stim, he despised the club's membership barriers. As he told one staffer, with disapproving sarcasm, the tennis club had "the nicest anti-Semitic restaurant in the city."

Seattle set out to shake the city, to question everything—the power structure; the attitudes toward civic entertainment; the received notions of what was good or bad about the city; all the conventions that society, with people like Dorothy Bullitt at the top, held to. *Seattle* had fun rubbing people's noses in their hypocrisy. It snorted at suburbanites; heaped scorn on Broadmoor, the walled enclave of the wealthy; and attacked the downtown club, the Central Association. That wasn't Dorothy's way—those association members were her friends, so she had reason to feel distaste for the magazine. To some, even some on the magazine staff, the trouble with *Seattle* was that it seemed to be looking for things to criticize. When it profiled improvements to the *P-I* under publisher Dan Starr, the otherwise glowing article had to point out that Starr was short and, when sitting, his feet didn't touch the floor. Piling it on, it also pointed out that he was somewhat deaf and unwilling to wear a hearing aid. Boeing, the city's dominant industry, made clear its displeasure with *Seattle*. When Bunzel tried to arrange interviews for a profile of the new 707 airplane program, a Boeing spokesman said *Seattle* was unimportant and Boeing executives had "better things to do." Such treatment reinforced Bunzel's view that Boeing and other powers only wanted a booster magazine. He cherished *Seattle's* identity as "a thorn in the community. We work hard at it," he wrote to a friend in New York.

One person's disapproval did make him squirm. Bunzel was too discreet to mention it, but one hostile presence was none other than Dorothy Bullitt, who he believed hated the magazine. Some of those pompous figures skewered in *Seattle* wanted to tear down walls. Worse, *Seattle* at times seemed to sneer at the very city she had told friends was like heaven. The fact that *Seattle* started out a money-loser, and remained so, only reinforced Dorothy's harsh view of the magazine. Yet to Bunzel's knowledge, Dorothy never interfered with the magazine.

From what outsiders saw, Dorothy Bullitt would defer to her son, the man in the family. In a tangled relationship that others sensed but could never understand, some thought they detected an antipathy between mother and son. Around others, Stim seemed excessively formal with her. As for Bunzel, he felt her disapproval. That was always an ominous issue, for she remained a powerful presence in the company, the controlling shareholder who was always checking expenses and revenues with the treasurer's office. He sensed that she didn't like him, which he never took personally. It was just her dislike for *Seattle*, he believed. And of course, the fate of *Seattle* always hung on the fragile relationship between mother and son. On the chilled ground between mother and son, *Seattle* existed in the Bullitt family DMZ.

Bunzel was even feeling static from a key member of the staff—Edward Hewson, a graduate of the Harvard Business School who served as business manager. Hewson had zero experience with magazines but he did have some specific thoughts about what could be done to make money. Hewson thought the magazine was unnecessarily confrontational. Although the two men had cordial relations, Hewson viewed Bunzel and the writers as too liberal. Hewson wanted to build circulation and advertising. He was convinced Bunzel and the writers just didn't care. When an ad salesman thought a meeting between Bunzel and an advertiser might help smooth things, Bunzel refused. Since Stim listened to Bunzel alone, Hewson was safely ignored. Bunzel was one of very few King Broadcasting staffers invited to Stim and Kay's Sunday dinners on Harvard Avenue, a location close to Dorothy Bullitt's home. By 1967 Bunzel was more than editor and publisher of *Seattle*. He was also Stim's administrative assistant, a position some saw as preparation for bigger responsibilities.

Hewson did not want to be ignored. In frustration he went to Stim.

"I think I should resign. I don't think I can do any more for your magazine," Hewson told Stim.

"I'd like to keep you in the company," Stim replied. Hewson was moved into a new division devoted to buying and building CATV, later called cable-TV, a system that sent TV signals through copper wires. The method was viewed as a means to extend the company's station signals beyond a transmitter's radius and to boost advertiser appeal. Eventually, those cables became a means of carrying a wealth of new programming that consumers would pay to get. Under Hewson's management, they would become extremely valuable—as valuable as the stations themselves.

Hewson wasn't the last business manager who wanted out. His successor, twenty-seven-year-old Thomas Bethell, wrote a mournful note to Stim and Bunzel: "I find myself in the awkward position of advocating that I be fired," wrote Bethell, the magazine's third business manager after Hewson and Roger Hagan. "The basis for this thinking is the simple fact that I am ill-equipped—temperamentally, educationally, or professionally—for the job of businessman." He went on to denounce himself as a "congenitally disorganized and volatile person." He said the magazine deserved better but so far it had yet to have a business manager familiar with magazines. Indeed, with the exception of one executive whose experience was only slightly relevant, no one in all of King Broadcasting had the qualifications, he said. Because of that, simple magazine-cost analyses took Bunzel and himself hours to do, "without any guarantee that the correct figures will result." Bethell argued that *Seattle's* lack of magazine-management skills was only matched by its commitment to spending. "Because of the large staff, our payroll alone exceeds the entire budget of Boston magazine."

Bethell pleaded to be replaced "at the earliest possible opportunity." In a separate note to Bunzel, he said he wanted to return to work as a writer-photographer: "Why write memos when we can talk about it?" Bethell asked. "Well, we really can't. For a lot of complex reasons, we've never developed the kind of rapport that lets me keep your attention span longer than a minute or so."

Bethell lasted one issue as business manager.

There was plenty of turnover at the magazine, but editors did a remarkable job of finding talented people who would work for the magazine at low wages, attracted to the challenge of a new kind of journalism in a young city. Many of the applicants were ushered down the narrow hallway to meet Stimson Bullitt, whom, they were told, protected the magazine from attacks inside and outside the company.

The writers found that meeting Stim was one of Seattle's more interesting experiences. Stim's office was lit dimly and had no windows. A framed portrait of the Florentine statesman and patron Lorenzo de Medici hung on the wall—a symbol, in one writer's view, of Stimson Bullitt's view of himself: a guy who wants to use his wealth and power to uplift the city, as de Medici did. Stim would ask some odd questions or simply say nothing, staring as the applicant squirmed in the silence and wondered if this was a method to force people to reveal their inner qualities. None of these people knew that Stim was shy to the extreme and a stickler for formality. Writer David Brewster made the mistake of calling him Stim. "We may eventually reach the point of using first names," Stim told him gently, "but we haven't yet."

Everyone talked about the time that talented writer Frank Chin was taken to see a "Mr. Bullitt" without any explanation of what was ahead. In the mix-up, no one told Chin that the man he was about to see was president of King Broadcasting. Chin thought he was seeing just another person in the company's elaborate hiring process. But there was a certain weirdness to the questions, particularly those about Ingmar Bergman, the Swedish filmmaker whose grim movies dealt with death and other weighty matters of the soul. Chin disliked Bergman's films but sensed the wisdom of keeping that to himself. Wondering what this was all about, he looked around the office and noticed a couch, which seemed to explain Stim's baffling line of interrogation.

"Do you mind if I ask you a question?" he asked Stim. "Are you the company shrink?"

"I beg your pardon?" Stim replied.

"What is your position in the company?" Chin wanted to know.

"I own it," said Stim.

Chapter 14   "More People Than Mr. Chips"

Near the end of 1966, Senator Henry Jackson returned from a visit to South Vietnam. Jackson by then was one of the nation's most powerful politicians, a key ally of the Defense Department, and a steady supporter of federal contracts for the Boeing Airplane Company, which employed 90,000 workers in the Seattle area.

The first identified casualty of American involvement in Vietnam was Army Specialist 4th Class James Davis of Tennessee, killed in an ambush in 1961. When Jackson stepped off the plane in Seattle five years later, the figure had grown to 6,047. But the pace of killing had slowed during a Christmas truce. To reporters in Seattle, Jackson declared that the bombing of North Vietnam must resume with more intensity.

The war in Vietnam was good for the Seattle area economy. It boosted Boeing's defense contracts, swelled payrolls at the Puget Sound Shipyard, and brought cash to businesses serving the expanded Fort Lewis Army Base and McChord Air Force Base. Regional business spent more on radio, TV, and newspaper advertising. (In a small way, the war also benefited a distant division of King Broadcasting, a plywood mill in Okinawa, where defense spending had also grown. Stimson Bullitt had merged the mill, along with other Bullitt Company assets, into King Broadcasting. The 1968 books for the newly combined company showed before-tax income of $2.7 million on sales of $24 million, more than three times what King Broadcasting's sales had been in 1963.)

Seattle boomed in other ways. Boeing had decided that year to build the world's largest jetliner, the 747. The old Orpheum Theater was being demolished to make way for a circular Washington Plaza Hotel, the city's first new hotel since 1929. The final section of the new interstate through Seattle to Everett and Tacoma was nearly complete. The region's employment was growing at twice the national average. State government was awash in nearly $99 million more in tax collections than had been projected.

In late December, Stimson Bullitt went to the barber and got himself a very short haircut. Stim preferred the clean-cut look, in marked contrast to the more shaggy look starting to gain favor among fashionable men in Seattle. The cut gave him an ascetic, almost monkish air that matched the seriousness of his intent. The meticulous president of King Broadcasting Company set about preparing himself for the most public moment of his life. He was rarely a self-revealing person, but he took care to warn his eldest son, Scott, that he was about to give a major speech. Scott, who hadn't yet turned eighteen, was impressed that his father had taken the time to alert him that something big was about to happen.

Stim had decided that the escalating Vietnam War was a mistake, and he would use King Broadcasting's stations to speak to the public directly. He sat down and wrote what would be his first editorial. For the broadcasting industry, it was already unusual for a station to do editorials, especially beyond bromides supporting Mother's Day. But Stim as owner was about to step forward and take a decidedly maverick position, one contrary to the views of thousands of viewers as well as Senator Henry Jackson and President Lyndon Johnson, who happened to appoint Federal Communications Commissioners.

Finally, the script was ready. Stim sat down to speak before the camera, which was taping him for broadcast later during the evening news. This would be the largest audience ever to see and hear Stimson Bullitt, more than a hundred times the readership of *Seattle*. As president of King Broadcasting, Stim could present himself or a viewpoint to that audience whenever he wanted, a power that any politician would envy. If only Stim had appreciated TV. He knew its power, all right. But to his way of thinking, TV had no class, no integrity, and possibly even no long-term future. Stim never felt comfortable defending TV to his circle of friends. It was ironic: his big moment was a TV moment, and its success would be judged in the context of that crude medium.

"Greetings," said Stim as the cameras rolled. "Until now, I've never broadcast an opinion for this company, but the war and its treatment in the news compel one to speak out. The intensity of our military action should be stepped down, and we should stop bombing North Vietnam."

He was awful. He was visibly nervous. He stammered through his text. One of the cameramen could not believe how bad Stim was. If this aired, he felt, it would be a disaster for KING. Roger Hagan, whom Stim had brought from Harvard to help the magazine, was called by a sub-ordinate who just happened to have been in the studio. You've got to look at the tape and get him to redo it, Hagan was told. He looked at the tape and was appalled. The performance was so bad no one would have heard the words; they would have remembered a man stammering through some speech. It was so bad he wondered if the studio crew had actually tried to sabotage Stim. Hagan knew that some in the TV division loathed Stim for his attitude toward television—to Stim, the cash cow for his personal projects; but to them, their life's passion, their chosen profession. Not long before air time, Hagan persuaded Stim to redo the speech.

By 1966 the greater Seattle area had more than 685,000 TV sets. On that night, KING-TV had at least a third of the viewing audience. In his address, Stim argued that the war was unjustified on many counts, yet he stopped short of calling for a pullout of U.S. troops. He called the war "repulsive to American ideals," a costly waste. "The more we claw the place into a plowed field populated by refugees, prostitutes and hostile guerrillas, the less we can achieve at helping them build the kind of society we would like." Keep the U.S. troops there, he suggested, maintain strategic positions, and let the South Vietnamese work toward a more representative government. North Vietnam might send in more troops, but they posed no serious threat, he argued. "And our new direction can assist us: first, to reduce the bloodshed—ours and theirs; second, to cool the overheated atmosphere of that miserable country as a step to enabling its inhabitants to make peace with each other; and last, to raise our standing among the nations and relax the tensions between the great powers until they can suppress those instruments which can, and may, wipe out the human race."

Those fine words went out over the airwaves and were picked up by antennae in citizens' homes. They did not start a revolution, however. The war continued. Henry Jackson was not persuaded, but he was enraged to be contradicted by people he saw as friends. Jackson was an old friend of Dorothy Bullitt's and at least a friendly acquaintance of Stim's—despite the hits from *Seattle* magazine. Although Jackson did not complain directly about the editorial, he let his displeasure be known through intermediaries.

Even with a second taping, Stim's performance was wooden. But many in KING's newsroom were proud of the boss. They agreed with his opinion and felt it showed courage to take such a stand, particularly in the bland world of broadcasting. They felt the city needed to hear it. Many in the community were equally impressed. Marvin Durning, a former Rhodes Scholar who had moved to Seattle to practice law, was one of many liberals who felt encouraged by Stim's stand. As he watched the broadcast, Durning felt like standing and applauding.

The last thing Stim wanted was for the community to see him as dictating an opinion to the masses. He hated the idea that anyone would compare him with William Randolph Hearst, the bombastic newspaper tycoon who used his properties to trumpet his shrill views. Even so, KING took an advertisement that ran on December 23 in the Seattle *Times,* which chose to place it not in the general news section but in what then was called the Women's Page. The *Times* carried the full text of Stim's message just below a recipe headlined "Flavored Milk Drinks" and *Hints from Heloise* (a tip on solving another social problem: how to make a fluffy meatloaf). The *Times* news department carried nothing on Stim's editorial. Dick Larsen, the Wenatchee reporter who became an aide to U.S. Representative Tom Foley, heard that some people in politics thought King Broadcasting had gone off the deep end. Advertising an editorial in a competing news medium struck some as excessive. To them, it showed too much zeal, an evangelism that had gone overboard. But Stim believed that opinions should be stated strongly and visibly, at junctures when a strong view could make a difference. Stim's editorial did not affect the conduct of the war—not that anyone would have expected it to—but it helped validate those who opposed Senator Jackson and President Johnson. And it forever colored people's opinions of him. Even his critics would judge it his finest hour, a moment of courage and thoughtfulness. Four years later, he did his only other editorial, criticizing the secret invasion of Cambodia.

Stim wanted King Broadcasting to set itself apart from the rest of the television industry and see itself as a tool for social change. Something good could be wedged between the deodorant and hemorrhoid ads, he figured. That much continued his mother's values. But he took it further. He wanted to see the company on the cutting edge of what advertisers, even viewers, would accept.

His mother saw the company as a means of improving the community. She did not endorse Stim's more radical moves. Had she been in Stim's position, Dorothy would never have done anything so bold, political, and confrontational as calling for an end to bombing North Vietnam. But because of her revered standing in the company and in the community, whatever was good about the editorials—that King Broadcasting stood for something—was attributed to her, while his eccentricity was all that many remembered about Stim. She got credit for Stim's courageous initiatives. She got credit for the hiring and promotion of women and minorities, for KING-TV having the city's first woman on-air reporter. But all those initiatives came from Stim—and they contributed to his downfall.

Stim wanted his company run by high ideals. He set forth his goals in a high-minded document called the "King Broadcasting Company Policy Manual," a manifesto for a new way to run an organization. The first edition came in 1965 and was written much like Stim's 1959 book-length essay on politics, *To Be a Politician*, with sprinkles of quotations and references to great figures in history. Perhaps no other company manual in Northwest history managed to quote Oliver Cromwell and Marshall Field on the same page. Because many at King Broadcasting had little direct contact with Stim, the policy manual provided the only chance to understand what he was trying to do with the company. To many, he was the blue blood who rode a bicycle to work and disappeared into his dark office—not at all like his mother, who invited everyone to her office to have a smoke and swap funny stories.

The first aim of the company, Stim wrote, was to achieve a profit. Only by achieving financial strength could the company be independent in its decisions. But beyond profit, what was the purpose of King Broadcasting? His answer was pure Stimson Bullitt, his own brand of idealism brought to the huckster's world of television: The purpose of King was in part to serve as teacher, leader, and guide, and in part to respond to popular tastes. "We aim to supply our audience with creations of our own, not just to hold up a mirror to the mob, not just to treat the public as the sun which we worship as though we were some shivering pagan or which we passively reflect as though we were a sort of electronic moon," he wrote. "The aristocratic element of our approach rests on our duty to provide something of our own; the responsive element rests on the public's right to have some of what it prefers; both necessary to hold our audience, the former over the long run, and the latter over the short."

King Broadcasting products, he said, should "express beauty and convey truth." The company should achieve a level of sophistication "located in a thin zone: above the expressed public taste yet below the limit of the public's realized capacity to appreciate. That is, just above what they ask for but below the line beyond which they will not accept." King should help raise Seattle's knowledge, understanding, and taste, just as Neiman-Marcus had elevated Dallas and Ralph McGill's newspaper had elevated Atlanta.

King Broadcasting afforded an opportunity, Stim told its employees. Each station was a combination theater, newspaper, debating hall, cultural center, and school. With it, King Broadcasting could make a difference. "With our instruments at hand we can contribute to setting the course toward points which range from extinction of civilized society to sunlit uplands with bountiful and fulfilling lives on a high plane for all," he wrote.

Stim put it more simply to a group of KING-TV journalists, whom he had called in to encourage them to aggressively cover government—You can shape perceptions. Your reporting is vital to a healthy democracy, he told them. The fact that he was not threatening their jobs, as he had done with Herring and others, suggested that Stim's view of the newsroom had improved. He now saw the newsroom for its possibilities.

"You people reach more people in a single night than Mr. Chips reached in a lifetime," said Stim, referring to the English schoolmaster in James Hilton's famous novel.

But great instruments required what Stim called "the best people."

Since the company could not afford to buy the nation's recognized talent, his strategy was to seek promising young people who could be hired cheaply, taught the business, and developed. "An employer is to some extent choosing blind. Like sandlot stars, these superior novices come cheaper than major league players both because they are not then of major league effectiveness and because no one knows which ones will develop it," Stim wrote.

But how to find the "best people"?

The company sent recruiters to meet graduating seniors from Harvard, Yale, Stanford, Dartmouth, and many other good universities. The goal was to identify people with "brains and general education." For managers, Stim even supplied a list of factors against which to measure a job candidate. Character and attitudes were a large factor. Grades were a smaller factor. Ethnic or social background were not factors at all.

Many at KING read the manual with shock. In their view, Stim wanted to fill vacancies with Ivy Leaguers who knew nothing about broadcasting or running a magazine. Just how, asked the managers, would a newcomer call the cues, pace a broadcast, or handle a studio camera without prior experience? Stim apparently regarded experience as a defect in an applicant. Old-timers at KING took the "sandlot" remark as evidence of Stim's contempt for the people who had built the station. To them, Stim was saying that the pioneers of Seattle broadcasting were second rate. They wondered: What does "Mrs. B" think? Is she going to let Stim ruin KING? Convinced that Stim had an interest only in Ivy Leaguers, they guffawed at his line that everyone in the junior ranks had a chance at promotion: "Every private should be given to know that he has a marshal's baton in his knapsack." Wasn't that something Napoleon had once said? they asked. It was false that you had to be an Ivy Leaguer to succeed at KING, but many employees thought they knew the score: If you weren't an Ivy leaguer, your baton was smaller than that of others.

Stim made room for the new by sweeping out many of the managers and others who had been hired by Dorothy, Henry Owen, or Otto Brandt. In 1966, all three station managers were replaced. "Do extend my congratulations to Stimmie. Unquestionably, he has lined up more brilliant Eastern talent to fill these roles," wrote a sarcastic long-timer who had been passed over for promotion and had left the station.

He made other changes.

In early 1966, Bob Schulman, the author of *Lost Cargo* and other KING documentaries that had helped establish the company's reputation, was called into Stim's office and told he should look elsewhere for a job. Schulman asked why, and Stim only repeated that he should look elsewhere. Schulman was devastated. He went to Ancil Payne, Stim's protégé and a social friend of Schulman's, for an explanation. Payne was working then as Henry Owen's assistant. When Schulman described the abrupt end to his career at KING, Payne simply replied: "That's Stim for you."

Schulman could only guess. Had Sam Sharkey, Stim's departed news director, secretly raised suspicions with KING management? What had happened? Was it Schulman's closeness to Al Rosellini, who served two terms as governor? What was wrong with being friendly with a governor who had appointed Dorothy Bullitt to the University of Washington Board of Regents? Schulman told people he suspected his firing had to do with his documentary work at KING. Stim had spoken vaguely to Schulman about doing documentaries in a new way, but Schulman had resisted doing anything artsy. He wanted to do journalistic documentaries, not feature films. He had thought he was secure enough to resist Stim, but he was wrong.

Schulman also went to Dorothy, but she made it clear she was not running the company. "Stim is in charge and Stim has the directions to make," Dorothy told him. "There's really nothing I can properly do about it."

So Bob Schulman was out, and he told people he never knew why.

Then another giant fell—Lee Schulman. No one ever said why publicly, but the man described in the *Times* as "Mr. Television," the man who had put KING on the air, was out. Lee Schulman had complained that Stim's hiring policies were impractical; Schulman wanted people who could operate a camera, not quote Cicero. If differences over hiring were the reason, neither Lee Schulman nor Stim would say so publicly. Lee Schulman was forced out of his post as KING-TV general manager, replaced by Tom Dargan.

Dargan's secretary, Janet Ruthford saw Lee Schulman come out of Otto Brandt's office. Schulman invited Ruthford to his office, closed the door, and began to cry. "It's over. I'm leaving," he said. Later, Schulman told his former aide, Kit Spier of the firing, and he invited Spier to go with him to a station in Chicago.

Everyone at KING knew Lee Schulman had been very close to Dorothy Bullitt. Seeing him go must have hurt her very much, they believed. They had to believe that. Wasn't the company a family? But if Dorothy were hurt by the changes, why hadn't she done something? Why was she letting this happen? Most of them could not accept or did not know the truth: that Dorothy Bullitt was far more informed than people realized. Since people wanted to believe that Dorothy would not approve Stim's firing of personnel, they had to believe she did not know. They could not embrace the aspect of Dorothy Bullitt's personality that had been a part of her success—a willingness to be ruthless to protect the company. As for her part, Dorothy was quite willing to let people assume her ignorance; it allowed her to stay on good terms. If her children would not praise her for her business success, at least her employees would.

But Stim was causing a more fundamental problem, and one that would arouse his mother to act. Stim's pet projects were draining the company. By May 1967, *Seattle* was facing an annualized operating loss of $160,000 as King Broadcasting Company's overall profitability was dropping. The company's before-tax income was down to 20 percent below budget projections. Year-to-date company revenue was $5.6 million, $400,000 below budget. Over three years, *Seattle* had lost $621,000, and no profit was expected the following year. Employees were upset that *Seattle* was burning money that they felt should be going into the company's pension fund. In their view, it was one thing for their president to cause snickers in the broadcast world, to ignore them and favor anyone who crossed Harvard Yard, but it was another for his whims to threaten their old-age income.

Moreover, even bigger losses were coming from Stim's other pet project, King Screen Productions, formed in mid-1966 to diversify the company but blissfully untainted by market research. Stim approved the division's first and most costly project before its general manager was even appointed. Stim had liked the work of filmmaker Michael Roemer and had agreed to finance his next movie, *The Plot Against Harry,* a black comedy about a middle-aged Jewish gangster that was to be filmed in New York.

To run the screen division, Stim picked Roger Hagan, who moved from *Seattle.* Hagan had no prior experience in film and yet was given the task of creating a film industry in Seattle. Hagan had to contact authors, sign up screen rights, and produce theatrical movies and feature-length documentaries. But films were expensive to produce and required Hollywood connections to finance and distribute; and Seattle was a long way from Los Angeles, where the deals were made. New York was then the only alternative to making feature films in Hollywood, yet Stimson Bullitt was going to make Seattle a third choice. It was a breathtakingly audacious idea, but it diverted money from the TV stations. KING-TV, the company cash cow, went begging for money for new cameras as King Screen hired writers, the broadcasters suspected, who took four-hour lunches. Now King Screen was run by a manager trying to learn the business while the division's annual operating loss reached $203,000.

The losses worried Otto Brandt. As vice president for broadcasting, it was his duty to safeguard and nurture the three stations that floated King Broadcasting Company. He tried to convince Stim to modify his policies. He tried to get more money into the broadcast operation. He sought more practicality in Stim's Ivy League hiring; it didn't make sense to expect liberal-arts grads to perform technical tasks. He tried to save people that Stim wanted out. Yet Stim was insistent that his hiring policies be strictly followed. Angered by foot dragging and by new recruits being made to feel unwelcome, in late 1965 Stim called a meeting of senior managers and warned that his policies were being sabotaged. Not one of you has the courage to refute it, Stim told them, his anger on full display. Anyone standing in the way would be removed. He regretted that he needed to speak that way; it shouldn't be said to reasonable men, he said.

Part of Stim's anger was directed at himself. He knew he had chosen the wrong strategy in dealing with subordinates. Trying to come across as nonthreatening, Stim had chosen a small office for himself and would visit his vice presidents instead of summoning them. But they took advantage of his modesty, he felt. Many would simply brief him on a proposal and expect him to sign an approval form. One executive chatted on the phone, letting the president of the company wait. Stim was certain that executives visited his mother, complained of his policies, and received encouragement to brush him off. As Stim held meetings, his mother would send in her secretary, who insisted that he call her immediately.

Unwilling to confront anyone, Stim tried to minimize the humiliation he felt by further reducing his contact with people. So he'd sit alone in the cafeteria, leaving others to guess about his thoughts. Visitors to his office suffered through long periods of silence. Wondering: Did I say something? Is he angry? Why is he staring at me? At age twenty-two, Jean Enersen met Stim for her first job interview. She walked into the room and saw a couch underneath a large light; in the corner was a small chair in the shadows. As Stim sat at his desk looking at her, she was confused about what to do—should she sit under a spotlight on the couch, or far away in the corner? It was all so strange that she decided it was some sort of subtle experiment in how she would alter her environment. Enersen's solution was to pull the couch away from the light and sit down. She got the job.

To some, there was something faintly ridiculous about Stim. He wasn't just eccentric, he was profoundly eccentric, a millionaire who rode a bicycle to work. He owned TV stations but forbade his children to watch television during summer. (They watched at friends' homes.) He ran King Broadcasting with high-minded seriousness but when he walked through the studio, technicians were certain he was about to trip over a cable. When he dedicated KGW's new building in 1965, he returned to his seat after a speech, leaned back in his chair, and promptly fell off the stage.

Part of what eroded Stim's authority was distrust of his motives. Many of KING's managers believed that Stim just didn't care about the basic business of his mother's company, an impression formed not long after he became president. In 1962, Stim was offered a briefing by the Blair Company, the national advertising representative. Blair sent half a dozen account executives from New York to give him an overview of the accounts that represented about 50 percent of company revenue. All of King Broadcasting's top managers came, including the station managers from Spokane and Portland. Stim arrived twenty minutes late, without explaining his tardiness, then he opened a notebook and read from it while the Blair people spoke. Before they had finished their presentation, he stood up. "I'm sorry, I have to leave," he said. He left a group of people who stared at one another. No one ever found out why he had left.

Another problem was his treatment of people, even those perceived as more valuable to the organization than himself. On rare occasions, he could be mean and cutting, especially if he perceived disloyalty. Otto Brandt may have been the longtime symbol of the class and integrity Dorothy Bullitt wanted at King Broadcasting, a popular figure in the company, but Stim did not hesitate to move against him. Brandt was King's ambassador to the networks (the Company had ABC and NBC affiliates). He was chairman of the board of the Television Bureau of Advertising, chairman of the NBC Television Affiliates Board of Delegates, and a board member of the National Association of Broadcasters. He knew everybody. Bob Sarnoff of NBC sought him out at conventions where Brandt, not Stim, represented the company. Inside the company, dozens of people thought highly of him and his wife Thelma.

Yet Stim began to humiliate Otto Brandt. He mocked Brandt to his face at meetings, to a point some found painful to watch. Peter Bunzel felt Brandt was being cruelly treated, even though Brandt was a major reason for the company's growth and financial success. Why? Brandt may have been simply a displaced target on the battleground between mother and son. Stim wanted to redo King Broadcasting completely, yet he was surrounded by Dorothy's loyalists or loyalists to the old way, chiefly personified by Otto Brandt.

The Brandt-Stim conflict had festered for years, flaring over big and small problems, in private and before other employees. For example, Brandt supported a $20,000 request to build a room for disc jockeys—whom Stim regarded as annoying "pipsqueak nonentities" representing the worst of broadcasting—to rest or prepare for going on the air. Stim often let requests languish without a response for weeks. This time Stim said he opposed the item. It had not been budgeted in advance. Besides, he was contemptuous of his AM station and felt the disc jockeys weren't worthy of creature comforts.

Brandt, normally unflappable, left one tense meeting with his face flushed with anger.

"I'm sorry you had to witness that," he told Eric Bremner, the corporate personnel director. "When Stim came in with his ideals and ideas, I was willing to accept that he was brilliant and there were some really good ideas. But I've come to believe he is wrong. He is just wrong."

It was inevitable then. One day in early 1968, Stim moved against Brandt.

"Either you go or I go, and I'm not going," Stim told Brandt.

Brandt went to Dorothy. He unburdened what had been years of frustration. He told the mother that her son was damaging the company. The seventy-six-year-old Dorothy would not break with her son. Not yet, at least. That deep voice rolled with the words that ended Brandt's career with King Broadcasting—after seventeen years.

"Blood is thicker than water, no matter how much I love you," she said.

The Black Panthers had Seattle scared. Led by their captain, nineteen-year-old Aaron Dixon, they wore black pants and leather coats, black berets on defiantly large hair, and dark glasses that hid their intentions. Everything about them seemed to say: *Don't mess with me, man.* But that's not how some in the Seattle Police Department took it. They wanted to mess with Seattle's Black Panther Party, the first chapter organized outside of California. To police, the Panthers were troublemakers importing ideas with no place in Seattle. Blacks had no reason to riot, many whites thought. Seattle was not Oakland, Los Angeles, or Newark. Anyone driving through the Central Area could see that: the modest but well-kept houses, the procession of well-dressed Negroes walking to Sunday church.

Seattle in 1968 exploded with economic growth. Boeing that summer employed more than 104,000 workers, the highest total in company history, a payroll that lifted the entire region's economy. Boeing was about to put into production the 747, an airplane that would usher in a new era of transoceanic travel, and there was talk of building a supersonic jetliner.

But there was discontent. Seattle's blacks felt untouched by prosperity, with an unemployment percentage double that of whites. They had trouble getting hired as high-paid union construction workers, as bus drivers, as police officers or fire fighters. Banks directed loans away from their homes or businesses. Blacks were discouraged from living outside an invisible line on Seattle's map. Ruling whites seemed to want it that way, having two years earlier rejected by two-to-one a proposed open-housing ordinance. The same condition existed in the schools. Most black children attended schools that were 90 percent black. Whites were pulling their children out of schools with a large share of black students. The city's reputation as a place of friendly race relations was a myth. The racial rhetoric was heated and at times ugly. "Pretty soon the white man is going to have to decide whether he wants to live with us, or to kill us," a black member of the Seattle–King County Economic Opportunity Board told a reporter for *Seattle* magazine. "And when that time comes, he won't be fighting just the teenagers—*he'll be fighting us all.*" The magazine concluded that "it is difficult to see how Seattle can escape the flames."

At Meany Middle School, there were regular incidents of interracial violence, fire bombings, even a stabbing. When a group of students, as a gag, rushed a teacher, her instinctive reaction was to hide under her desk. Tensions were already rising that year when the Reverend Martin Luther King was murdered in Memphis in April 1968. In Seattle, it touched off what became a months-long series of protests, sit-ins, scattered violence, and overreaction by police, who were mistrusted by blacks. King County Prosecutor Charles O. Carroll, for his part, inflamed things by seeking maximum penalties.

That summer, *Seattle* carried a special issue devoted to one topic— white racism. In a note to readers, publisher Peter Bunzel said he had had qualms about approaching the topic because of the distrust blacks felt for the Seattle press, which by necessity included his all-white staff. His reporters circulated in the black neighborhood expecting to get roughed up. The magazine's photographer, Frank Denman, was physically expelled from Garfield High School by "a group of angry young militants."

Dixon and his Panthers felt blacks had good reason to be angry, for they saw themselves as victims of systematic white racism. Tired of milder pacifist approaches to promote civil rights, they adopted the radical views they found in Che Guevara's *Guerrilla Warfare* and Mao Tsetung's *Red Book*. They drilled, military style, in the Madrona playfield, carried guns, and spoke of violence. They were the vanguard of what *Seattle* called "the violent Negro revolution." Ten of them had marched into the office of the principal of Rainier Beach High School carrying unloaded rifles to protest the beating of three black students by a large crowd of whites. They followed Seattle police cars through the Central Area to monitor police treatment of black people. They called the police "pigs." Unlike the Oakland Panthers, who lived in California ghettos, the Seattle Panthers mostly lived in decent homes, reflecting the comparatively milder conditions in Seattle. Instead of living in a burned-out tenement, Dixon lived in a modest but comfortable two-story house on 33rd Avenue, about two blocks from the Panther headquarters at 1127-1/2 34th Avenue. The son of an illustrator at Boeing, Dixon was a sophomore English major at the University of Washington, where he wrote prize-winning poetry. But Dixon and other militants had convinced Seattle police that a true uprising was at hand. "The panther never attacks first, but when he is backed into a corner, he will strike back viciously," Dixon told reporters. "You see, we've been backed into a corner for the last 400 years, so anything we do now is defensive." He spoke vaguely of restaurants being burned down. Other Panthers encouraged blacks to get guns.

Whites driving through the Central Area, even police, could be pelted with rocks. Once in a while, a sniper took a shot at a police car. The windshield of Mayor Braman's car was smashed by thrown rocks and soda bottles. Firebombs were tossed into buildings. When fire trucks came, they were firebombed, too. In July alone, thirty-nine police were injured and one-hundred black youths and adults were arrested. Police Chief Frank Ramon, who worried about diminishing property values in the Central Area, responded by flooding the area with extra patrol cars and tear gas, blockading entire blocks of the Central Area and sending overhead a new police helicopter that swept houses with powerful search lights. The effect of all this was to give Seattle's black neighborhood the distinct feeling of a prison near riot. Assistant Chief M. E. "Buzz" Cook authorized helmeted police to move against crowds swiftly: "Use all necessary methods to effect arrests or dispersal," he said.

This fascinated Ted Bryant, a King Broadcasting long-timer who had replaced Charles Herring as KING-TV's news anchor in 1967. Bryant emulated the Edward R. Murrow style. Like Murrow, Bryant had graduated from Washington State University, had a wonderfully dramatic, resonant voice, good looks, and an elegance and polish that viewers, especially women, loved. Like Murrow, Bryant often lowered his face when talking to viewers. There was a quality to Bryant's presentation that suggested brains, whiskey, hard work, and honesty. He looked like a guy who used his fists to get a story. Bryant, though, was more than an image. He was a superb journalist and Seattle loved him. He had a degree of authority over the newscast that no anchor before or since would have. Unlike most anchors who simply came in and read what others had written, Bryant produced and wrote the newscast. He was not completely independent; he reported to News Director Warren Guykema, but he had a great say in what shaped the newscast, more so at KING than even the granddaddy of anchors, Walter Cronkite, did at CBS. Bryant came to KING in 1956 from KTNT in Tacoma. He had anchored the late newscast for years before taking over the 5:00 P.M. newscast in 1967. With his huge share of the TV audience—at that point, typically half of viewers during the news hour—practically everyone in Seattle recognized him. People in restaurants wanted his autograph. He was the face in their homes.

In July 1968, Bryant invited the newest employee in KING's news department to go with him to the Central Area to check out reports that any black in a leather jacket would be harassed by police. Bryant wanted proof. He asked twenty-nine-year-old Bill Dorsey to join him in a stakeout.

It was no accident that Bryant had approached Dorsey. Although lowest in KING seniority, Dorsey brought to the story a special dimension— he was black, one of the first two African Americans to work at KING news.

Bill Dorsey had recently been discharged from the army, where he had worked as a combat motion-picture photographer. After three tours in Vietnam, Dorsey had become disillusioned about his intended goal of a career in the military. He settled in Seattle and looked for work. King Broadcasting appealed to him because it had a screen division, but after an interview he found there was no job at KING-TV. The company, however, told him about a possible opening at KGW. They flew him down to Portland, where he met with Ancil Payne and others, but again there was no job.

Just as he was about to take a job at KOMO, he got a call at home from a man who identified himself as Stimson Bullitt with King Broadcasting. He asked Dorsey if he could come over and discuss job prospects at KING-TV. Sure, said Dorsey, who had no idea who Stimson Bullitt was. But during their conversation, Stim made it clear who he was and how King Broadcasting would offer Dorsey an opportunity to work in several divisions on interesting projects. Stim said that his was the only local station in the nation to come out in opposition to the Vietnam War, and that he was prepared to take a similarly strong stance on the civil rights issue.

Dorsey was impressed. They talked for more than an hour. Dorsey liked the shy patrician who had come to his home. He felt Stim's intentions were genuine. And they were. Even more than Vietnam, civil liberties defined Bullitt family beliefs. After World War II, Dorothy Bullitt had served on the Civic Unity Committee to promote racial harmony and had become friends with Ruby Chow, a prominent activist in the Chinese American community. During World War II, Stimson Bullitt wrote to each member of Washington's Congressional delegation urging that Japanese Americans be allowed to join the military. (The internment of Japanese Americans took a personal toll by forcing the relocation of Edward Ohata, a close friend from boyhood whose father had been C. D. Stimson's longtime chauffeur. When Ohata was taken away, it was one of very few times in his life that Stim broke down and cried.) After the war, Stim had fought red-baiting and saw it take a toll on his friend John Goldmark. He found racial discrimination disgusting. One time, he struggled to avoid punching a building agent who had refused to rent an office to a physician friend who happened to be black. He quit the Rainier Club in protest over what then were racist and anti-Semitic policies. He refused to join the Seattle Tennis Club for the same reason.

Dorothy Bullitt came from a different age. She and Henry Owen employed perhaps two or three blacks and a few Asians, but Stimson Bullitt threw the weight of his company presidency into hiring and promoting minorities. Although many of his managers supported his goal, Stim was rarely satisfied that the company was moving fast enough. There was a business purpose to his goal: a command from government to end discrimination in broadcasting. In 1968, the FCC warned TV and radio station owners that they faced possible loss of their licenses if they discriminated against blacks. But no one doubted that Stim's interest in racial justice was genuine. The Bullitt home was a shrine for civil rights. Stim introduced his children to James Meredith during a visit to Seattle by the activist. When Stim drove past the Daughters of the American Revolution building on Capitol Hill, he told his children that the national DAR had barred Marian Anderson, a black woman, from singing before its membership. Stim tutored his children on the history of blacks in America, including the fact that his own forebears in Kentucky were slave owners. The children were instructed to call their cleaning lady by the respectful "Mrs. Lilly," never by her first name as adult slaves had been addressed.

No Bullitt lived the cause more ardently or at such personal cost that year than twelve-year-old Dorothy C. Bullitt, a student at Meany Middle School. Many of her white friends had fled the school. White boys who remained were often beaten, but Dorothy at that young age saw herself as playing a part in a larger struggle. She knew that if she and other white students stuck it out, the schools would not be forgotten by the white majority. She was proud of the fact that she had black, Asian, and white friends, but she paid an almost daily price of suffering petty harassment, extortion, insults, slaps, punches, clubbings, and hallway fondlings from some blacks who saw her as just another white. She rarely told her parents of her trouble. She figured she could handle it and make herself a soldier in the cause of integration. Like her father, she was stubborn. Being a victim of black racism just reinforced her view that racism of any sort was wrong.

Stim's energetic wife, Kay, ran an interracial day camp each summer for her own children and children of the inner city. She enrolled her children in a Freedom School at a black church where they learned civil rights and black history. She organized a petition drive to push integration of Seattle's public schools. When a black friend was looking for an apartment, Kay brought her daughter Dorothy to join them in the search; Kay figured it would be harder to reject a black person when two whites were looking with him.

Kay served on the board of the Seattle Urban League, whose aggressiveness in promoting civil rights made for an uneasy relationship with its financial supporter, United Good Neighbors. Kay was a good friend with the League's executive director, Edwin Pratt. A rising star in the national organization, Pratt was widely known around the city for his quiet effectiveness, charisma, diplomatic ability to press business leaders for opportunities for blacks, good humor, and jokes about his constant struggle to control his weight.

"When are you going to start firing black employees?" Pratt asked a startled Ancil Payne. Payne replied that King Broadcasting had very few black employees, so it couldn't afford to fire any. Besides, said Payne, Pratt and the Urban League would raise hell if he did.

"That's just the point," said Pratt. "Until you feel free to fire black, you are never going to feel completely free to hire one."

Payne took that as the best advice he had ever received on integration.

Stim made a point of never interfering in the operation of King Broadcasting's newsrooms, but it was certainly no accident that the newscast had a liberal reputation on civil rights, a tradition begun in 1961 when KING had stirred controversy with *A Volcano Named White. Seattle* magazine covered civil rights with so much sympathy that some readers complained its editors had become intoxicated with black revolutionaries. When Stokely Carmichael came to Seattle in 1967, KING thoroughly covered his appearances and carried a talk show afterward that analyzed the impact of his visit. Civil rights was a big issue in every newsroom in Seattle but especially so at KING, where commentator Herb Altschull regularly championed the cause, driven largely by his own views of civil justice, but also to prove wrong what he had heard when he arrived in Seattle—that the city could not have a "Negro problem" because the black community was small and quiet. Altschull pushed the open-housing ordinance, causing some outraged real-estate interests to protest to KING management. In 1968, he produced a major documentary, *Color Me Somebody,* which told white Seattle residents that their black neighbors were ordinary people who held jobs, cared for their children, and aspired to dignity. The program brought Seattle viewers into the kitchens of black residents to hear them discuss the city, their future, and the possibility that racial unrest could lead to more violence. It took pains to show that the black community had a spectrum of views, as represented by Pratt, a Black Panther, and other members of the community. The show caused a flood of calls, pro and con. Some hostile callers insisted that radical blacks were planning an uprising, that Seafair would be disrupted as a part of a plan to embarrass Seattle in front of the nation's eyes. Altschull felt KING was the strongest voice pushing civil rights in Seattle, which is why it was so important for Stim to get blacks working in KING's newsroom. It was the right thing to do, but the execution was a little shaky, as Bill Dorsey found when he arrived for his first day at KING in 1968.

"Why are you here?" Dorsey was asked.

"I'm supposed to go to work today," he replied.

Stim had neglected to tell anyone of Dorsey's hiring, nor did he know another black photographer had just been hired. Gil Baker, a still photographer working at Boeing, had been hired, too, but had not yet started at KING. Baker filled the one opening in the newsroom. Both men were slightly apprehensive of how they would be treated at KING. They knew they had the support of Stimson Bullitt, but how would the lower-level managers treat them? They both discovered that, although KING was the most liberal of Seattle's stations, it was not free of racism. Both detected slights and got the distinct feeling from some older news staffers that blacks were not acceptable. Because of his combat experience, Dorsey already knew what he was doing. Baker was vulnerable because he lacked training in motion-picture photography. But that didn't eliminate the slights, and worse, felt by Dorsey. He would return from an assignment, only to find his film had been surreptitiously opened and ruined, or the sound head on his camera had been disabled. (Within a year, KING's news department had five blacks—two reporters, two cameramen, and a librarian.)

On that night in July in 1968, Ted Bryant and Bill Dorsey took a KING car into the Central Area, accompanied by a couple of young Panthers whom Bryant had met earlier. They had agreed to act as guides. People at KING thought Bryant, as a white man, was showing courage by going into the racial hot zone. Dorsey, as a resident of the Central Area, thought the perceptions of violence in his neighborhood had been vastly exaggerated. Dorsey was not afraid, not after combat in Vietnam.

It wasn't long before they saw the flashing lights of a police car racing to a scene a few blocks from Garfield High School. Ten to fifteen police officers were out of their cars, and it looked to Dorsey that they were clubbing someone on the ground. Dorsey was out of the KING car in an instant, filming with his hand-held camera. There was just enough light to capture what was going on. Suddenly, the police noticed the KING crew and did something that Dorsey had never before seen and would never forget. Several of the officers started backing toward him with three-foot-long batons held backward at their sides, pointed at him. The policemen were careful not to turn toward him, so Dorsey could not get their faces on film. They closed in and began jabbing him, hard. The blows dented the camera and bruised Dorsey's hands, but he kept filming until their backs made it impossible to record anything else.

The next day, Stim took the unusual step of reviewing the footage before it was aired. Bryant did a piece that night that included an interview with Dorsey.

Seattle had never seen anything like it. Most residents refused to believe that their own police department had members who would brutalize anyone, but KING had filmed evidence. Residents refused to believe that police would actually interfere with the press taking pictures of an event on a street—KING had ample evidence of that as well. Now Bryant brought those photos into the homes of Seattle residents. It was an important moment in the city's journalism: something that only TV, with its sound and moving pictures, could bring. KING gave Seattle's middle class a sense of life on the streets. The reaction was sensational. Ted Bryant got calls that night and later from journalists at other stations, congratulating him on his job. Mike James, a reporter who had just moved from radio to the TV news department, was awestruck. To James, Bryant had raised Seattle TV journalism to a new level. KING wasn't relying on what the designated "black leaders" were saying, or quoting only what police said, as journalists often did; Bryant had cultivated Black Panthers who were taking him to places that most Seattle reporters wouldn't see. But it was still TV journalism. The Bryant story stood out in part because TV journalists rarely spent more than two minutes on a story, hardly the detail and perspective that a print writer, if motivated, could offer. The episode was perhaps Bryant's greatest

As one of Seattle's foremost businessmen, C. D. Stimson helped to build much of the city's downtown and to shape its social and cultural organizations. He tutored his daughter, Dorothy, in principles of business. Stimson died in 1929. Photo courtesy of the Seattle *Times*.

The Bullitt family in 1928, posing for a campaign picture by the pool at Greenway, the house in The Highlands given to them by C. D. Stimson. From left to right: Stimson, Harriet, Dorothy, Scott, and Patsy. Photo courtesy of the Seattle *Times*.

Twenty-year-old Stimson Bullitt listens to his mother during a social outing in 1939. In his writings, the son revealed that he rarely felt his mother's approval, especially in his role as president of her company. Photo courtesy of the Seattle *Times*.

Not long after King Broadcasting was formed in 1947, a friend of Dorothy Bullitt persuaded Walt Disney to create a logo for the company. Disney charged $75 for "King Mike." Courtesy of King Broadcasting.

As director of programming and later as station general manager, Lee Schulman, left, put his stamp on every KING-TV program. His driving personality often infuriated engineers, but they considered him a genius. The man at right is engineer Clare Hanawalt. Photo courtesy of King Broadcasting.

In 1952 King Broadcasting moved from its cramped studios at 310 Second Avenue West to 320 Aurora Avenue, a converted furniture store. On the right can be seen King's mobile news-gathering vehicle, "The Bread Truck." Photo courtesy of King Broadcasting. Photograph by Webster & Stevens.

A Seattle *Times* photographer found one downtown commuter, attorney Stimson Bullitt, who was unaffected by a 1956 Seattle transit strike. Five years later, Stimson Bullitt became president of King Broadcasting. He continued to commute on his bike. Photo courtesy of the Seattle *Times*.

Ruth Prins, as "Wunda Wunda," earned KING-TV its first national award: a Peabody Award in 1957. Working with Gloria Chandler, Prins followed Dorothy Bullitt's mandate for high-quality children's programming. Prins sang, danced, and read stories—but never showed cartoons. Photo courtesy of King Broadcasting.

Stan Boreson had a long run as host of the children's afternoon program, KING's Clubhouse." Photo courtesy of King Broadcasting.

Charles Herring, left, and Robert Schulman, center, often teamed up to cover the Legislature in Olympia. Robert Schulman created *Lost Cargo* and other documentaries that established King Broadcasting's reputation for in-depth reporting. The photographer at right is unidentified. Photo courtesy of King Broadcasting. Photograph by Merle Junk.

Dorothy Bullitt's personal lobbying of NBC Chairman David Sarnoff, center, helped persuade that network to switch in 1958 from KOMO to KING. At left is Otto Brandt, whose ties to the industry helped land the network. The man at right is Bill Jahn, TV writer for the Seattle *Post-Intelligencer.* Photo courtesy of King Broadcasting.

Dorothy Bullitt at her desk at King Broadcasting in 1961, the year her son became president of the company. Photo courtesy of the Seattle *Times*.

Ted Bryant became KING-TV news anchor in 1967 and brought a greater degree of aggressiveness to the newscast. During rioting in Seattle's central area, he investigated complaints of police misconduct—one of many times KING displeased the Seattle Police Department. Photo courtesy of King Broadcasting.

As a reporter and later as a columnist, Don McGaffin wanted to shake up Seattle, which he saw as smug about social problems. He was equally aggressive in protecting what he felt were KING-TV's journalistic standards. Photo courtesy of Don McGaffin.

Commentator Charles Royer skewered politicians and then decided to become one. His departure from KING to run for mayor of Seattle created an awkward situation for the newsroom. Photo courtesy of King Broadcasting.

Some in KING's newsroom saw Jean Enersen's promotion to anchor as a surrender to entertainment values. But she survived constant turnover in news management and emerged as the last icon of KING's quality tradition. Photo courtesy of King Broadcasting.

News anchors Jean Enersen and Jim Harriott interviewing Dorothy Bullitt at the 1973 ceremony honoring King Broadcasting's Twenty-Fifth Anniversary. Photo courtesy of King Broadcasting.

Dorothy Bullitt in 1979. She built King Broadcasting into a great Northwest institution and held hopes that the company would stay in the family. It was difficult for her to face the fact that none of her children loved the company as she did. Photo courtesy of the Seattle *Times.* Photograph by Ann E. Yow.

Promoted to the presidency during a company crisis, Ancil Payne grew King Broadcasting into one of the West's largest media organizations.

Left to right: Ancil Payne, Dorothy Bullitt, and NBC news anchor John Chancellor, who was visiting King Broadcasting to honor the 1980 opening of its new headquarters. Photo courtesy of Ancil Payne.

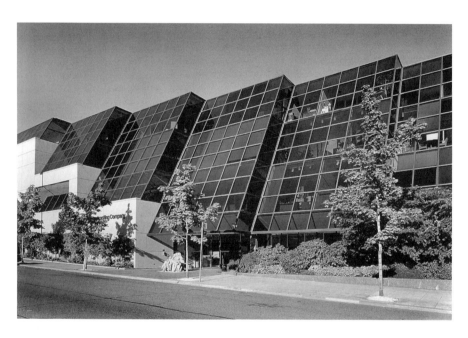

In 1981 King Broadcasting remodeled and expanded its headquarters. The $18-million venture enlarged offices and studios, but created heat problems on sunny days for workers under the glass. The sculpture in front was placed there as a barrier after a former employee drove a Porsche into the lobby. Photo courtesy of King Broadcasting.

Dorothy C. Bullitt, granddaughter of King Broadcasting's founder. Highly regarded in the business community, young Dorothy was thoroughly prepared to step into the executive office, but her aunts wanted to sell the company. Photo courtesy of the Seattle *Times*. Photograph by Betty Udesen.

Soon after their mother's death, Harriet Bullitt and Patsy Collins, left to right, sold the King Broadcasting Company. The Bullitt family was out of the communications business. Photo courtesy of the Seattle *Times*. Photograph by Betty Udesen.

contribution to KING's reputation for journalism. But his passion for the news done his own way was soon to end his career at KING. He would go in his typically dramatic way.

Bryant had no trouble working with news director Warren Guykema, an easygoing personality who shared power in a loosely run newsroom. Each day, a list of planned stories was prepared and reporters would pick the one they wanted. The Bryant-Guykema newsroom seemed to run well, and Guykema thought his place was secure. He'd been told that he had been identified as a possible future station manager. But the word came without warning, and Guykema was out as news director, replaced in 1968 by Robert Hoyt, a former Neiman fellow at Harvard. Don't worry, Guykema was told. You'll move to a corporate position with responsibilities to be defined later. The decision to replace him, Guykema was told, was just Stim doing another quirky thing. The assembled news staff was still numb from the abrupt change when Stim personally brought in his latest news director. Stim made a little speech, introduced Hoyt, and asked if there were any questions. There were none. Hoyt said nothing.

Robert Hoyt was strong-minded and faced a newsroom that was ungovernable, a tradition at KING that would continue long after Hoyt was gone. But Hoyt was determined to make some changes. Although Hoyt had had some TV experience, he had never run a TV newsroom. One of his first acts was to tear down a wall that separated commentator Herb Altschull from the rest of the newsroom. Hoyt wanted control over everyone, Altschull included. No one was going to refuse an assignment. Secretary Janet Ruthford thought Hoyt looked like Humphrey Bogart and she was impressed by his forceful style, his slow, deliberate way of talking, and his intelligence. On the other hand, Barbara Stenson, a KING reporter, found Hoyt vulgar and rude.

Whether Hoyt was right for KING, he had plenty of ideas and he pushed them on the newsroom. Central to his planning was to scale back the authority of the anchor—Ted Bryant—to writing and reading. He announced that Bryant would no longer have responsibility for producing the newscast and no authority over the content of the show. Bryant was outraged, and soon decided to quit. He told the new KING station manager, Eric Bremner, that he was leaving unless Hoyt was fired. Bremner tried to talk his friend out of a hasty decision. He offered

Bryant a vacation—not Hoyt's head, though he privately regarded Hoyt as a disaster in the newsroom. Bremner employed the city's top anchor, but something important was at stake: management authority. Bremner knew that if he capitulated to Bryant's demands, the role of the news director, regardless of who held the title, would be undermined. Not long after that, Bryant stunned his viewers by announcing at the end of a broadcast that it would be his last.

Bryant had no job to go to. He later told print reporters that he was quitting because Hoyt's system didn't work and led to errors. Hoyt appointed Gene Wike and Bob Faw as co-anchors. Bryant's departure hurt KING morale, but it also hurt the company's bottom line. KING's ratings, which had been slipping prior to Bryant's departure as KOMO's newscast improved, took a sharp drop. KING-TV, the station that had originated television journalism in Seattle, fell behind KOMO.

The company's turmoil paralleled the escalating disorder and trauma in the city. Seattle was alive with protests, rumors of violence, and racial tension. But no incident would so horrify the city as the one that caught the attention of President Richard Nixon. It happened on a cold night—January 26, 1969—with the city blanketed in three inches of snow. The snow seemed to absorb all sounds. It was after 8:30 P.M. At the home of the Urban League's Edwin Pratt, just north of the city limits, Bettye Pratt was putting the couple's five-year-old daughter to bed when she heard a noise outside, as if someone were thumping the side of their house. She went to a window while her husband went out the front door. She saw two men crouched in the yard, both of whom looked like six-foot-tall white juveniles, one of whom was holding something.

"Look out!" Bettye shouted to her husband. "They've got a rifle!"

Too late. One of the men aimed a shotgun at Edwin Pratt and fired at close range. A large slug—a special kind that worked in shotguns, weighing about as much as five 25-cent pieces—tore into Pratt's mouth, shattered his teeth, and severed his spinal column. A chunk of the slug broke off and lodged in his lung. Pratt, at age thirty-eight, was dead. The men jumped into a Buick Skylark and raced off. The weapon was a kind often used in assassinations because there are no ballistics on the bore of a shotgun, as there are on a rifle. The slug in Pratt's body had no telltale marks. No one knew who killed Edwin Pratt or why, but the King

County Sheriff declared the incident an assassination.

In more than a year of bombings, snipings, protests, and more, Seattle had not seen anything as chilling as this deliberate murder of a civil rights leader. It stunned adults and children, white and black. It revealed an element that many had thought absent in Seattle, the city isolated from the polluting elements of other parts of the country. The killing underscored a point that Pratt himself had made: that there was a huge gap between what Seattle thought about its progress in civil rights and the reality. Every day, business leaders spoke against discrimination yet remained members of such clubs as the Seattle Golf Club and the Seattle Tennis Club that banned blacks by policy or indifference. "Hypocrisy is rampant," Edwin Pratt had said in a speech shortly before his death.

Someone came to the Stimson Bullitt home and told Kay Bullitt that Edwin Pratt had been murdered. Kay had seen Pratt just two days earlier at the Urban League's annual meeting. She was horrified at the news and began to cry in the doorway. Later, Kay hosted a reception following a memorial service for Pratt at his church, St. Mark's Episcopal Cathedral. Among those gathered at the Bullitt home were the Reverend John Adams, pastor of the First African Methodist Episcopal Church and the city's most prominent black religious leader; and Whitney Young, head of the national Urban League.

The King County Commissioners voted to offer a reward, which added to a $10,000 fund established by local businessmen. A fund to assist the Pratt family was also created. Acting Mayor Floyd Miller declared an official day of mourning. The state Senate rushed through a resolution of condolence for the Pratt family. President Nixon met with Attorney General John Mitchell to be briefed on the investigation. A "considerably upset" president sent Mrs. Pratt a sympathy card, aide John Ehrlichman, a Seattle native, told Seattle reporters.

The FBI entered the investigation. Police questioned 100 witnesses and chased down dozens of leads, but with no success. The killers of Edwin Pratt were never brought to trial. The young man in the dark glasses, Panther Aaron Dixon, was quick to tell white Seattle that the killing was part of a national pattern. "We feel this is another assassination by whites to slow down the black people of the country," he said. The prospects of racial harmony in Seattle seemed more remote than ever.

With his control over KING's newsroom strengthened by Bryant's departure, Bob Hoyt was free to direct the news as he saw it. Hoyt, however, knew little of Seattle's geography, much less its racial climate.

In May 1969, Hoyt asked Janet Ruthford, who had given him some earlier tours of the city, to show him around the Central Area. One night they drove there in an unmarked white car. He wore a black suit, she a green dress—symbols, Ruthford would say later, of the well-dressed Establishment.

It was a little past 5:00 P.M. when they drove by Garfield High School and Hoyt looked ahead. He saw a threat.

"There's going to be a problem," said Hoyt, who had been to Selma during civil disturbances. "I can't say what, but anytime you've got more than three people on a street corner, you've got trouble. What I see up there is a whole lot more than three."

They kept driving. Hoyt slowed as a crowd of black youths walked in the street toward the car, blocking the way. "I can't hit anybody, because if I hit anybody, there'll be a riot," he told Ruthford.

Suddenly, something big hit the windshield, which splintered into a million pieces and sagged toward them. Then someone was pounding on the side of the car. Angry faces approached the car. Ruthford was horrified. A hand reached through her open windshield and began to yank a ring off her finger.

"What have I done?" Ruthford asked. "Let me take it off." But she couldn't. She noticed that someone had opened Hoyt's door and he was being dragged out of the car. "Don't let them get you out of the car or they will rape you!" Hoyt shouted, as someone began to beat him with a baseball bat.

Then she heard another voice.

"We're from CAMP!" said a voice, referring to the Central Area Motivation Program. "We're going to get you back in the car." Someone helped Hoyt into the passenger's side and Ruthford took the wheel. "Go, but go slow," Hoyt told her. Ruthford drove and soon noticed a large group of Seattle Police officers, dozens of them, who had been watching her during the most awful experience of her life and who, measuring whether their involvement might escalate the incident, had done nothing.

That night, a rattled Hoyt was given a Scotch and was treated by a doctor for his injuries. Ruthford was uninjured. The next day, a bullet hole was found in the car two inches from where her head had been.

KING-TV did not report the story. In a city enduring months of bombings and riots, the story of two white people getting roughed up was not a major story. Management concluded that Hoyt had shown bad judgment in bringing a woman into the city's hot spot. The incident weakened his position in the newsroom. But in the aftermath, that was the least of the station's problems. KING's news ratings continued to slide to the point where KING was running a poor second, and KIRO, whose newsroom was run by a small staff with shabby equipment, was becoming a threat. KING station manager Eric Bremner, convinced that his newsroom was in a shambles, soon decided that Stim's news director had to go. The problem lay in convincing Stim.

Chapter 16 Darkness at the Center

His nose looked puffy from drink, his eyes unfocused and vacant, his lips slightly pursed and twisted off center. With his hair slicked back, his broad jaw tilted slightly downward, King County Prosecutor Charles O. Carroll looked like a husky thug in a lineup, about to be fingered by a victim. His face was framed in a poster glued to a brick wall. The banner over his head screamed: REMOVE THE COUNTY PROSECUTOR.

Seattle, the publishing arm of King Broadcasting Company, had decided to take on the most powerful figure in Washington state politics— Charles Oliver Carroll, kingpin of Seattle's courthouse, ruler of King County's criminal justice system, the darling of the Seattle *Times.* Everything about the presentation, from the photo to its alarming headline, suggested that Carroll was a public menace. The magazine all but called him Scarface.

This was perhaps the most fundamental attack on the ruling Old Guard of a city already on edge. Going after Carroll said much about King Broadcasting and Stimson Bullitt's tenure. It was one thing for Robert Schulman to go after a weak Seattle Port Commission; it was another to launch an assault on a politician who had real clout, useful friends, and the means to fight back. Just as the Vietnam editorial had set a high mark for Stimson Bullitt personally, the attack on Charles O. Carroll represented the company's most ambitious effort to date—and would prove to be its clumsiest failure.

That summer of 1968, Seattle reflected both local and national tensions over race, crime, politics and war. Long hairs, newcomers, blacks and others were calling for change and new ideas, but the City Council, dominated by septuagenarians, fretted over bond ratings. The new hip crowd wanted to save Pike Place Market; the downtown crowd wanted to raze it. Neighborhoods demanded attention as the city's population shrank. A group calling itself Choose an Effective City Council (CHECC) was trying to clean out City Hall. Two council members had already been ousted. The rest were doomed. A new sort of city government was being born.

It was an exciting time. But some were simply frightened by the pace of change and the unraveling social fabric. Hippies openly bought and sold drugs on The Ave in the University District. Planning was underway for the Sky River Rock Festival and Lighter than Air Fair, a Labor Day rock festival that would draw 20,000 to a party colored by rain, mud, LSD, and a fleeting sense of communal ecstasy.

Country Joe played rock at the Eagles Hall. Be-ins were held at Volunteer Park. Scruffy writers for the underground newspaper, *The Helix*, gave young people a sympathetic view of the counterculture that was missing from the pages of the *Times* or *P-I*. Black Panthers brandished guns and called for revolution. A new radio station, KOL-FM, was among the nation's first to play rock in an album format. Hubert Humphrey, campaigning that September for the presidency against Richard Nixon, suffered the worst heckling of his campaign and, during a mini-riot, was driven from the speaker's platform at Seattle Center. The next day, Humphrey would deliver a speech divorcing himself from Lyndon Johnson's Vietnam War and pledging a halt to the bombing.

It was a year of challenging those in power, and no one better symbolized Seattle's version of old-style politics than Charles O. Carroll.

Since 1948, Charles O. Carroll—the "O" distinguished him from Democratic City Councilman Charles M. Carroll—had built a political machine that converted deputy prosecutors into campaign doorbellers, intimidated most political adversaries, and made for easy victories when Carroll stood before the voters. From the day he had entered politics, Carroll was already a big man in the city, the All-American running back who had led the Washington Huskies in 1928 and 1929, the "human battering ram" honored by no less a fan than President-elect Herbert Hoover, who had invited him to dinner after a game at Stanford.

His parents, Thomas J. and Maude Carroll, moved to Seattle from the Midwest in 1881—eight years before C. D. Stimson bought his Ballard sawmill—and began what became a comfortable jewelry business in downtown Seattle. Born in 1906, Charles was an early success, a sixteen-letter athlete at Garfield High School, where he was editor of the school newspaper and president of the senior class. After graduation from the University of Washington, he went on to its law school, where he was an average student. In his first run for public office, he lost in the Republican primary in the 1938 race for King County Prosecutor.

He got the prosecutor's job in 1948 when King County Commissioners voted to appoint him to the vacancy created when the incumbent accepted a judgeship. It was not a unanimous vote. One of the three commissioners had wanted candidates screened by the Bar Association. But in an indication of Carroll's style of politics, the forty-two-year-old lawyer had allied himself with King County Sheriff Harlan Callahan, who lobbied the commissioners. As soon as he took office, Carroll began to organize support for the 1950 election, which he won handily. He soon established policies that favored the *Times,* which had the largest number of readers in King County. His staff timed big announcements for the *Times*'s afternoon press runs, and his secretaries waved *Times* reporters into Carroll's office without an appointment. The *Times,* in turn, produced a steady stream of articles—Carroll's duck hunting, his hunt for diapers for his newborn son, tributes from admirers, and his occasional interest in running for governor. Aided by his friendship with fellow yachtsman Ross Cunningham, who was for years the *Times*'s chief political writer; and by conservatives such as Bill Boeing, Jr., and County GOP Chairman Ken Rogstad; and by claims of a 90 percent conviction rate, Carroll easily won a series of reelections (except for the 1958 race, when a chirpy-voiced Democrat, Brock Adams, gave him a scare).

Cunningham and others believed that Carroll was the centerpiece of Seattle's efforts to keep out The Mob. Cunningham, who later became editor of the *Times*'s editorial page, said Seattle officials had taken harsh steps to keep East Coast mob figures from establishing operations here, including, he hinted, tossing some organizers into Elliott Bay. Protected from corrupting influences from afar, Seattle could not be unclean.

That Seattle had its own form of organized gambling, with payoffs going to police and other public officials, was somehow proof that Seattle was untainted—because Seattle's vice was supposedly a less virulent breed, being small-time, controllable, and less corrupting. As former Mayor Gordon Clinton once told a reporter, the most you could ever lose gambling in Seattle was the price of a candy bar. But that may have more reflected gambling in his neighborhood than elsewhere in Seattle. It was no secret in the city's establishment that the police ignored high-stakes gambling, despite state laws against it. The premise underlying the so-called tolerance policy was that officials could contain vice and therefore monitor it. Despite the fact that gambling was openly advertised in parts of the city, Carroll said there was no such thing as a tolerance policy: "There is no tolerance policy and never has been. If enforcement agencies want to make arrests, we will bring charges."

Arrests would have been awkward. Many of the people who could make arrests were either on the take or knew about payoffs. As court testimony later showed, more than 10 percent of the city's 1,000-member police force took money, including some of the department's highest-ranking officers. According to the *P-I,* the payoffs represented a vast apparatus set up to skim cash from citywide gambling, which generated $5 million a year in betting. Since city officials could unofficially wink at gambling, that gave police and other officials the arbitrary power to tolerate or close an establishment and the right to be paid for making the choice. Patrolmen were the collectors and enforcers. Four, five, even seven officers would show up at a bar and ticket patrons for minor violations of the state liquor regulations, such as standing while drinking. Or they'd ticket customers as they left. They forced operators of barrooms and gambling dens to turn over $200 or more a month, which was collected and distributed up the chain of police command and to other city officials. A police captain, then making some $13,000 a year, could almost double that income with his take of payoffs. The payoffs kept most cops away, but occasionally one would show up and demand hundreds of dollars on the spot to let a gambling game continue.

Carroll was not the sort who boasted publicly about his power or what he did with it. There was no need to. He showcased his clout at an annual Christmas party at the Olympic Hotel which drew a large number of elected officials, including the entire State Supreme Court. If anyone from his staff failed to buy a ticket and appear, he would personally call and ask why. He was known to have an explosive temper, worsened by the pain he felt from a bleeding ulcer and a weak heart. "Maybe you'd better not work here anymore," a secretary said she was told by Carroll when she refused to work in his campaign. If he didn't like what a judge was doing, he didn't hesitate to call, even to the point of chewing out a judge he called "gutless." To stay in contact with sources in city and county government and in the political world, he kept two phone lines in his home and seemed to hear every whisper in King County. After two Seattle *Times* reporters spoke to a source in Kent who claimed to know of public corruption, they were called into an editor's office and handed a transcript from a tape recording of the entire interview which, the editor said, had been sent over by Carroll. The prosecutor reputedly taped conversations in his office and kept investigative files on rivals and enemies. Reporters learned it was safer to butter Carroll than to burn him.

Perhaps the clearest demonstration of how his links to the news media kept him in power had occurred in the 1962 election, when Carroll was facing a weak challenge from Democrat Dan Brink. That year Carroll had proclaimed that King County was "as clean from organized crime as a community can be." But instead of getting the top "superior" rating from the influential Municipal League, Carroll was designated "above average," while Brink was labeled "superior." Carroll heard about the ratings before they were announced and demanded a reconsideration. Rallying to his friend, Ross Cunningham called C. A. Crosser, the League's executive secretary, and said Carroll had been a bulwark against the influx of gangsters and, while Brink was honest, there was no guarantee that Brink would show the same vigor in resisting promoters of vice. Cunningham also threatened not to publish the ratings unless Carroll was upgraded. A special meeting of the League's trustees and the ratings committee was quickly convened, attended by Cunningham and Richard Auerbach, former head of the Seattle FBI office, as witnesses for Carroll. Although only eight of the league's twenty-five trustees were present, Carroll's rating was changed to "superior." A Republican rival of Carroll's and a member of the trustees quickly filed a lawsuit, but a judge refused to block publication of the revised candidate ratings. Carroll crushed Brink in the general election.

The payoff system seemed entrenched even when witnesses came forward with public complaints. In 1967, two tavern owners said several police officers regularly came around with demands for money—hardly the "clean as can be" situation described by Carroll. An embarrassed Mayor Dorm Braman formed a blue-ribbon committee to investigate the police department and put to rest the rumors once and for all. Without subpoena power, the group invited witnesses to mail statements. Few people came forward. Cops figured the investigation was a sham, particularly because the department liaison was none other than Assistant Chief M. E. "Buzz" Cook, the operating head of the police department. That was an easy conclusion for Inspector David Jessup to make because he received payoff money from Cook, he later told prosecutors. Since Jessup knew of Carroll's information network, he figured Carroll knew everything about the police department. Cops suspected he was either part of the system or a fool. And no one believed Carroll was a fool. To no one's surprise in the department, the blue-ribbon panel concluded that there was no organized payoff system.

The payoff system and Carroll seemed invincible until one morning in late August 1968, when the Seattle *Post-Intelligencer* splashed across half of its front page a photograph of Ben Cichy, the head of the pinball association, entering Carroll's home at 10th Avenue East on Capitol Hill. Reporter Orman Vertrees had been watching Carroll's house for weeks and had discovered a suspicious hour-long meeting between the head of the gambling establishment and the county's top law enforcement officer. Several articles detailed Carroll's volatile temper, his techniques of pressuring lawyers for support, his edgy relationship with Governor Dan Evans and other moderate Republicans, his influence over King County Commissioners, and his lax enforcement of anti-gambling laws.

In a report uncharacteristically aggressive for a Seattle daily, Vertrees revealed that Carroll and Cichy, "on opposite sides of the fence of life," had regular monthly meetings at Carroll's home. "What could possibly be the nature of such liaison between men of such diverse callings, a prosecutor and a pillar of the pinball fellowships?" Vertrees wrote. The article stopped short of accusing Carroll of taking payoffs—even though publisher Dan Starr and others at the *P-I* believed it—but it left that impression by noting four actions by Carroll's office that had favored pinball interests. Rather than policing the gambling interests, Carroll had acted more like "a den mother," Vertrees wrote.

In a column, executive editor Louis Guzzo told readers that the paper had been investigating Carroll for two years. (Guzzo left out a tantalizing anecdote: at a meeting in Washington, D.C., Guzzo and Starr had personally told FBI Director J. Edgar Hoover of their suspicions about Carroll. Hoover listened politely and did nothing.) The following day, the *P-I* carried a headline quoting Governor Evans as saying that Carroll should come up with some "substantial answers—fast."

It was clear what the *P-I* was doing. It wanted Carroll out. The *P-I* was a powerful presence in the city's politics, but it was not a member of the city's inner circle. Over the years, the *P-I* had gradually shifted from Republican policies to a more centrist Democratic view. Hard as the *P-I* publisher might try, he was always an outsider, an employee of Hearst headquarters in New York. The *P-I* publisher could never travel in the circles of the publisher of the Seattle *Times*. The *P-I* wasn't a full-rank member of Seattle's ruling elite, so it was in a good position to go after Charles O. Carroll, the friend of William Boeing and Ross Cuningham.

A few days after the *P-I* carried its exposé, *Seattle* hit the stands, with the cover photograph of Charles O. Carroll that made him look like Public Enemy No. 1. Bunzel told readers that *Seattle* had begun an investigation of Carroll independently of the *P-I,* and that when reporters from *Seattle* discovered that the *P-I* had already been working the story, Bunzel had decided to join forces. It was an interesting, unusual, and ultimately wrong decision. "Normally, this is quite unheard of," Bunzel wrote. "Newspapers and magazines are usually in competition for readership, for advertising, for 'beats.' Here, though, the community interest transcended customary journalistic considerations, and so we agreed not only to share information but to coordinate a joint approach."

KING-TV was a bit player in the investigation. Without the muscle of a meticulous prober like Bob Schulman, KING-TV's newsroom at that point lacked the resources to probe Carroll thoroughly. The best it could come up with were some quick stories. Its coverage of Carroll during this time was not memorable; KING-TV was about two years away from doing hard-hitting political-investigative stories. KING's most powerful public outlet, its airwaves, carried little on what Bunzel regarded as one of the city's most significant problems.

The exposé of Carroll was intended to be *Seattle*'s and, by extension, Bunzel's finest hour. Bunzel had long sought a big story that would perform a major public service and thereby establish *Seattle* as a major force in the community. Nothing would have felt better than to take out the man who seemed to be the town's most corrupt public official, the big fish who also happened to be close to that symbol of the kind of Seattle journalism so distasteful to both himself and Stimson Bullitt—Ross Cunningham. After that, presumably, nobody would turn away *Seattle*'s reporters as the Boeing publicists had done. Frederick & Nelson couldn't resist buying ads in the most-discussed journal of the city. Bunzel wanted *Seattle* on the map.

Stim played no direct role in the Carroll investigation. He encouraged Bunzel to stay on the story, which involved months of work and nearly the entire magazine staff. The story had gone through many revisions and careful consultations with lawyers for King Broadcasting. The story had to be bulletproof. Any error or misstep would have handed Carroll a weapon to use against King Broadcasting, possibly leading to a libel suit tried before a judge friendly to the prosecutor. But Bunzel and the rest of his staff had little experience with investigations. Bunzel felt himself under intense pressure. He and others at the magazine, fearful of Carroll's power, worried that the prosecutor had tapped their phones as he picked up details of their questions. They had the tiger by the tail, as Bunzel put it later, but what would happen?

"Prosecutor Carroll should be removed from office forthwith," declared the article in a self-described "indictment." To the right of the text was Carroll, in what was obviously a surveillance photo, looking haggard, defeated, as if he were ready to go quietly to jail. "THE CASE AGAINST CHARLES O. CARROLL," declared the headline. The article set forth charges against Carroll: that he had failed to enforce statutes against gambling and other vices; that he had inflamed racial tensions in Seattle with overzealous prosecutions of blacks; that he had pressed for excessive bail and sentences. The article's tone was severe—"few men are so disliked as Chuck Carroll"—but *Seattle* just didn't have the goods, or at least not in what it delivered to readers. Instead of claiming that Carroll was the spider in the middle of a conspiracy, as many suspected, *Seattle* lamely said that Carroll's lax enforcement policies "are making the county a sitting duck for the Mafia." That old chestnut, the Mob from Outside, must have brought a sardonic laugh to the bar owners who had long been extorted by a Seattle mob wearing badges.

The article actually had two themes: police payoffs, and Charles O. Carroll's career. Each was told in fascinating detail, but the article didn't make a convincing connection between the two. It only noted Carroll's "inaction" in the face of twenty years of payoffs. As a political profile, it was brilliant—full of telling details of Carroll's harsh treatment of black defendants; his vindictiveness over perceived slights, however small; his attempts to dominate whomever sat in the governor's chair. It was elegantly conceived and written, as good as anything ever published in Washington state on a major political figure. Graceful writing was a hallmark of Bunzel and *Seattle*. But it was not jugular journalism. As if the editors were acknowledging that they lacked hard evidence, the article came to a mushy conclusion: "Even if Carroll is finally absolved of illicit conduct, he should still be removed on the grounds of being a bad prosecutor," the magazine declared.

Bunzel knew he was putting King Broadcasting at risk. As the article was being prepared, Carroll, who had dodged requests for an interview, sent telegrams to *Seattle* accusing the magazine's writers of malicious intent—a legal term used in libel lawsuits. In a letter to KING, his private attorney made hints of Carroll taking his case to "an appropriate and impartial forum."

Seattle called for Carroll's ouster. The *P-I* kept the story on page one. What would Governor Evans do? He had the power to direct the state attorney general to investigate Carroll. But Evans was up for reelection and his opponent was none other than the Democratic Attorney General John J. O'Connell. To win, Evans needed support from Carroll's wing of the party. That left Evans with a tough choice: give a headline-making issue to his political rival, or look bad by not investigating Carroll.

Evans scheduled a meeting in Seattle to talk directly with Carroll. After a 75-minute closed-door meeting, Evans emerged to face waiting reporters. The press loved Evans. He was always friendly, his aides talked, and he made good copy. *Seattle* had once put Evans on its cover with a shot taken at dawn of the handsome mountain climber doing pushups, a grin on his face.

Evans announced that Carroll had told him he had known Ben Cichy but there was nothing hidden or unusual in their relationship. He then described Carroll as "a man who has served in office with the highest degree of integrity" and said it would be premature for the attorney general to probe Carroll. That stunned the reporters. Had Evans decided to back off? What had Carroll said to Evans? The reporters never got the answer. From that moment on, Evans stood in a neutral corner. After days of delay, Evans announced he would leave it to the judges of King County Superior Court to decide if a grand jury should be convened. O'Connell was outraged. But the matter stayed before the judges who, after Evans' reelection, announced that they lacked investigative authority to do anything.

Carroll said he had done nothing illegal in his twenty years as prosecutor. Much of the news media rallied to his defense. *Argus* charged that *Seattle* and the *P-I* had performed a hatchet job on Carroll. Radio KVI called *Seattle*'s indictment of Carroll "asinine" and demanded that the magazine "get off Mr. Carroll's back." Others complained that *Seattle*, once again, was looking for people or things to put down. In protest, some retailers canceled their advertisements and newsstands refused to sell the magazine.

The case against Carroll was fizzling.

In his column in the magazine's next issue, Bunzel tried to defend his judgment: "Our angriest critics ripped into us because we had failed to prove that Carroll had committed any criminal acts, and when we point out that our main concern was with his public record, many launched into a defense of Carroll as epitomizing 'the best there is in Seattle,'" Bunzel wrote. Bunzel vowed that his magazine would stay on the story, "persisting to uncover the facts." Privately, he viewed the fact that the Carroll story angered some major downtown advertisers as further proof that Carroll "was the creature—and handmaiden—of important members of the downtown Establishment, as was the tolerance policy itself."

Bunzel left out one significant disclosure. Contrary to critics who saw the *P-I* and *Seattle* as cohorts, the *P-I* initially had resisted *Seattle*'s getting involved in what it saw as its story. The "coordinated effort" was little more than an agreement to run their stories at about the same time. *P-I* Editor Lou Guzzo felt that the magazine's probe had uncovered nothing substantial and was alerting Carroll before the newspaper had a chance to get its facts fully assembled. In private, Guzzo complained that Bunzel was a loose cannon who had forced the *P-I* to run its story prematurely. Guzzo felt *Seattle* had blown the *P-I*'s schedule and possibly the best chance to remove Charles O. Carroll.

Bunzel felt he had failed. What *Seattle* had published was not as tough as he had wanted. He blamed King's attorneys for watering down the article. He realized that it had been a mistake to work with the *P-I*, for that fed the perception that the magazine was pursuing an agenda rather than facts. Running the piece close to elections also fed the perception of a political smear, even though Carroll himself was two years from his next race. In the draft of a note to a complaining subscriber, a demonstrably more humble Bunzel confessed that the tiger gripped by *Seattle* had bitten him.

After that, *Seattle* stayed away from Charles O. Carroll. Bunzel seemed shaken and humbled. "I think all of us in journalism should be careful about being too sure of themselves, for 'facts' and truth are hard to come by," Bunzel wrote in an unpublished letter. "Robert Frost put it pretty well in this couplet:

> *We dance around a ring and suppose,*
> *And the secret sits in the center and knows."*

But the center would soon fracture.

On a September night in 1969, when Police Chief Frank Ramon was out of town on vacation, a group of officers disgusted with the tolerance policy raided Charlie Berger's Lifeline Club on First Avenue. Eighty-six people were cited and twelve were arrested by the thirty-four officers who busted the club, which had been flagrantly violating the law for years. Berger, a convicted felon, was arrested and taken to jail, along with eleven employees. Officers discovered more than $7,000 in cash, and books that showed that the club collected $1.5 million to $2 million a year. The Lifeline was cut off.

Ramon rushed back from vacation and ordered Berger released. He also ordered the return of a gun to Berger, who, as a former felon, got a weapons permit only through the unusual intervention of a sheriff's deputy. Ramon announced that there would be no more raids on bingo parlors. The arresting officers figured they had an easy felony gambling case against Berger, but instead the case was filed in the municipal court, where Berger was charged with a misdemeanor ownership of gambling devices. Evidence in the case was returned to Berger—but not before much of the paperwork had already been photocopied by a tough TV reporter who had been working the payoff story for a solid year. Don McGaffin, a KOMO reporter, had been waiting for the big break to blow open the payoff story, and he finally had it—bank records and canceled checks from the Lifeline showed payments going to some of the biggest politicians in Seattle.

McGaffin, thirty-eight, had arrived in Seattle in 1967 from a TV job in San Francisco, and had quickly discovered Seattle was in denial about its police department. Even reporters at KOMO who showed McGaffin evidence of open violations of gambling laws insisted that the police department was clean. McGaffin, who loved a good fistfight, saw a chance to give what he regarded as smug Seattle a poke in the eye. Now he had the evidence. He went on TV and read off the names of politicians receiving campaign contributions: three county councilman, a city councilman, seven legislators, a congressman, and a former sheriff. A $1,000 check to the Sheriff Jack Porter dinner committee. Berger supported campaigns in five counties.

In his report, McGaffin confronted Seattle with its failure: "One of the peculiar and sustaining myths of our times is that bingo is a game played by gray-haired little ladies in church basements for prizes such as electric blankets or toasters. This is the purest kind of nonsense. Practically every knowledgeable vice squad detective knows that bingo long ago turned into a huge commercial gambling operation."

Outraged over Ramon's handling of the case, three assistant chiefs—Eugene Corr, A. C. "Tony" Gustin, and George Fuller—in 1969 walked over to Mayor Floyd Miller's office, described the extent of the payoff system in the department, and demanded that the mayor either oust Ramon or that they each be demoted to the civil-service rank of captain. Within a few days, Chief Frank Ramon resigned. From that point on, the payoff system began to unravel. An aggressive U.S. Attorney began seeking indictments. Among the first to be tried and convicted in 1970 for lying about his knowledge of payoffs: Buzz Cook.

In 1970, a politically weakened Carroll said he would run for reelection. He still had the backing of the old lions of the GOP establishment as well as the Seattle Police Officers Guild. Carroll must have expected an easy win; he made few appearances and the phone number for his campaign was unlisted. Two Democrats filed against him, as well as a Republican assistant attorney general named Christopher Bayley, a founder of the CHECC reform group and an aide to Slade Gorton, a close ally of Dan Evans. Backed by the Dan Evans wing of the GOP party and some reformers in the police department, Bayley, at age thirty-two, beat Carroll and went on to win the general election.

One of the new prosecutor's first investigative targets was Charles O. Carroll. In July of 1971, a King County grand jury indicted Carroll for bribery and participation in a conspiracy to promote extortion and illegal gambling. The grand jury indicted eighteen other current and former police and government officials, including the former president of the City Council, the former King County Sheriff, the county license director, the former chief of police, one former and one current assistant chief, a police major, and three police captains. Several other high-ranking officials, including the former mayor of Seattle, Dorm Braman, and others were named as being involved in meetings or campaign contributions, but were not accused of any crimes. The indictment said Carroll had met with Braman to arrange political contributions to Braman from gambling figures.

Carroll got special handling at the courthouse. He was arraigned by the court at an unusual hour that would minimize publicity. While under indictment, Carroll found time to serve as program chairman for a testimonial luncheon for retiring U.S. Representative Tom Pelly, the conservative Republican who had beaten Stimson Bullitt in 1952.

The case against Carroll was severely weakened by the absences of a few key witnesses, including Ben Cichy—who had drowned in five feet of water, fifteen feet from his Yarrow Point home, less than a year after his association with Carroll had been disclosed. At a trial in 1973, Judge James Mifflin surprised some observers by dismissing the indictments against Carroll and most of the defendants. Like several other judges, Mifflin had served as a former deputy to Carroll. At a dinner three years before the Carroll trial, Mifflin had said he didn't believe a payoff system existed. During the trial, he stunned courtroom professionals by complimenting one defendant for not cooperating with investigators. "I think you showed a degree of honor by not ratting on the other rats," the judge said. Dismissing the charges, Mifflin said the prosecution had lacked sufficient evidence to prove a conspiracy. "I believe the grand jury brought in the wrong kind of indictment—it should have been bribery and not conspiracy," said Mifflin.

Even with the unexpected outcome of the indictments, the case as a whole brought significant change: a host of weak or corrupt public officials were forced out of office, the tolerance policy was dead, and a thirty-year-old payoff system inside the Seattle Police Department was out of business. After that, it would be hard to dismiss gambling as a harmless civic pastime or to claim that City Hall had never been corrupt. More important, the ground had shifted in Seattle politics.

Seattle had played a role in those changes. With cover stories on Carroll and on troubles within the Seattle Police Department, the magazine showed its best and worst qualities. It had the courage to grab sensitive topics. It explored how the city's leadership acquired and used power, how it faced or ignored problems—and why. Departing from the dry he-said-she-said style of daily journalism, it brought a brilliant voice and style to the issues of the day. But though driven by noble intentions, its performance disappointed its admirers. It moved too quickly on the Carroll story, and then did not stay with it. It raised issues, only to drop them when more fashionable concerns appeared. The lack of follow-through was one reason why *Seattle* never became a heavyweight in Seattle journalism. Another reason was its size. With just 30,000 readers, it lacked the resources, circulation, and daily presence that the *P-I* (with 205,000 daily readers) brought to the Carroll story. *Seattle* was read by an elite, not the masses.

On the Carroll story, however, the magazine's brashness served an important purpose. While the *P-I* only called for Carroll to answer questions, *Seattle* went further and called for his removal from office. Foolhardy or courageous, the magazine took an extreme position about what it saw as a serious problem. *Seattle* was never shy about pointing fingers. By attacking Carroll directly, it risked the ire of a downtown establishment devoted to Carroll, but more important, it gave sustenance and validity to a liberal vanguard seeking power in the city. Carroll's defeat was not the first victory by reformers in King County. But the loss of the prosecutor's office was the biggest post war defeat for Seattle's conservatives. Thereafter, liberal rule in the city would go unchallenged for years.

Peter Bunzel felt a sense of vindication watching Carroll turned out of office, but his thoughts in the fall of 1970 were dominated by a gathering gloom over his magazine. It was losing more than $100,000 a year. Fiddling with the mix of stories, sharpening the covers, softening the covers, resizing the magazine, adding business news, seeking new advertisers—nothing had worked. Inside King Broadcasting, pressure was mounting to sell or close the magazine. Stim's vote as president was the only vote Bunzel needed to keep the magazine going. But behind the scenes stood Dorothy Bullitt, who kept checking the monthly figures. Increasingly, it appeared that the magazine was hurting Stim within the company and, more ominously, within the Bullitt family. Peter Bunzel sensed the danger to his friend, but he was exhausted and wanted out.

On a warm day in late April of 1971, Stimson Bullitt and a secretary from King Broadcasting visited Seward Park, a secluded tree stand in south Seattle on the shore of Lake Washington. It was one of few spots in Seattle where old-growth trees had been spared. A pleasant road circled around the park, and Stim and his secretary were looking at the lake, as they said later. He was fifty-two. She was twenty-seven.

Three youths approached the couple. One displayed a gun that wiggled in his nervous hand. Give us your money, they said. The three took $35 from his wallet, $1.35 from her purse. The robbers directed Stim to walk into the lake; when the water reached his knees, he turned around and saw them run into the woods. Stim later called the police, gave a report, and, in a request that reflected how little he knew about actual news gathering, asked that the incident be kept private—unaware that reporters routinely combed through crime reports. The next day, a four-paragraph story appeared in the Seattle *Times*.

The item caught the eye of political columnist Ed Donohoe, one of the most feared writers in the city, who could blend lacerating put-downs with inside gags from sources all over town. He loathed reformers and ridiculed the police officers who had risked their careers to end the payoff system in the department. His column in *The Washington Teamster* was the best read in Seattle. Donohoe pulled no punches with Stim. "The Duke of Aurora," he wrote, had once again proved his place in "the lexicons of psychiatry. . . . Being in a secluded park with his secretary may raise a few eyebrows, but my considered guess is that the relationship was platonic, and they were just there for their mutual interest in flowering dogwoods, dandelions, and the godawful view of the Kennydale burn." Donohoe called Stimson Bullitt a failure at King Broadcasting. "The trouble with Stimmie (unlike Harry) is that he is running out of flops. One of these days, he is going to do something right and it will be a shock to us all."

To some people at King, the incident damaged Stim's authority within the company by crystallizing what they saw as his foolishness. The company's self-styled paragon of probity had tainted his name with hints of hypocrisy and moral wrongdoing. For a man uncomfortable both with people and with business, the incident probably worsened Stim's sense of isolation at King Broadcasting Company. But Stim was tough. He was not a quitter. He didn't like failure.

By this point, Stimson Bullitt had been president of King Broadcasting for a decade.

He had changed the company in ways his mother could never have achieved or wanted. He expanded the number of women and minority employees and insisted that they be promoted and given meaningful jobs. He campaigned early and courageously against the Vietnam War. He made it onto Richard Nixon's enemies list, probably for his 1970 editorial protesting the United States invasion of Cambodia.

Stim's 1968 merger of the Bullitt Company into King Broadcasting brought a diverse collection of assets: C. D. Stimson's beloved 1411 Fourth Avenue building, the Logan Building and other properties; timber concessions in the Philippines; a plywood mill in Okinawa; a minority interest in the Hing-Shing Shipping Company; joint-venture partnerships with the Hanwa Steel Company of Japan. The Asian investments grew out of efforts to improve supply and distribution for the Okinawa mill, which had become a chronic problem. None of the Asian investments, however, was a significant money maker.

But with the real estate division as a base, Stim was able to launch a visionary project for Seattle's downtown, the payback of which would take many years. Beginning in the late 1960s, Stim began a secret, aggressive effort to buy up parts of nine blocks in a dilapidated area around First Avenue in downtown Seattle. The bargain purchases made King Broadcasting the landlord of sleazy businesses along a street made famous for its porno parlors in the movie *Cinderella Liberty*. King tried to replace those tenants when their leases expired, but it took time. Senior management feared that some investigative reporter, possibly even one at KING-TV, might do some digging and disclose the company's relationship to porn. But the collection of land holdings made possible Stim's goal of an urban development grander than anything conceived by C. D. or his mother—a massive redevelopment built on the premise that people would someday return to live in Seattle's downtown.

Stimson Bullitt had launched *Seattle* and King Screen and had pushed for the purchase of cable-TV properties in the Los Angeles area and elsewhere. He saw King Broadcasting as a diversified communications company, not a mere broadcasting enterprise—a vision that other TV companies would not embrace for decades. He considered buying the Portland *Reporter*, a newspaper published by striking employees of the *Oregonian* and *Journal*, both owned by Newhouse. He came close to merging King Broadcasting with the Walter Reade Theater group, a New York company with twenty-six East Coast movie theaters, a shopping mall, and a large inventory of film. Stim killed the deal, partly because of warnings from some in management that taking on a movie chain across a continent was a mistake. The Reade company was probably too big a gulp, but Stim remained committed to expanding the company, broadening its business focus, and raising it from the "lowbrow influence" of television.

He brought an original approach to company hiring. He looked for the smartest amateurs he could find. Those with brains, youth, and no broadcast experience were perfect: they were unspoiled. The recruits from Harvard, Yale, Princeton, Reed, and other fine schools were like seeds for a new culture. Existing employees were offered free tuition to study at Seattle's colleges and universities. He wanted learned people. He reminded them that the public's attention was a public trust and that much could be done by focusing the public on political and social problems.

One of his most ambitious ideas was a series of prime-time reports on the architecture and geography of the Seattle area. The intention was to promote a new perspective, to promote the notion of beautiful design. One goal of the "Remake Seattle" public affairs program was to push for the dismantling of the Alaskan Way Viaduct, which cut off the downtown from the waterfront. Stim hired attorney Marvin Durning to run the project, but Durning was given no specific guidelines or direction. Durning turned the project into a grass-roots discussion of urban social problems. Broadcast as *The 8th Day,* the program ran over several nights, focused on serious issues facing the Puget Sound region, and brought thousands of people together for the first time to talk about solutions to problems. The program won several awards, including the Sigma Delta Chi Award and the *Saturday Review* Award in 1971 for "distinguished programming in the public interest."

Although there was chronic grumbling about the King Screen division, the company's filmmakers achieved some high honors. With thirty-five people, King Screen made dozens of commercials and several industrial films per year as well as a number of socially conscious documentaries, including *Huelga* on migrant workers, *Advise and Dissent* on Senator Wayne Morse, and *Napalm* on a war materiels company. But nationally, there wasn't much of a market for independent documentaries, and King Screen was losing hundreds of thousands of dollars per year. A big check once came in that pushed the division briefly into the black. But the picture of profit was a mirage. The division failed to show a profit at year's end.

In 1968 King Screen's general manager, Roger Hagan, thought its documentary on the California redwoods had a chance to win an Academy Award in the short documentary category. Hagan found a semi-retired, cigar-smoking Hollywood publicist who called in some favors and got *The Redwoods* screened with another film that Academy voters would want to see. And to everyone's amazement, the film actually won an Oscar. Stim did not go to Hollywood for the presentation, however. It was not his style to be much involved. Typically, he'd look at a movie made by the division, thank everyone, and leave without comment.

Stim had less luck with the first movie he had agreed to finance: *The Plot Against Harry.* Director Michael Roemer took years to complete the film, a dark comedy done in black-and-white when movies had long since moved to color. It starred unknowns. It was not easy to watch, given its dark humor and slow pacing. The lead actor, Martin Priest, looked weary in every scene. After the film was completed, Hagan tried to get a distribution deal in Hollywood. "You're screwed," a marketing executive told him, explaining to Hagan that distribution deals were done before filming so the distributor had a stake in the film's success. *The Plot Against Harry* got its world premier in Seattle in 1971, played one week at the rented Blue Mouse Theater to nearly empty houses, and disappeared. That year, King Broadcasting recorded a $340,000 loss from the project. The failure of *The Plot Against Harry* amplified company complaints that Stim was wasting money.

Stim believed in movies, but television was gaining ground with the public. By 1971, the TV stayed on in U.S. homes for an average of six hours per day. In Seattle, the number of TV stations had grown to eight possible channels. (In radio, Seattle had twenty FM stations and thirteen AM stations.) KING-TV viewers could watch *Twilight Zone, Laugh In,* Bill Cosby, Dean Martin, *Walt Disney* and *Bonanza,* as well as early-evening and late-evening newscasts. KING followed NBC's hit *Today* program with its own *Telescope,* a program of celebrity and author interviews and cooking tips.

Network TV journalism was at a high point.

CBS and NBC battled for journalistic supremacy by producing costly documentaries and investigative reports. Responding to *CBS Reports,* NBC gave viewers its sixty-minute *NBC White Paper* news specials. Other NBC reports dealt with foreign policy, race relations, and the energy crisis. Although the networks lacked the courage of the Edward R. Murrow era, they still took pride in the prestige of quality journalism. Big topics sometimes got a full three hours of prime time, so generous were network news budgets.

But a serious financial issue faced both the networks and the affiliates.

In Washington, D.C., anti-smoking forces had finally prevailed on Congress to ban cigarette advertising from the public airwaves effective January 2, 1971. Ironically, Stim for years had wanted to get cigarettes off KING's stations, but there was no practical way for an individual affiliate to screen out certain ads. Now he was getting his wish, but the ban threatened a large chunk of King Broadcasting's revenue that the company could budget for each year. Once cigarettes were gone, a chain reaction would force ad rates down, weakening every TV station's revenue.

Everyone at King Broadcasting knew this was coming. They had been warned in 1966 by Senator Warren Magnuson, chairman of the committee that oversaw the Federal Communications Commission. Dorothy Bullitt could not talk him out of the ban because political winds were forcing the change. Magnuson himself had worked to keep liquor ads off the airwaves.

"You're going to lose cigarette advertising. It's gotta come off the air," Magnuson told Dorothy Bullitt, who was smoking during the conversation.

"Now Maggie, you know it's a legal product," Dorothy replied.

"I don't care. You've got five years. That's just about when it's going to come to a conclusion, because cigarettes kill a lot of people," said Magnuson.

Meanwhile, demand for Boeing planes was falling and Seattle's largest employer began cutting its work force by the thousands. Boeing's high-paying jobs had numbered 95,000 in 1968; in just a few years this would drop below 40,000. Unemployment reached 12 percent or higher in 1971, double the national average and the worst in any major city since the Depression. One hundred thousand people were out of work. Congress killed Boeing's supersonic airplane, the SST. "We are losing buckets of blood," declared Miner Baker, chief economist for Seattle-First National Bank. As a wry joke, two real estate agents bought a billboard on Pacific Highway South that read: "Will the last person leaving Seattle please turn out the lights?"

King Broadcasting was hurting. After years of steadily improving balance sheets, annual profits before taxes had begun to slip. Profits were $2.7 million in 1968; $2 million in 1969; and $1 million in 1970. The next year would show a significant loss, if projections held.

Another problem loomed. None of the family members had ever pulled substantial dollars from the company, but Patsy and Harriet were pushing for a change. Their wealth was largely tied up in King Broadcasting stock that paid modest dividends. Bankers were reluctant to make loans on stock for which there was no market and thus no easy valuation. Unlike their mother who took relatively little from the company, they wanted more cash, and they had Dorothy Bullitt's support for that goal. Stim knew there was no way of giving his sisters more money without a significant turnaround in the company's finances. He needed help. He turned to the person in the King organization whom he trusted most: Ancil Payne.

Ancil Horace Payne was a perfect contrast to Stimson Bullitt. Where Stim was shy, withdrawn, and formal, Payne was outgoing and relaxed. He could talk to anybody—and did. In this way, he was like Scott Bullitt. He was an engaging mix of sophistication—his penmanship had the grace of a professional calligrapher (acquired from an early job as a sign painter)—and folksiness. He never took coffee in his office, for example. He took it in the cafeteria and made a point of sitting with everyone, from floor directors to managers.

Given his background in politics and his way with people, many thought Payne should have run for office. Some nicknamed him the Senator. He could walk through a room and, one by one, leave people laughing. A masterful storyteller, he changed voices to play different characters, paced the telling for dramatic effect, and ended with a punch line that left people howling, no matter how many times he told the tale. It was easy to assume he was a mere backslapper. But the jokes and laughter masked a subtle and clever intellect. If the subject shifted to a serious topic, he could focus on a speaker with intensity. His manner was unsophisticated, but in fact he was well read, had a supple mind, and could master the essentials of business. More important, he had an uncanny way of reading people and knowing how to manage them. He was especially skilled at working with the Bullitt family, three of whom were fiercely independent women. The father of three daughters himself, Payne joked with a writer from *Broadcasting* magazine that he was the one male in a harem. "We finally got to the point where we got a male dog," he said, "and the son of a bitch ran off. He couldn't stand it either." That was the sort of vivid quote that no writer could resist, and Ancil Payne knew it. He understood the instincts and behavior of journalists better than most of them did themselves.

Ancil Payne grew up in The Dalles, Oregon, where he attended public schools. His mother was a teacher; his father a house painter. In high school, he was elected student body president. After the Navy, he earned his degree from the University of Washington and was elected to Phi Beta Kappa. In college and afterward, he was active in the liberal groups, including the ADA and Young Democrats. As a liberal, Payne and others were sometimes called Communists, but in fact he battled regularly with Communists who wanted to take over the Democratic Party. Payne met Stimson Bullitt in Seattle at a Young Democrats meeting. The two men were bright and on the move, both sharing the more left-wing views of Democrats then. In 1948, Payne worked Hugh B. Mitchell's successful campaign for Congress. As Mitchell's top aide in Washington, D.C., he learned to work with big egos that flared from time to time. He learned how to get things done, including when to do something, when to go along, and when it was smart to share credit. At Mitchell's office he met Valerie Dorrace Davies, who became his wife. Payne ran Mitchell's failed campaign for governor in 1952, the year Stim first ran for Congress. After that, Payne spent three years in Alaska managing a truck company and serving as president of Operation Statehood. Some there expected him to become one of Alaska's first senators. Instead he moved to Portland, Oregon, where he managed an investment company.

In 1959, Stim invited Payne to meet his mother. Payne accepted a job as Henry Owen's assistant, with the understanding that Owen would be retiring soon and that Payne would then be elevated to the job of vice president for business. Owen stayed on longer than expected, delaying Payne's promotion until 1963. In 1965, Stim reorganized the company and sent Payne to Portland as a corporate vice president and general manager of KGW. Serving in Portland gave Payne experience running a station and kept him at a distance from the conflicts that raged between Stim and Otto Brandt. Although Payne technically reported to Brandt, Payne had a large degree of independence, aided by the perception that he was the closest of managers to Stim. When Dorothy Bullitt had trouble understanding her son, she at least felt there was a reliable friend who did.

"You're the only one who understands Stimson," Dorothy Bullitt told Payne.

"No, Mrs. Bullitt," replied Payne. "I'm the only one who knows he *doesn't* understand Stimson."

In Portland, Payne continued King Broadcasting's liberal tradition of editorializing. He led a staff that urged preserving Oregon's beaches from development, criticized the smear of an Oregon legislator named Monroe Sweetland, and chastised downtown employers for not hiring blacks. KGW's first commentator, Tom McCall, went on to become Oregon's governor.

In 1970, Stim offered Payne the newly created position of chief operating officer. Payne would return to Seattle to take charge of King's day-to-day operations, freeing Stim from the hassles of management. Payne, however, was reluctant to leave Portland. He had his own little kingdom and he worried about accountability. If all the department heads reported to Payne, and Payne reported only to Stim, one of them would become superfluous, he figured. If trouble broke out, the board would quickly want to eliminate one of the two positions, and it certainly wouldn't be the man who owned a third of the stock. So Payne stalled until Stim finally implied that he would look for someone else if Payne didn't take the job.

Over a period of weeks, they discussed their respective duties. It was Payne's understanding that he would run the store while Stim focused on long-range issues. Stim and Payne both agreed that King had to do something about its money losers. So after he moved to Seattle, Payne methodically went about eliminating or reorganizing several units, including the mobile TV company and the plywood plant in Okinawa. Payne was willing to continue to subsidize *Seattle* magazine, but only if Peter Bunzel would stay on. Bunzel, however, would not agree. It bothered Bunzel that the magazine was losing money. Bunzel went to a company board meeting in 1970 and outlined the options. He recommended closure. The city was too small and its business leadership too conservative to support a magazine like *Seattle*. "Any of us who don't recognize this fact are living in a dream world," he said. The board accepted his recommendation. The magazine closed publication with the December 1970 issue. Its cover showed a gravestone honoring a brief life, 1964–1970. The jaunty man with an umbrella was now buried with a view of the city's skyline.

Earlier, in September, Stimson Bullitt had posted a note:

> Seattle magazine will be brought to an end after the December issue. In starting the magazine, King planned to contribute to our community, and in this aim we have succeeded. However, although Seattle was not expected to make big money, it was intended to become self-supporting. A business enterprise cannot be justified unless it offers services for which users will pay enough to let it stand mainly on its own feet. Despite efficient operation, some loyal supporters and almost seven years' tests, the magazine shows no prospect of approaching independence of a subsidy. The Company is proud of Seattle's present quality, and we regret to close it down.

Afterward, a dinner-wake was held for the magazine's staff. "You'll be poisoned!" Payne's wife, Valerie, told him in mock seriousness. He went anyway. Payne told people that Bunzel had acquiesced to the closing of Seattle. Payne never got a specific signal from Dorothy Bullitt to close the magazine, but sensing her moods was one of his skills, and he knew she condoned the decision. Peter Bunzel soon left town and wound up at the Los Angeles Times. Many Seattle magazine staffers were absorbed into other divisions of the company. Payne liked to joke that a shrewd manager kept his fingerprints off the musket. If Payne had orchestrated the death of Seattle, where were the fingerprints?

For several months, things worked smoothly between Stim and Payne, but bit by bit, problems began to surface. Stim would start to suggest something, only to be interrupted by Payne. "That's my problem," Payne would say firmly. Gradually, Stim began to express unhappiness. The pace of hiring or firing, of bringing in minorities, and other steps was too gradual for Stim. Their relationship began to deteriorate.

"You're angry with something, and I have to know," Payne said to Stim one day. "The smoke is coming out from your door." Stim stammered that there was no problem, but Payne knew Stim's stammering worsened when he was upset.

Others took note of the shift—Roger Hagan, for one. Payne was no longer backing Stim when objections to Stim's ideas surfaced. Payne was particularly hostile to the "Remake Seattle" project. There were even moments, it seemed to Hagan, where Payne was cutting and rude to Stim.

Payne was a believer in moving a group of people gradually. He saw it as important to send the right signals to the employees, who, if angered or disillusioned, could cripple initiatives. Stim was more willful. If he didn't like someone, he wanted that person gone. One day, Stim told Payne that he wanted an individual fired. Payne said he wouldn't. Stim pressed the point. Payne went back to his office and wrote a letter of resignation. He was careful not to let anyone see the note; talk of such things would have spread rapidly. The letter said Stim had failed to live up to their agreement, so he had no choice but to resign. While Stim was out, Payne dropped it off on Stim's desk, went back to his office, picked up his personal belongings and went home.

Payne was making a calculated gamble. There was a good chance that his career at King Broadcasting was over after more than a decade in the company. But he also knew there was a chance that things would go his way. Stim's credibility in the company and within his family had been weakened because of the financial problems. Forcing Otto Brandt and other long-timers out of the company had caused controversy and lingering bitterness. The sisters wanted more money for their needs. Perhaps Payne was the path toward that end. Where was Dorothy Bullitt in all this? She was the controlling shareholder. She had the power. She was warm to Payne; she always visited him at KGW when she was in Portland visiting grandchildren at Reed College. Her views of broadcasting, as a practical balance between education and entertainment, were closer to his than to Stim's, or so Payne felt. Stim wanted to challenge Seattle in ways that made Dorothy feel uncomfortable. But she had always been publicly committed to supporting the man of the family. As she had once told Payne during a conversation in Portland, "I don't care what happens. I am completely behind Stimson."

That was the facade. For years, Dorothy had been quietly working through her daughters to pressure Stim to make changes. Just as she used Henry Owen to fire people or report unpleasant news, she urged Patsy and Harriet to lobby their brother. Throughout the 1960s, she would ask that they "do something" with their brother. She disliked *Seattle* criticizing her friends, and Stim's decision to merge the Bullitt Company into King Broadcasting. She thought some of his new writers were unmannerly. She accepted her son's efforts to hire minorities and women, but thought it a lot of work for such small results. She even hated the crown logo Stim had picked for the company's letterhead. But she rejected the daughters' suggestions that she confront her son. She insisted she didn't want to interfere.

In 1971 she became alarmed at Stim's interest in selling King Broadcasting in exchange for stock in Times-Mirror, owner of the Los Angeles *Times'* parent company. Stim saw the deal as a means of giving shareholders liquidity and achieving his goal of getting out of broadcasting. Dorothy called the sisters, who agreed that King Broadcasting's weakened finances made it a poor time to sell. Harriet finally called Stim and told him he had to call off the discussions. Once again, Stim felt the disapproving presence of his mother.

There was another factor at play. Unbeknownst to Payne or Stim, one of the long-time board members had been quietly lobbying Patsy and Harriet to scrutinize their brother. He kept this activity secret, but over a period of months, he gently urged them to get some independent advice about Stim's investments of King Broadcasting's money. This board member did not think highly of Bagley Wright, whom he felt had too much influence on Stim.

But what did Stim want? Payne believed that Stim was unhappy—that he did not enjoy running King, and never had. Payne realized that there was a chance that Stim would leave the company, perhaps nudged by his sisters, whose own motives could have been a complex tangle of sisterly love for a brother, a desire to end tensions at the company and within the family, and also a practical need for cash. At the center was Dorothy Bullitt, who was getting close to another family schism. She was torn between loyalty to her son and the survival of her other progeny, the King Broadcasting Company. Decades earlier, she had worked through the split between Scott Bullitt and her brother Thomas. If another split was coming, this one would be hard to keep quiet. King was closely followed by full-time TV writers at the newspapers. Any rancor at the top of King could wind up as embarrassing headlines.

Whatever was done had to be done quietly.

Payne had only been home a few hours when the phone rang. It was not Stim. It was Henry Owen, retired from King but still a close advisor to Dorothy Bullitt, calling to ask about Payne's resignation. Owen and Dorothy kept offices in a little brick building across an alley from King. The fact that Owen had called was a good sign. He and Payne had deep affection for each other. Owen pleaded with his protégé not to act swiftly. "Let things cool down," he told Payne. Payne knew that his close ally would lobby Dorothy for him. Outside of the family, no one was closer to Dorothy Bullitt than Henry Owen. Maybe Ancil Payne still had a career at King Broadcasting.

Later, a call came from Harriet. She was very upset. Payne did not know her well. She had launched an environmental newsletter, *Pacific Search*, which she edited in an office across from King Broadcasting. She and Payne were friendly but not close, and Payne knew her as someone who looked at life in her own way. If things didn't interest her, she wasn't listening. But this matter between Stim and Payne had her full attention. Harriet was bright and, when she wanted to be, she could be extremely focused. She urged Payne not to make a rash decision. She said she knew there had been a problem. Payne got the feeling that there were ongoing talks between the sisters and their mother and brother. And he knew that whatever solution emerged, it had to go beyond Stim and engage the entire family. Therein lay the risk and the opportunity. Would they side with Stim, no matter what? Or would they take a larger perspective and see the company at risk? Would they see Payne as the solution to the company's and to their brother's discomfort? And which way would Dorothy Bullitt go? Dorothy had still not called Payne, nor he her. He was trying to read her mind through what Harriet was saying. Payne listened carefully, but the conversation did not resolve anything. Payne was still guessing.

A few days later, Payne came back to King Broadcasting for a meeting with Stim. The burden of ten years of running the company bore down on Stimson Bullitt. Payne was the person inside the company he felt he could most trust. And now came a parting between the friends. "I can't run the company with you, and I can't run the company without you," Stim said to Payne. "So I'll get out."

The next meeting of King Broadcasting Company's board was brief. The atmosphere was tense. Everyone knew what was going to happen. One of the company's lawyers started to read the minutes, but he was overcome by the suppressed emotions of the occasion and began to choke up. Stim then made a simple announcement that he was resigning as president of King Broadcasting.

Sitting there at a boil was Stim's long-time friend, Bagley Wright. Wright believed that Stim had been done in. Not by Stim's sisters. They were unsophisticated in business. He suspected Ancil Payne, who was sophisticated, skilled at finessing people, an expert in palace politics. Payne had convinced the sisters that the sky was falling and their brother had to go. And the mother could have stopped this, but didn't. She never really understood her son, Wright felt. There were fingerprints on the musket. He strongly believed they belonged to Ancil Payne. Wright couldn't take it. He lost his temper and walked out.

Mrs. Bullitt said nothing. What could be said? Her son, her only son, was leaving for the good of the company, and perhaps for himself as well. It was so painful. The meeting lasted a few more minutes. Ancil Payne was elected president of King Broadcasting. A press release was issued saying Stimson Bullitt had been elected chairman of the company. But for all practical purposes, the Bullitt prince was out, and with him went his uncompromising vision and ideals. Despite whatever gloss was put on Stim's departure, the episode would stain the family image. All the future celebrations of King Broadcasting's progressivism would honor Dorothy Bullitt, not her son. Dorothy Bullitt would never reveal to Ancil Payne what the family had discussed prior to Stim's departure. Even within the family, the subject was off limits. Some of Stim's own children felt a vague sense of shame or failure about Stim's departure and, despite all the rumors and questions, they would never raise the subject with either their father or grandmother. They could only wonder if their father had felt betrayed. Was this a repeat of what Dorothy Bullitt had done years ago, picking the company over her children? In the enforced silence, the tangle of questions never would be resolved.

In his last act at King Broadcasting, Stimson Bullitt cleaned out his belongings from the president's office and accidentally locked his keys inside.

Her son was out. She was eighty years old. Now the issue was Ancil Payne.

Payne went to see Dorothy Bullitt. He came quickly to the point, but he sweetened it with humor.

"We either get married or get divorced," he said.

Payne, fifty-one, made her laugh. He told good stories. He was fun. Unlike her son, he seemed to enjoy being with her and seeking her views. She was ready to trust him and make a commitment. Plus, he had the support of her old ally Henry Owen. Dorothy's children didn't think much of Henry Owen, but she still did. And Owen had pushed for Ancil Payne.

When Payne took over at King Broadcasting in 1972, his biggest problem was company finances. Seattle was teetering, hemorrhaging jobs. The city's recession dampened local advertising, and national advertising revenue had still not recovered from the loss of cigarette advertising, which had caused a drop in profits starting in 1970.

The company was perceived to be in trouble. Business leaders detected a sense of crisis at King Broadcasting. Payne represented continuity, strength, and a fresh start all at once. When Payne came up from Portland eighteen months earlier, he had cut an enviable deal for himself with Stim: a ten-year contract. Now he wanted from Dorothy Bullitt an even better deal—a guarantee of fourteen years of pay.

"Fine. Work it out with Dick Riddell," said Dorothy. Payne hired a lawyer, and the deal was done. He was guaranteed an income until he turned sixty-five, when he planned to retire.

With Stim gone, Payne moved swiftly to close down the remaining operations that were money losers, including King Screen. He then ordered a 10 percent reduction in staff, assuming privately that the real cut would come in at 5 percent. King was fundamentally a strong company, virtually debt-free. Payne was convinced that finances would turn around once national advertising improved, as seemed inevitable, and King Broadcasting cut down its fixed costs, which he was doing. Of the company's divisions that he kept, only one—KING radio—was a money loser, but Payne believed it could be made profitable.

Payne assumed that his trickiest problem would be to work out the formal split of King Broadcasting between Dorothy and the sisters and Stim. But actually, it was easily decided that Stim would get the properties. There, after all, was where his heart lay. Dorothy Bullitt would remain controlling shareholder of King Broadcasting, and his sisters would remain large shareholders. The split was negotiated secretly and delicately. There was no rancor, yet Dorothy Bullitt wondered why the split had to be so complicated. Why couldn't everyone pick from a list as she and her brother had once done when C. D. Stimson split his company? But, she was told, there were now tax laws and legal considerations. For one thing, the split had to be done so that all stockholders, including non-family members, were treated fairly.

The next step was to accomplish the split in such a way that none of the Bullitts were taxed. The IRS had to view the two companies as completely separate—different boards, no shared assets—with each becoming more profitable apart from the other. Payne worried that John Ehrlichman, a former Seattle resident and President Nixon's domestic policy adviser, would see an opportunity to hurt a liberal opponent and would pressure the IRS to create problems for King. In anticipation of that, Payne went to see Warren Magnuson a formidable ally in case of trouble. But there was none. The IRS wanted only one adjustment: a King-owned cable-TV system in Montesano, Washington, had to be sold because of an FCC rule against broadcast signals overlapping regions where the same company held a cable franchise. A $150,000 asset, it was quickly sold. The deal sailed through and was formally approved by King Broadcasting's board in April 1973. King, in effect, bought back 23 percent of its stock from Stimson Bullitt for assets valued at $6.4 million.

Stim's assets became Harbor Properties, with a new board and eight of King's former employees. King Broadcasting still held a sizable stake in Safeco, the insurance company C. D. Stimson had helped launch. Safeco stock that had cost $38,214 had increased in value to $7.8 million.

For the Bullitt family, the effect was to take Stim's children out of King Broadcasting and make them heirs to Harbor Properties. Stim's withdrawal from King Broadcasting was total. Ever the stickler for principle, after the split, he wouldn't even enter company headquarters.

Stim had six children. With Carolyn, he had Ashley, Scott, and Jill; with Kay, he had Dorothy, Ben, and Margaret. Of Stim's older children, Scott Bullitt did the most to create an identity of his own. Dropping out of Reed College after one semester, he spent much of a year traveling America, staying with people in the counterculture movement, before deciding to begin a career as an artist. In 1969, at age twenty, he started calling himself Fred Nemo because he didn't want his planned career ever to embarrass his family. The name "Nemo" appealed to him because in Latin it meant "no man." From his time studying classics at the Lakeside School in Seattle, he liked the story of Ulysses stabbing Cyclops's one eye. When the creature roared in pain, he told his supporters that "no man" had stabbed him. Scott—now Fred—admired Ulysses's cunning. Besides, in changing his name, Fred felt he was giving the name Scott Bullitt back to his grandfather. As Fred Nemo, he performed as a dancer with a rock band. In a family of eccentrics, he topped them all.

With Stim out of the company, Patsy and Harriet stood to inherit control of King Broadcasting. Both were remarkable women, but Patsy at age fifty-two, and Harriet at forty-eight, had little interest in business. From the day he took over, Payne believed he worked for one person, Dorothy Bullitt. He had made that clear to the sisters, as well, but they would prove to be a challenge for him.

Even as a mature woman, Harriet remained very much the youngest child. She was a free spirit, given to whims, indulged by her mother, attended by men who were attracted to her high cheekbones, bright smile, and athlete's energy. Some admired her independence and style. A few saw her as willful, self-absorbed, and thoughtless. When she was asked to do something she didn't want to do, she simply changed her mental focus and, as one person put it, just floated away. She was seven when her father died and her mother buried herself in work. Harriet spent much of her time with a nanny whom she learned to manipulate or avoid. Harriet herself considered her behavior with the nanny devious, but it was a survival skill. She became very good at circumventing household rules. As a teenager she grew tired of living up to her mother's moral standards, the commandments to bathe regularly and always be honest. She complained that her mother never liked her friends, who were never good enough.

Harriet was brainy. During the war, she studied chemical engineering at the University of Washington. She was interested in pursuing a medical degree but ran into sexism. One day, a professor told her not to use the library because she was distracting the male students. She wound up at Bennington College, which she quit to marry a medical student, William Brewster, a handsome Dartmouth graduate. The marriage ended in divorce after eighteen years, and Harriet returned to Seattle, where she eventually married three more men. Her relationship to her mother was complex and mystifying to outsiders. She told people she felt close to her mother, yet some people detected a residue of anger. She never could get over feeling abandoned. "To mother, family came first . . . though that doesn't mean acting on it," Harriet later told a reporter. She added, "She was not motherly in the conventional sense, but she was warm."

Patsy was the plain, dutiful daughter, the weed puller. As a baby she was so frail that doctors feared for her life. After Vassar she fell in love, becoming engaged to Lawrence Norman, an Army Air Corps bombardier. In 1944, Norman's plane disappeared over Germany. Plans for their wedding were canceled, as Patsy spent months trying to find proof of his death. Three years later, she married Josiah "Joe" Collins, a graduate of the Thacher School and Yale, a Seattle blue blood, and a family friend for many years. Collins's father had been the chief of the Seattle Fire Department who had earned a place in city history by being on vacation in June 1889 when the Great Fire broke out. The marriage to Collins ended in divorce; Patsy did not remarry.

Patsy had a good sense of humor and liked to tell stories that left her erupting in laughter almost before the story was completed. Yet she had a serious side as well. She felt deeply about world peace, volunteering to help burn victims in Japan after World War II. She donated vans and money to orphanages and hospitals around the world, joined international peace groups, and help found the Christians for Peace in El Salvador. On a trip to the Middle East, she caused a row with NBC by saying the American press had an anti-Arab bias. Like Harriet, she was impulsive and given to testing limits. In the mid-1960s, teachers warned Patsy not to take her children out of school, but one night she announced at dinner: "Let's take off." And they were gone nine months on a world tour that included the Soviet Union.

Both sisters resisted Dorothy's influence over their lives, but Patsy had less success than Harriet. When Patsy married Joe Collins, the couple wanted to move into a houseboat. Dorothy instead gave them a house next to her own, picked out the furniture and moved her servants into the home's second floor. Dorothy retained title to the home, which she called The Annex. One day, Patsy came home to find the door painted Chinese red—Dorothy's idea. Joe, who worked for the Bullitt property company, passively accepted his mother-in-law's dominance, while Patsy sullenly nursed her resentments. Patsy wanted independence but also wanted to avoid a scene with her mother. In 1949, when Dorothy was out of town, the Collinses moved to Bellevue. Later, they moved to San Diego.

Ancil Payne believed that the sisters wanted nothing to do with running the company, other than continuing as little more than functionaries on the board of directors, as they had for years. (The sisters would dispute this, saying Payne regarded their involvement as interference.) Sometimes they didn't even attend board meetings, where the eleven-member group discussed but generally ratified whatever Payne and Dorothy Bullitt had decided. A few times, one or the other of the sisters would be gone and no one on the board knew where they were. But their departures were understandable, their friends said. The sisters were bright, dynamic people forced to the sidelines at King Broadcasting. Sometimes, said King executives, the sisters showed up and fell asleep during a presentation.

Beyond Patsy and Harriet's involvement, there was the issue of their children. With Brewster, Harriet had a daughter, Wenda, and a son,

Scott. There were no other children from her later marriages. With Collins, Patsy had three sons: Jacques, William, and Charles.

Among that group of five young adults, who would want to come into the company? Would any of them want to run King Broadcasting? How would family succession be handled? It was a critical question, for it affected not only Bullitt family dynamics, but also the company's employees and its commitment to public service. Keeping the company within the family would not be easy. In such situations, family ownership typically ended before the third generation because of business downturns or family members losing interest. King Broadcasting needed to know its future and prepare. Payne believed it would be disastrous for the company to fall to grandchildren who were untrained for leadership of a large company.

"You have to tell me what you want to have done with the children," Payne told Patsy and Harriet. "It's logical, reasonable, and right that they should be brought into the company. If you want this kind of succession, I can place them around the company where they can learn something of the business. It's going to be a hardship unless they do that."

According to Payne, Patsy and Harriet told him that none of their children had the combination of interest and capacity needed to run King Broadcasting. A few of them might hold odd jobs at the company, but none was considered executive material. Not one of the five grandchildren was ever to be brought onto King's board. Unlike the Blethens, who owned the Seattle *Times,* or the Fishers, who owned KOMO, there was no commitment by one generation to groom the next. Patsy and Harriet had grown up feeling burdened by the social position and business responsibilities of their mother. They made sure none of their children felt that. But that decision meant that the next generation had no strong identification with the company and its place in the community, and thus no reason to fight for its survival. To Harriet and Patsy's children, it was a property that could be bought or sold. It was not, as it was for their grandmother, a legacy to be preserved. Dorothy could influence her children, but this was one area where she did not interfere.

Payne arranged with Dorothy a system for handling Patsy and Harriet. If the sisters wanted anything, they brought the matter to their mother. If it was something Payne did not want to do, Dorothy would back him and explain that even she had a hard time with the stubborn Payne. It was Dorothy's way of keeping herself out of the conflict and subtly conveying her wish that he be left to run the shop. So long as Payne kept her informed of major issues and sensitive personnel matters, he was free to make his own decisions. For her part, she would sit in her office and receive visitors or greet employees in the cafeteria. She was growing very old. She kept an eye on things, but she trusted Payne, perhaps even more than she trusted the judgment of her daughters, who surely must have resented the arm's-length treatment.

Payne called himself the foreman of the company, a joking reference to the sprawling Texas ranch owned by the King family. But no foreman had so much authority. He rarely had a disagreement with Dorothy, and one time when he did, he made it plain to her what the cost of interference would be. Dorothy became upset when she heard allegations that a KING-TV reporter had visited the relative of a murder victim and had supposedly rummaged through letters on the relative's desk. Furious, the relative called KING to complain. When Dorothy heard of it, she wanted the reporter fired.

"We don't know if the story's true," Payne told her.

"No. Fire him," said Dorothy Bullitt.

"He's in a union. We can't arbitrarily fire him."

"That's what I want."

Payne stood his ground.

"We have to decide who runs the company," he told her. "I've been an assistant before, and I don't want to fire him."

The reporter, who denied the allegation, kept his job.

Stim's departure from King Broadcasting generated talk within the business community. Why did he leave? What would happen to the company? One Seattle businessman approached Dorothy about buying the company. He talked loudly, thinking the eighty-year-old woman was going deaf. Like many others who misread Dorothy Bullitt, he figured he had to walk her through a business discussion.

"Mrs. Bullitt, we want to pay just enough to get sufficient return on our investment," Dorothy later quoted the man as saying.

"Who wouldn't?" she replied. She said the company was not for sale.

One of Payne's most significant moves was to reach out to the city's business community. Payne felt that Stim had withdrawn from the community, and that this ultimately had hurt the company. Like Otto Brandt, Payne believed that goodwill in the business community benefited the company in the long run. Payne wasn't afraid of offending people. In fact, he enjoyed controversy. But he wanted King Broadcasting to be a player in the community, a recognized force for good. When the downtown business community launched a campaign to offset the negative national image created by the Boeing recession, King Broadcasting was among the first to join, helping to produce a documentary called *And Now the Good News from Seattle*. Payne shared Otto Brandt's view that the company grew if Seattle grew.

Payne saw himself as sharing Stim's overall social and political goals for the community, but he believed a practical approach would be more successful. Like Stim, he realized the power of a medium with an audience of 500,000 each night. Unlike Stim, Payne was comfortable with the notion that public service and news had to be entertaining, too. Moreover, he wanted King Broadcasting's documentaries and news to be regarded as fair, reasonable, and based on facts, not prejudice. He wanted people to believe that the company would always at least listen to their objections or problems. To that end, he set out to regain the confidence of business leaders. He joined the boards of the Greater Seattle Chamber of Commerce and the Pacific Science Center. He also joined the Chamber's Community Roundtable, a group of business and political power brokers who met to promote consensus on issues. For the Chamber, he joined a task force that promoted mandatory busing in the Seattle public schools. Payne told the news department that he would not give news tips to the company's reporters, nor were they to give his presence any special treatment, either by ignoring it or emphasizing it. Other King Broadcasting executives joined community groups, but no one in a news or policy position at King was allowed to be involved in a partisan or political group.

David Brewster, the former *Seattle* writer who wound up at the *Argus* weekly, took note of changes under Payne in a 1973 article marking the company's twenty-fifth anniversary: "King has been busily retrenching since 1971, pulling in its horns somewhat, starting to resemble conventional stations more than before, and drifting out of the magnetic field of the Bullitt family."

Brewster was right. King Broadcasting was changing, though Payne fiercely disagreed that the company had lost its sense of mission. But it had stopped speaking as a company directly to its viewers. Not long after Stim stepped down as company president, KING-TV stopped doing editorials, largely because Payne wanted time to get things under control. Later, Dorothy Bullitt wanted the editorials to resume and thought Payne, as company president, should deliver them. He submitted a list of issues and how he thought the company should stand—his indirect way of locating any areas of disagreement. They had no differences, so about three years after taking charge, Payne began writing and delivering the editorials himself. His philosophy was simple. Editorials should not be used on issues where the proper conclusion was obvious, so no Mother's Day editorials. He only wanted to take a stand where the issue was important and its outcome could go either way. He wanted to be a voice for constructive change and to reverse King Broadcasting's image as a "a community scold."

Payne campaigned for traditional liberal causes. As editorialist, he supported a freeze on nuclear testing, opposed U.S. intervention in Central America, supported civil rights protection for gays, denounced an anti-pornography proposal as a threat to free speech, praised an initiative that would remove the state sales tax on food, called for cuts to military spending and controls on hand guns. The editorials also supported the traditional community causes: school levies, civil service reform, bonds for improvements to streets. Most editorials supported proposals for higher taxes. Occasionally, his editorials upset key business figures, whom Payne often soothed with humor.

As a performer, Payne was a better editorialist than Stim. He sat upright and gave his message like a Calvinist preacher telling his flock to dig deeper into their wallets. He came across as sincere, intelligent, and an upright member of the establishment, but none of his charm, wit, and easy laughter made it through the cathode ray tube. Payne performed better on the balance sheet.

By eliminating money-losers, Payne could pour the savings into the broadcasting operations, which had been starved for years under Stim.

KING-TV got new cameras and other equipment. New management was brought in. By the time Brewster wrote his article, KING-TV news had regained the number one news rating. They celebrated with a champagne party.

Over the next several years, Payne expanded the company's holdings. He bought cable and radio stations, spending $18 million for an independent TV station in Honolulu and $8 million for KYA-FM and AM in San Francisco. He vetoed the purchase of a cable system in New Jersey because he worried that King would be forced into dealing with sleazy politicians who would want payoffs. When the FCC held a lottery for cellular-telephone licenses, King Broadcasting filed on some twenty licenses and wound up with a fraction of a license in Tacoma. Since Dorothy preferred 100 percent ownership, King sold its share to a group that included a company founded by Elroy McCaw's son, Craig. King managed to make a huge profit in one cellular deal with investor George Lindemann. King gave Lindemann roughly $6 million to help him buy cellular licenses, and sold its interest two years later for a profit of more than $60 million.

NBC had long been a respectable second to CBS in ratings and profitability when Ancil Payne became chairman of NBC's board of affiliates in 1975. CBS led in the entertainment programs, and NBC dominated the news and the morning and late-night talk programs. NBC had gained a lead in news with the marvelous pairing of Chet Huntley and David Brinkley, who put viewers in the habit of turning to NBC during major breaking news. But its prime-time lineup was beginning to look stale, and ABC programmers, led by Fred Silverman, began to gain viewers. Owners of affiliates knew that sagging ratings would cut their advertising revenue. Gaining affiliates at NBC's expense, ABC would nearly triple its profits in 1975, surpassing NBC's profits. NBC was in a tailspin that would last through 1981.

CBS was so successful that it gathered its affiliates and told them what was coming each season. Any affiliates who didn't like it were free to drop their affiliation. ABC was so weak that it had to listen to affiliate demands. NBC was in the middle, but it had a clever way of softening up affiliates each year. NBC would fly the nine members of the board of affiliates to New York City, host them at an exclusive restaurant, and pour drinks until a late hour. The business meeting would start the next day at 9:00 A.M. Network representatives would launch into detailed, lengthy briefings for the fatigued or hungover board members. The presentations were carefully scripted, each ending with promises that there would be time for questions at the end. At noon, the network president would say the buffet was ready, but if anyone had a question, they would hold the food. Rarely were there detailed questions.

When Payne became chairman of the board of affiliates, he was determined to raise substantive issues. He sent out a letter asking each board member to describe his problems and concerns regarding the network. He persuaded the members to come a day before meetings to seek a consensus on issues. Each member was assigned a specific issue, so no one dominated the discussion.

At the next briefing of affiliates, NBC ran through a detailed presentation on its program lineup. As Payne later retold the story, NBC President Julian Goodman then asked: "Do you have any questions?"

Payne replied, "Julian, we don't have any questions. We'd like your people to leave the room so we can discuss this among ourselves."

NBC was stunned. An NBC staff member operating a recording machine dropped the thing on the floor. Goodman came back after lunch and asked, "What's the trouble?"

"Julian, I have been asked by the [affiliate] delegates to tell you that the delegate organization has lost faith in the leadership and the programming of the network," Payne said.

Goodman picked up the phone to his secretary. "Keep everyone out of the office and keep the door closed."

And they all had a long talk.

The next year, the affiliates gathered on the day of an awkward headline for NBC in the New York *Times*. Page one carried a story saying NBC's most popular interviewer, Barbara Walters, was jumping to ABC, where she would co-anchor the news with Harry Reasoner at a salary of $1 million a year.

"We've got a problem with her," Goodman told Payne. "We can hold her if we make her co-anchor. What do you think?"

Each of the nine board members said it would be a mistake. Walters went to ABC.

NBC got wind of a provision in Walters's new contract which said that when ABC went to a sixty-minute newscast, she would get certain considerations. NBC was determined to go first with an expanded broadcast, but it wanted affiliates to give up the extra half-hour from local programming. NBC would, in effect, pay rent for that extra time, but NBC would get all the advertising revenue for the half hour. Affiliates realized they would lose money in the process but, after several meetings, many said they were willing to go along.

Slowly, the momentum was moving toward the sixty-minute newscast until an executive of NBC news made a little speech to the affiliates. The executive said the half-hour was needed to inform viewers. Local news did not cover the news adequately, he said. Without NBC documentaries, the public wouldn't know about problems in education. The board members took this as an insult, including Payne, who was very proud of King Broadcasting's documentaries on education and many other issues. The speech hardened opponents.

Later, NBC Vice Chairman David Adams took Payne aside.

"Forgetting all the rhetoric, isn't it just dollars? Adams asked.

"You bet it's dollars," said Payne. The affiliates wanted to sell some of that time and keep the revenue.

Adams insisted that the network needed all of that revenue or it couldn't afford the extra half-hour of news. They both repeated their positions.

"In that case, that ends the subject," Payne said flatly.

NBC's sixty-minute newscast was dead.

When ABC learned of NBC's decision, it too dropped plans for its sixty-minute newscast. Had either network gone forward, all of them would have been forced to meet the competition. At CBS, journalists complained that NBC affiliates had killed the industry's expansion of TV news. Payne thought that was unfair. It was just wrong to saddle stations with so much of the cost, he felt. He was a strong supporter of TV news. He felt he had the best, toughest local newscast in America. He had the lawsuits to prove it.

He was more like an Irish cop than a TV reporter. He didn't care about his looks. His dull brown hair might have been plastered down by a flat hand and spit. His jaw defined everything. It stood out wide, big, and solid. Don McGaffin was a tough guy. The trench coat looked right on him. Unlike the blow-dries found so often in TV journalism, he really worked stories. He drank with cops and crooks. He didn't think much of journalism in Seattle, especially as practiced by local TV journalists. TV as a whole was fluff and entertainment, run by people who didn't read much and who rarely asked hard questions. Working at the Fishers' KOMO, he commented on an article he had read in *The New Republic*. Nobody had heard of the publication.

He sometimes refused to wear makeup. He wouldn't let anything phony get between himself and the viewer as he told the story in simple, ten-cent words. He was a journalist lifted from Damon Runyon, although in fact he was a graduate of Columbia University. His familiarity with the educated and moneyed classes made him all the more contemptuous of the typical owners of a broadcast license. In his mind, they held a public trust and their job was to get out of the way of the journalists on their payroll. To him, it was outrageous that mere ownership of a TV station gave a person the right to edit his copy.

McGaffin was anxious to leave KOMO in 1970 when he got a call from Norm Heffron, the news director at KING. Heffron was a shy, monkish man who recently had been moved up from KING's sister station in Portland, KGW.

KING news was recovering from the brief tenure of another manager from KGW, Forest Amsden, a close ally of Ancil Payne. Amsden, who had come in as temporary news director, made no secret of his distaste for KING's loose structure and anti-establishment tilt. He toned down a report by Mike James on the way business interests were influencing the siting of the new Kingdome sports complex. He insisted on changing the conclusions of a report by Bob Faw which raised doubts about a rapid rail proposal being pushed by a coalition of civic activists, bond lawyers, and unions. Faw reacted to the interference with disgust. Responding to what he saw as an abrupt end of independence at KING-TV news, Faw quit and wound up as a network correspondent. It wasn't the last time that the news staff would bristle at someone's trying to control them. After KING's news staff got its jolt, Amsden went back to Portland, where he became general manager.

When Heffron arrived, KING-TV news was running a weak second in Seattle during the city's worst recession in decades. Under Payne's influence, however, money was going back into broadcasting, particularly into TV news. Payne was determined that KING take back the lead from KOMO. He wanted Heffron to try something new, to bring in new faces and establish KING as the best. Beyond that, Heffron was given no specific instructions. Heffron treated McGaffin the same way. McGaffin wanted freedom. He wanted to be taken seriously in a profession that constantly struggled between entertainment and journalistic values.

The next big hire was Charles Royer. Royer had been a political reporter for KOIN, a Portland TV station, and had left to take a fellowship at the Harvard/MIT joint Center for Urban Studies. After a year there, he contacted Amsden about the KING commentator job that Herb Altschull had left to become a journalism professor.

Royer was just turning thirty-one when he arrived in Seattle in August of 1970. Growing up in a small apartment in Oregon City, Oregon, Royer was a jokester, a second-string athlete, a skinny kid with jug ears and a hook nose. No one expected him to go anywhere. The nose was what they kidded him about—the hurtful nickname: Nose.

The man who walked into KING on Aurora Avenue had filled out some. He was still thin, the nose still prominent. But in the way that time sometimes softens a person's looks, Charles Royer had become a darkly handsome man. There was a polish and elegance about him, a gracefulness in his walk and the clever way he used words. Women especially found him attractive. He came to KING to what he would call one of the greatest jobs in the world. Every night he would speak his mind on the issues of the day—local, regional, whatever. KING was his soapbox. On the air, he jabbed, needled, and ridiculed with a prickly sarcasm. A city proposal for a West Seattle freeway was an example of government's low regard for people. President Ford was a "benevolent prince" in pardoning Nixon. A proposed domed stadium for professional sports was a dubious use of public dollars.

KOMO and KIRO had their own brands of commentary, each reflective of station ownership. At KOMO, general manager Bill Warren was conservative politically and personally. He was not comfortable with commentary, according to one news director, but nonetheless the station in the early 1960s brought in a succession of University of Washington professors to offer analysis (as opposed to opinion) of news events. The professors' scripts were not screened in advance but there was no need to do so. Their material was thoughtful and earnest but generally tepid stuff, certainly not as overtly liberal as at KING. Commentary never became a strong point in KOMO's news broadcast. While Ancil Payne wrote and delivered his own editorials, Bill Warren had a public affairs director deliver KOMO's views, which generally were calls for civilians to do the work of fire-department paramedics, or for more frequent lawn mowing at city parks. While Payne criticized President Richard Nixon and discussed national ideas, Warren felt national issues "were being competently addressed by the network." He broke that rule when Nixon resigned; KOMO called for national togetherness.

In 1963, Saul Haas sold KIRO-TV, AM and FM for $5 million to Bonneville International Corporation, a unit of the Mormon Church. Five nights a week, management editorials were written and delivered by Lloyd Cooney, KIRO president. Cooney's editorials were full of opinion, bluntly delivered, laced with a boot-strap conservatism lampooned by the *P-I*'s TV writer Frank Chesley. Cooney tended to have a simple solution for every problem, be it striking teachers, government-funded abortions, or body-painting parlors. During Watergate, Cooney defended Nixon and criticized the Press, calling on CBS to reassign correspondents

Dan Rather and Daniel Schorr. Cooney said one reason he did editorials was to make it easier for his reporters "to distinguish between opinion and fact." Cooney was colorful and folksy, but his hip-shooting was not persuasive.

Royer, by contrast, did his homework. He selected his targets and skewered them. Royer praised KING management for not requiring him to submit his commentaries for advance review. Not only was that tradition among KING's commentators but it also worked for Payne's interests. As he worked to improve King Broadcasting's relations with the business community, Payne could always tell those who disliked a Royer commentary that he hadn't seen it—Ancil had his cover if Royer drew blood. That gave Royer a rare freedom in a business that typically favored the inoffensive over the blunt. "It's an oasis in a really crummy business," Royer told an interviewer. "The idea is complete independence, so that you can take a hard position, an unpopular position—it might not be terribly popular with one of the downtown stores, for example—and not be subject to any pressures from the sales department operations manager."

The remark implied that commentary elsewhere was influenced by sales managers. Like McGaffin, Royer had general contempt for broadcast journalism. Both felt KING was an exception. Under Heffron, Royer and McGaffin felt free to pick the stories they wanted to do and say the things they felt needed to be said. They couldn't believe their good luck in working for KING. They made full use of the station's expectation that a person do something important with the instrument of television. In a larger sense, they became almost as much an emblem of King Broadcasting as Dorothy Bullitt herself, the young men who seemed to operate on a different level from other local-TV journalists. It was impossible to see them together at any other Seattle station. Much later, they too would become part of King Broadcasting's mythology, the sense that the past was better. And even then, Royer and McGaffin felt the present was as good as it got.

To them, the good flowed directly from that old woman, Dorothy Bullitt. They saw KING as the embodiment of her values, quality, and courage. They nearly worshipped her. They savored every moment they had with her, either in conversations in her office or during encounters in the stations' cafeteria. Royer and McGaffin both felt they had a special closeness to Mrs. Bullitt. Of course, Dorothy Bullitt gave many people that impression. She was a very sympathetic listener.

Heffron remade KING-TV news by hiring people who came across through the airwaves with distinct personalities, in contrast to the general blandness found at KOMO and KIRO. To replace anchors John Komen and Al Wallace, he brought in a likable personality named Jim Harriott, who came from ABC radio. Harriott had a guy-next-door style that pleased viewers and balanced with the strong characters who sat next to him during the newscast.

The following year, Heffron brought in another distinctive personality, Ray McMackin, to do sports. McMackin was smart, quick-witted, and determined to get attention. You don't have to love me; just watch me, he said. He criticized sacred cows and enjoyed the controversy. He suggested that longtime UW football coach Jim Owens was past his prime and should move on. A native of Kirkland, a Seattle suburb, McMackin had grown up listening to KING's Bill O'Mara describe the first hydro races. Like thousands of other kids, he dragged a shingle behind a bike and imagined himself a hydro driver. But he considered Seattle, for all of its pretensions, a hokey little town with good salmon fishing and little else. He had a way of irritating everybody and a flare for the outrageous. Once, in the men's room before air time, Royer urged him to hurry up at the urinal. Without saying anything, McMackin turned and finished on Royer's shoes. When McMackin and other sportscasters made a promotional appearance at Memorial Stadium for a soccer game, he brought his seven-year-old son. When the announcer introduced the sportscasters, the crowd cheered KOMO sportscaster Bruce King. Many booed McMackin. "Daddy, why doesn't anybody like you?" his son asked.

By 1971, Heffron was thinking about a totally new look for the 11:00 P.M. broadcast. He got an idea from a public television station in San Francisco, where the reporters sat around discussing the news as if they were in somebody's living room. He decided to bring back Jean Enersen. She had been moved from news to the program department, where she co-hosted the *Telescope* program. Previously in news, she had been stiff, a little clumsy, and not very good—sent to do vegetables at the

Public Market. But in the talk format, she was relaxed, warm, and attractive. The camera loved her. It brought out her natural personality and brains. She had earned two master's degrees at Stanford. Jean Marie Stanislaw Enersen was Polish, Irish, Slavic, and Russian, but to many viewers in Scandinavian Seattle, she looked like another blonde Norwegian. Around the office she was friendly, but she stayed out of the cliques. McGaffin didn't care much for her. He saw her as the type who got into television for fame and glamour. But Enersen had remarkable poise. She always said the right thing to reporters and, most of all, to Ancil Payne and Dorothy Bullitt, who both adored her. She would talk respectfully of the KING tradition and how lucky she was to be there. She told people she felt like she was part of "a playpen of the most obstreperous five-year-olds" who had been given this amazing equipment and the freedom to invent ways to communicate.

Heffron wanted her for the late-night format. He thought she was qualified and could do it. But at that point, few women anchored the news anywhere. And this format was shockingly different: no anchor desk; no formality. Enersen and Harriott would chat back and forth. Hopefully, the viewers would detect a genuine chemistry between them. Some in the KING news department asked how could a third-string reporter, a personality from the entertainment side of KING, be given a senior journalistic position? And the format? They sneered that it was "Chatty Cathy and Her Boy Friend." It was fluff. At KING, this change was viewed by some as a sorry chapter in the history of King Broadcasting, a cave-in to ratings, entertainment values, and appearance over substance.

Viewers felt otherwise. Almost from the first broadcast in late 1972, KING's late-night ratings took off. And no one credited the set or Harriott. It was the blonde. People liked her. There was something sincere, sexy, and intelligent about her. Both men and women liked her. Young career women were particularly pleased to see a woman in a leadership position during a newscast. Women were very important to advertisers. KING's ratings got stronger. Bigger ratings meant more money to the station.

Heffron later moved Enersen to the station's main broadcast at 5:30 P.M., but not immediately as anchor. He made her a consumer reporter for *Call for Action* and moved McGaffin from that job to a full-time columnist role—a second commentator for the broadcast. Inevitably, Enersen moved to co-anchor the 5:30 show, and the ratings grew. She became the leading symbol of an energized KING. *Argus* dubbed her "KING's Queen." The woman McGaffin had once dismissed as the Zucchini Reporter soon became irreplaceable.

Heffron had his team. KOMO and KING had roughly the same size newsroom, about thirty-six people each, and KIRO employed thirty-one. As part of the changes, McGaffin got promoted, partly out of recognition for one of the most memorable stories ever broadcast on Seattle television.

One morning in 1972, McGaffin spotted a small article in the *P-I* about an eight-year-old girl being treated at Children's Hospital for burns suffered when her pajamas caught fire. Her parents had tried to smother the fire but the cotton burned fast, scorching more than 50 percent of her body. McGaffin thought there might be a cautionary tale in how the girl was injured. At the hospital, he saw the girl in bed, covered with bandages drenched in saline to keep her flesh moist. He watched nurses peel bits of bandages away from her skin as she whimpered in pain. From nurses and doctors, McGaffin learned how dangerous sleepwear can be, catching fire from a spark and burning rapidly. Each year 1,000 children were burned to death and another 40,000 to 50,000 seriously injured, he was told. McGaffin learned that Senator Magnuson wanted to ban flammable sleepwear, but the cotton industry had blocked the legislation. McGaffin was outraged and energized.

After getting permission from the girl's parents, McGaffin and photographer Phil Sturholm took two days to produce thirty minutes of riveting television. McGaffin knew he was violating some rules of television: Never show a naked child, especially a girl. Never show a child in pain.

Two hours before air time, the executive producer of the newscast, Bob George, came in and said he wanted to see the report. McGaffin played the report. George watched the camera lingering on the girl and her pain. She didn't scream but whimpered. The scene of the girl went on for eight minutes—a very long time in TV news—and George became upset.

"You're not going to put this on my newscast," he told McGaffin. George said it was too graphic. People would be watching this during their dinners, he said. They would be revolted. McGaffin and he argued. Finally, McGaffin took the issue to Heffron, who said the report would be aired. George stormed out.

The tape was broadcast. McGaffin ended his report with a live commentary. His blue eyes flashed with rage. Viewers could make a difference, he said, by writing the Secretary of Commerce, who was misidentified as Paul Petersen. (The correct name was Peter Petersen.) Petersen's address stayed on screen for a long interval. Royer followed the report with an ad-lib commentary. "Perhaps my emotional response is too strong to try to talk rationally," Royer said. He and McGaffin discussed what government could do. The camera switched to Harriott, whose only comment was, "Write, please."

Viewers did. KING received 4,500 letters. The mail was forwarded to Petersen, who called KING to find out what the report had said. When the call was put through to McGaffin, he thought it was a joke and hung up on the Secretary of Commerce. Petersen called back. "What the hell did you do out there?" he asked McGaffin. He invited McGaffin to bring his program to Washington, D.C. Petersen was moved by what he saw. He told McGaffin that he was the father of two girls and would do what he could to help. Thanks to continued pressure from Magnuson and others, Congress soon passed a law imposing stricter flammability standards.

The day after the broadcast of *The Burned Child*, George apologized to McGaffin. He said his own son had been standing at the fireplace when his bathrobe had caught fire, and the boy had been hospitalized. George said he had been wrong. Privately, McGaffin saw the incident as one more time when someone who didn't understand journalism got in his way.

Later that year, McGaffin got on to an explosive political story. One night in late October of 1972, he got a call from an ambitious young lawyer named Keith Dysart, the top aide to Attorney General Slade Gorton. Dysart, a rising figure in the GOP establishment, had a hot political story for McGaffin: possible evidence that Al Rosellini, the former governor, had ties to organized crime.

As the November election approached, Rosellini was leading in the polls in a comeback race against the incumbent governor, Republican Dan Evans, a friend and political ally of Gorton. It was a tough campaign and there was a score to settle: Rosellini had been denied a third term as governor when Evans beat him in 1964.

McGaffin was wary. The story had to do with Rosellini, as a private lawyer, helping someone linked to a convicted criminal get a liquor license. McGaffin made no commitment to go with the story, only to look into it. He checked with Heffron and Payne, who urged caution so that KING would not be manipulated to smear Rosellini. Meanwhile, Dysart was also talking to the *P-I.*

McGaffin made some calls and concluded there wasn't enough evidence to justify a story. But Gorton made the matter public by announcing he had suspended Dysart for "working on an investigation with the King Broadcasting Co. and the Seattle *Post-Intelligencer.*" Any candidate has a right to investigate an opponent but Dysart's activities, Gorton insisted, were totally unauthorized and in direct violation of Gorton's orders. Over the next several days, both newspapers put pieces of the story on page one. The *Times* carried a story detailing what KING had known, hinting that perhaps the station had sat on a worthwhile story. In another story, Gorton said Dysart was working with KING. Evans said he hadn't known of Dysart's activities. Rosellini said he was being smeared with anti-Italian innuendoes.

McGaffin was furious that KING's ethics had been questioned. He, Heffron, Royer, and others were convinced that they had been used by Gorton, who they believed knew all along what Dysart had been doing, despite Gorton's assertions. Gorton insisted he hadn't known and had felt betrayed by a trusted aide. The controversy carried up to the election, where Gorton and Evans won their races. Rosellini got 43 percent of the vote to Evans's 51 percent.

Royer was disgusted.

"We the people have tremendous appetites," he said on TV after the election. "And it's a good thing. Because we are asked to swallow a lot. . . . Dysart, we are told, did not do anything unlawful. And I guess we have to swallow that. Dysart, we are told, planned on resigning way back in August, anyway, and I guess we have to swallow that. Dysart, we are told, violated an office rule, but his yearly salary of $25,800 will continue to be paid until the end of December when his 'resignation' becomes effective. And I guess we have to swallow that.

"And the ultimate mouthful: Dysart says the voters on November 7th, by reelecting Slade Gorton and Dan Evans, confirmed his good judgment and high motives in deciding to sell that baseless smear to a sympathetic press. And that, my friends, we do not have to swallow. The Dysart smear—known to high operatives of the Evans campaign . . . was an effective smear. And Mr. Dysart has earned his extra two months of salary."

Royer quoted a reliable poll that showed how Rosellini's standings in the polls fell sharply after the Dysart affair hit the papers.

"We have to swallow a lot, but we do not have to swallow Dysart's contention that the voters proved the worthiness of his cause. All the vote proved is that smear politics, like polite white-collar crime, pays off."

McGaffin remained irritated with Gorton, whom he believed had tried to draw KING into a political scheme that compromised the station's independence. But from another perspective, the incident underscored how far television and KING had come as a presence in politics. The fact that Dysart had gone to KING as well as the *P-I* demonstrated the enhanced status of television. McGaffin and Royer wanted that status. They wanted people's attention. They wanted influence. They wanted to pressure the bad guys and support the good. And they couldn't have achieved their personal status without having had the time and authority to do distinctive work. No other TV journalists in Seattle had their independence, which was the source of their power.

In 1975 they went after the single most powerful man in the legislature, August Mardesich, majority leader of the state senate. Mardesich had been acquitted of charges of extortion and tax fraud, but his case had generated a wealth of testimony about how a bill really became law in Olympia, Washington's capital. The details were sensational but not what TV needed. TV needed pictures, things happening. These were words on paper. So Royer and McGaffin improvised. For *The Bucks Stop Here,* they hired an artist to draw scenes people had described. They used a blackboard to show how people were linked. One cartoon showed a politico, at a desk piled with heaps of cash, lighting a cigar with a dollar bill. They called Mardesich "the chief executive of the Senate branch of the money machine." They spoke of lobbyists laundering payments. "Washing is a good term," they told the audience. "Washing is what you do when something is dirty or something smells bad." It was biting, sarcastic, brutal. They told viewers that special interests had bought their legislature. They told them to get it back. Three months later, Mardesich resigned his leadership position in the senate, blasting "a third rate Seattle newspaper, the *P-I,* and muckraking KING, hungry for improved audience ratings." The report won a national award from the Society of Professional Journalists. And more important, it strengthened KING's reputation as a place that did its homework.

There were many other stories. KING had become a special place. Not just for McGaffin and Royer, but for others as well. With the freedom they had, it did feel like a playpen. Most in KING's newsroom were thirty-five or younger and thought of themselves as smart and right about things. Seattle was alive with ideas and they were part of the action. They were the elite. When Royer led an investigation of Insurance Commissioner Karl Herrmann, he was openly contemptuous of the Seattle press for not following the leads he had uncovered. "Will you tell me where the rest of the press is in this town?" he asked. Royer accused the print press of being asleep at their typewriters.

McGaffin saw Royer as his spiritual kinsman. They became close friends. They partied together. They went to bars together. They talked about stories and ideas, other writers, even *The Federalist.* (McGaffin was surprised that Royer had read it in college.) Royer would host Sunday morning breakfasts at his home for a group that included McGaffin, reporter Mike James, and Charley Royer's brother, Bob, whom Heffron had hired as the political reporter. McGaffin hosted Royer and others for Monday Night Football. McGaffin and Royer rarely worked together on stories, but they spent hours talking about issues and how they should be covered. Both had a major effect on Heffron, who looked to them for ideas. In some ways, Royer and McGaffin ran the newsroom. They set the tone, gave it the connections, the drive, and the passion. They gave speeches, often in tandem, to community groups about the importance of journalism at KING. They believed what they said. They thought they were very good, maybe even the best. In their view, they were certainly the best in local TV journalism in any U.S. city. Journalists in television often felt insecure about what they did, that the people in print were the real thing and they were pretenders. Charley Royer and Don McGaffin had no such insecurity. They felt they could match anyone in print. It was their brains, their hustle that set them apart, lifted their reports from the bland assemblage of facts that characterized most TV reporting. They were stars in Seattle. When they went into a restaurant, people knew them. They showed up in the item columns of the *Times* and the *P-I*. Women found them sexy. They had influence and glamour. And power.

The closeness between McGaffin and Charles Royer wasn't matched by the relationship between McGaffin and Bob Royer, four years younger than Charley. Bob Royer and McGaffin didn't like each other, even though their social and professional interests placed them close. They would see each other at press conferences and Bob Royer would even attend parties at McGaffin's house. But Bob Royer thought McGaffin was a sloppy journalist. McGaffin thought Bob Royer was a dim bulb. Sometimes, the tensions boiled over.

After a golf game in the early 1970s, Mike James called out everyone's scores, with McGaffin as the winner. Bob Royer grabbed McGaffin, made a cutting remark and accidentally tore McGaffin's shirt. McGaffin dropped his golf bag and made ready to fight, but Charley Royer stepped between them. When Bob Royer refused to pay for a replacement shirt, McGaffin vowed to get even. He did so several years later, during another golf game with Bob Royer. At a lunch break that day, McGaffin excused himself, went out to the golf carts, poured gasoline into Bob's bag and set it afire.

"That's my bag!" Bob Royer shouted.

"You should have bought my shirt," McGaffin replied.

McGaffin wanted it to go on forever at KING. Journalism was his life. Journalism was not Charley Royer's life; he was feeling restless, though it wasn't clear in his mind what he wanted to do. He told McGaffin that the idea of running for political office was starting to attract him. After a meeting with Seattle Mayor Wes Uhlman, Charley Royer came away thinking of Uhlman as nothing special. So it was a short leap for Royer to see himself as matching what Uhlman had done. He didn't want to be an observer anymore. He wanted to get into the mix. He felt he had an idea of what the city's problems were and a vision about where the city should go. Having covered a lot of campaigns, he figured he could win. Unlike McGaffin, Royer was never satisfied that journalism was a lifelong career. Royer deeply admired Oregon Governor Tom McCall, who had served as a commentator for King Broadcasting's station in Portland. McCall believed that journalists should go into politics because they had experience in public life and had a good sense for politics. Royer simply thought he could do better in politics than a lot of the politicians he met. His restlessness was coinciding with his brother's determination to leave KING.

One night late in 1976 at a bar near KING, Royer brought the matter up again. He and McGaffin were scheduled to speak later to Fremont neighborhood Democratic Party activists, an evening launched with some Bloody Marys. Am I crazy? Royer asked McGaffin. He was getting closer to a decision, he said. They went to the hall—McGaffin brought his unfinished drink—and began their talk. McGaffin was always one to say things just to get a rise out of people. This time he had a good one. Shortly after the talk began, McGaffin made an announcement, pointing to Royer: "Ladies and gentlemen, let me introduce, with the grace of God, the man who will be your next mayor." People began applauding, some even on their feet. Many were ready to volunteer.

Royer was stunned. He hadn't completely decided. He hadn't told anyone at KING, but it wasn't long before word got back to the newsroom, and Royer, as candidate, was in the news. When word got to KING's newsroom, reporter Carol Lewis wrote Royer a check for $50, his first contribution. As she recognized later, what she did was wrong. Journalists weren't supposed to be helping candidates, but she was twenty-five and naive and thought her friend would make an exciting mayor. It was the first of many awkward moments with candidate Royer.

He stood before the crowd packed into the small Serbian Hall in south Seattle and it was all just perfect. Charles Royer, thirty-seven, never having served in elected office, was about to declare officially his candidacy for mayor of Seattle, just seven years after moving to the city. His only previous administrative experience had been as an assistant advertising manager of a Portland Sears store. At KING-TV, he had done a lot of talking about city government, and now he wanted to run it. Some of his colleagues at KING thought him crazy. But Royer had quit his job in December 1976 and was working full time out of the basement of his View Ridge home. He was not only a campaign novice but also was opposed by one of the city's most powerful political forces, the police union. Seattle police had once considered Royer troublesome enough to warrant making him the subject of a secret investigative file. Many in the city's downtown establishment saw him as unknown or untrustworthy. But he and his brother Bob, who also had quit KING, had done their advance work well. The crowd of several hundred looked bigger than it was. Some had to stand outside and look through windows to see the speech. The gathering of Jews, Slavs, Blacks, Asians, Native Americans, Scandinavians, Irish, and others was a powerful statement, one built on the deep ties Charley's wife, Rosanne, had to her Slavic and other ethnic communities. The strong showing at Serbian Hall signaled that the Royer brothers knew how to organize in the grass roots. Since they couldn't expect big money or big endorsements—those were going to others in the race, nearly all of whom were City Hall veterans—they were going to make a virtue of their weakness. They would run as outsiders, with Royer as the candidate of the neighborhoods; everybody else represented the old ideas of the establishment.

"My training," Royer said, "is in journalism. And it is good training for government. . . . Reporters spend most of their time listening to people. People who have been damaged by government, or angered or hurt by it. Or disappointed by it. People with ideas government won't listen to. That is my experience. Listening to people. Caring about people. And communicating with people."

Among the crowd listening with pride were journalists from KING-TV. It was something no one had seen in recent Seattle history: Journalists on hand to cheer a colleague running for mayor. Journalists were supposed to be fair-minded, but did that mean they couldn't watch their friend make history? One of them had crossed over. And in a way it was completely predictable that some day, someone from King Broadcasting's newsroom would enter politics, embracing a mantle of activism that, in one sense, had passed from Scott Bullitt to Stimson Bullitt and now to Charley Royer. At Serbian Hall that night, among those from KING was news director Norm Heffron, who saw himself as present only to give support to a friend, not as a working journalist. The people from KING had known Royer for years. He was a drinking companion, a fellow duffer, a leader in the newsroom, a mentor. It would have been difficult to stay away. They planned to cover him as they would cover anybody else. At least that's what they thought. It would be an interesting test of KING's ethics. A few journalists would leave KOMO and KIRO and wind up in public office, but never in a position as central and as visible as mayor of Seattle.

A sentimentalist at heart, Don McGaffin felt a sense of pride at seeing his friend stir the crowd. Royer was so good at this. His charm worked more powerfully in person than on TV. He was witty, warm, and thoughtful; people found him approachable. McGaffin saw the bright young people who had joined the fledgling campaign and felt he was witnessing the start of a Seattle Camelot. At the same time, he felt rueful over his friend getting out of journalism. There were so few good journalists that they needed to be protected and encouraged. Seattle was about to lose a good one. He's not one of us anymore, McGaffin thought. He and Royer represented different outgrowths of Dorothy

Bullitt's progressivism, each seeking a special role for himself in public life as a caretaker of values, certain about his purpose and direction.

But then, there was another message implicit in Royer's entry into politics, that journalism had its limits for anyone committed to public service. He'd certainly get a debate on that point from McGaffin, yet that discussion would focus on a style of local-broadcast journalism soon to be obsolete in a competitive industry. The question would be less whether KING would remain a golden island in a mediocre industry than whether KING could financially resist those changes and still hold viewers.

In 1976, broadcast journalism was at the beginning of a transformation that would significantly alter the daily habits in every TV newsroom in America. The kind of investigations and lengthy reports on issues that Royer and McGaffin preferred became harder to do, a change driven by industry finances, technology, and a perception that the tastes of viewers had evolved. By the time of Royer's candidacy, cable had penetrated nearly 20 percent of American homes, and it would eventually transform the distribution of content for television. As cable increased the number of channels, profits and audience declined for the networks. Within four years, Atlanta's Ted Turner would found a twenty-four hour news service, Cable News Network, that would directly compete with network newscasts. Ultimately, a network newscast became less a public service and more a profitable product that could be produced at reasonable cost. That meant greater pressure to create news programs with a hot emotional appeal in order to grab and hold audiences. The network response to these forces was accelerated in the mid-1980s by changes of ownership or control at CBS, NBC, and ABC, all of which sharply cut their news budgets.

The gadgetry of television news was changing as well. The arrival in the mid-1970s of Electronic News Gathering (ENG) equipment meant that TV journalists could quickly record and edit sound and video. Live transmissions became simple. TV journalists could do more stories, faster. Live was immediate and "hot," so it had a strong appeal to viewers. As newscasts carried more live stories, even traffic jams, journalists at a scene had little time to research a situation and often could only ad-lib answers to questions from the anchor desk and hustle off to the next story.

For a local station adapting to the new approach, the effect of these changes was to toss out most stories about government or issues and switch to topics that had live, interesting visuals, such as the scene of a fire, a crime, a catastrophe. At the same time, news broadcasts became very attractive to advertisers and thus more profitable. The combination of greater demand for news programming and the ease with which it could be produced made for an increase in newscasts. As coverage broadened across many time slots, it also got shallower or at least not any deeper. Stories would be recycled through the day. Feeds from the networks or other sources would be used to fill time.

But that was television's future, not Royer's moment. This was politics and Royer's bid to take over city hall. As Royer gave his speech at Serbian Hall, Richard Larsen watched with wry amusement. One of the state's shrewdest political observers, Larsen had become a political writer for the Seattle *Times*. Looking over at Heffron and the others from KING, Larsen felt repulsed and sympathetic at the same time. The sight of all those journalists applauding a candidate was unseemly, bush league. But then, this was as new to them as it was for him. No one had training in how to handle such a situation, so Larsen did not judge them too harshly. Covering Royer as a politician would be both awkward and interesting.

Although Royer ran without support from the downtown establishment, and the newspapers fretted about his inexperience, he had a huge edge in the familiarity of his name and face. Dispensing wisdom nightly on KING gave him an advantage over the five other major candidates, all city council members or city department heads. Royer set himself as the neighborhood's candidate and won the primary. In the general election he faced attorney Paul Schell, who had run the city's Department of Community Development.

Covering the race was a walk on a tightrope for KING's news department. To cover Royer, Heffron assigned its newest reporter, Lou Dobbs. To cover Schell, he assigned reporter Carol Lewis. He did not know—and Lewis did not tell him—that she had contributed money to Royer's campaign. What's more, Lewis was interested in working in city government, whichever man was elected mayor. She liked both candidates. Heffron figured he could watch coverage of the campaign very closely to ensure that it was balanced and unbiased. Oddly enough, no one in the Seattle press corps explored the unusual situation of KING covering an old friend and co-worker. The closest thing was a story in the *Times* reporting a sharp exchange between Lewis and Schell at a press conference. Schell's call for KING to release Royer's commentaries drew what the *Times* called "argumentative questions" by Lewis, who was covering the press conference. "They'll be old stances," the *Times* quoted her as saying. The *Times* reporter knew of the Lewis-Royer friendship but failed to pursue the issue, thinking it a private matter.

Inside the Royer campaign, Bob Royer and Charley Royer thought KING was going out of its way to be tough. Inside KING, anchor Mike James thought his station's coverage was too harsh. McGaffin decided his best course was to write no commentaries on the mayor's race, but that didn't mean he ignored it. When Royer was asked about a rumor that had spooked the Seattle police—that he had a secret plan to make McGaffin chief of police—Royer made a joke of it. He said McGaffin always wanted to wear a hat with a spinning red light on top. When the joke got back to KING, McGaffin was furious. Despite his gruff exterior, McGaffin craved respect. He hated to be trivialized. The Royer gag hurt, and it created a small fissure in their relationship. They would remain friends for years after that, but McGaffin would mark that as the beginning of the end. It may have been impossible for the friendship to last— McGaffin had too much aggressiveness toward office holders. For his own political survival, there were things that Royer couldn't tell McGaffin. More important, there were things about Royer that McGaffin couldn't tell his viewers.

Royer painted Schell as an operative of the downtown establishment, which favored a new Interstate 90 bridge across Lake Washington and a mall that would fill much of a proposed Westlake Park in the downtown. The strategy worked. He received 94,738 votes to Schell's 71,034 votes. After the election, Royer and McGaffin went out to dinner and discussed how they could protect their friendship. The only answer seemed to be to give no favors to the other. Royer would never give a story to McGaffin. And McGaffin would never give Royer, the mayor, a break. The arrangement worked most of the time, but they felt the tangle of conflicting missions.

In 1978 Royer became mayor of a city that had shaken its political past. The city was no longer ruled by any one faction, except perhaps for an influential group of residents, all recent arrivals, who had mastered its neighborhood politics. Power in Seattle was balkanized, with neither the mayor, nor the city council, nor one political party dominating. Ideas would be considered at length, circulated to the many neighborhood councils for discussion by participants sitting on hard chairs. Seattle at that point had lost some population, slightly under 500,000 compared with its peak of 557,000 in the 1960s. The suburbs were growing, fueled by cheap housing, malls and new schools without busing. Yet the city was fast acquiring a national image as a special place. In the past, tourists had come to Seattle for its outdoor scenery, but now the urban landscape offered good restaurants, museums, interesting bars, and concert halls that were celebrated in *Harpers* and other national publications. The local *Weekly,* founded by ex-*Seattle* writer David Brewster, was read by young professionals exploring the many attractive options. The city had professional sports—the Seattle Seahawks football team and the Seattle Supersonics basketball team, which was soon to win a world championship. A half-million visitors would see the "Treasures of Tutankhamen" at the Seattle Art Museum. The economy was changing. The old jobs of timber and fishing in King County disappeared, replaced by a host of jobs with service-oriented companies, including Microsoft, a new computer-software firm. Boeing turned the corner in 1975 and by now employed 55,000 people in the Seattle area.

Royer faced tricky questions of dealing with electrical-power needs, picking a new police chief, and working with the city council and labor unions. But he was as confident as his young city. "I've never been awed by this job," he said, just before taking office. "It's controllable. I have confidence in myself, and I understand government."

Soon after taking office, Royer decided to hold informal twice-weekly talks with the press, a casual give-and-take on what the new mayor was trying to do. To keep things relaxed, his office decided that no TV cameras would be allowed. But that was like telling newspaper reporters they couldn't bring pens and notebooks. TV reporters must have footage—and Mayor Royer knew that. Or at least Royer, the journalist, would have known that. A new KING reporter, Linda Brill, decided to crash the event in the mayor's office, cameras rolling. She caught the new mayoral aide Carol Lewis (the ex-KING reporter) rushing the camera, trying to block KING's entry. KING aired the footage and even the New York *Times* picked up the hilarious story of the mayor squabbling with his former employer. Lewis later concluded that she and the other KING alumni at City Hall, including Deputy Mayor Bob Royer, were naive to think they could talk informally with the press. To the Royers and Lewis, it seemed that their old drinking buddies in the press had turned on them. It took a while to get over that sense of betrayal.

There were other awkward moments. McGaffin went after Donald Dudley, Royer's nominee for director of the Department of Human Resources. McGaffin reported that Dudley had drawn more than $30,000 in checks from two of his companies for personal items such as mortgages and school tuition. Dudley got the job, but he was damaged goods. In a later report card on their new mayor, KING gave him low marks, especially for his appointments of department heads. Royer was brought into KING's studio for a live broadcast without any word in advance of what would be said—standard journalistic fare, but Deputy Mayor Bob Royer, for one, felt they had been bushwhacked. He wondered if McGaffin, who had helped write the program, was doing another macho thing: Can you take a hit, big guy?

McGaffin and Royer together took a shot from the news media over a lawn party McGaffin had helped organize one warm August Sunday at the University of Washington. To celebrate the wedding anniversary of two friends, the group decided to have a picnic. And because the date also commemorated the start of World War I, which historians mark as the end of the Edwardian era, McGaffin and several friends decided to dress in Edwardian garb: the women in long gowns and the men in vintage tuxedoes. They were entertained by two violinists. The meal featured May wine, sugared strawberries, Cornish game hen, deviled eggs, and caviar served on linen tablecloths with crystal and china. Unfortunately, the picnic caused a nearby drama group to call the campus police twice, complaining of its loud noises. The fact that the mayor had briefly attended made it news—on page one of the Seattle *P-I*. The newspaper account suggested a rowdy, boozy event held by snobs. The *P-I*'s star columnist, Emmett Watson, saw it as a tasteless celebration of the start of a war: "Channel 5, living up to the monarchical tone of its call letters, advanced the cause of elitism. It was in the tradition of an evening last spring when anchorman Mike James played KING's piano while a lesser employee turned out counterfeit money on the company printing machine." Royer, denying that the group ever got rowdy, complained of "shoddy journalism." McGaffin vowed that he would punch Watson and the *P-I*'s city editor. No doubt some of the *P-I*'s readers enjoyed seeing both Royer and McGaffin, two KING commentators who had often flamed others, get their own turn on the media spit.

With Royer out of KING, Ancil Payne needed someone to fill The Chair, his nickname for the commentator job. Two candidates emerged. One was Bill Prochnau, a former writer for the Seattle *Times,* an aide to Senator Warren Magnuson, and the editor of a new Bellevue daily, the *Journal-American*. Prochnau was a gifted writer who had a deep understanding of Northwest issues but no TV experience, and he spoke with the speed of poured bunker oil. Another candidate was being pushed by McGaffin: Bob Simmons, an award-winning Los Angeles TV political reporter who had an interest in the environment and in explaining government to people.

A courteous, careful journalist, Simmons first encountered KING in 1968 when, as a reporter for KNXT-TV in Los Angeles, he visited Seattle to cover Bobby Kennedy's presidential campaign. He saw KING's newscast at that time and was impressed with the intelligence of the program, especially its straightforward opposition to the war in Vietnam. He called his wife. "You wouldn't believe what they're saying on the air," he told her, adding that if he ever left Los Angeles he wanted to work for King Broadcasting.

During their interviews, neither Payne nor Heffron specifically asked Prochnau or Simmons about their political views, but both men saw themselves as liberals, and their tilt was apparent in how they covered issues. KING wanted someone whose views would be noticed, as Royer's had been. Helped by his friend McGaffin, Simmons got the job.

Simmons started at KING in March 1977, knowing he couldn't and wouldn't be another Charley Royer. Royer was unequaled in his ability to leave ideas in viewer's minds. Simmons told Ancil Payne that he would be his own man. His approach would be more analysis than commentary. His pieces would roll out facts that spoke for themselves. New to Seattle, Simmons wanted to know more about the city before expressing opinions. From time to time he might ask Payne or one of the Bullitt sisters for guidance. He didn't want to step on any mines. Almost always the answer was the same: you're the commentator, you decide what to say. He felt astonished that, even though management and ownership of KING got heat for some of his statements, they didn't try to influence him.

One of the city's most powerful businessmen, Ned Skinner, owned a Pepsi Cola franchise and vigorously opposed a bottle-recycling bill. In an early commentary, Simmons spoofed the opponents' argument that the bill would lead to sanitation problems. The plague would break out, said Simmons, if people recycled bottles. Not long after the broadcast, Dorothy Bullitt approached Simmons in the company cafeteria.

"I think you should know that Ned Skinner is very angry with you," she said.

Oh-oh, thought Simmons. Here comes the end of my great job in Seattle. After the commentary, he learned that the Skinner and Stimson families had known each other for generations. "I'm sorry. I didn't intend to embarrass you in front of your friends," he told Dorothy Bullitt. "It never occurred to me there was a close relationship there."

"Oh no," she replied. "I thought you might want to hit him again."

Simmons felt relief and happiness that he had found a rare place in TV journalism. It was one of many demonstrations of the support he felt from the Bullitts and Ancil Payne.

Only once did Simmons stumble into a sensitive area, when he attacked Harbor Properties for opposing height restrictions on some downtown property it owned. Patsy Collins showed up at his desk. Since her brother had left the company, she held the title of chairwoman of King Broadcasting. She kept an office at KING on the executive's fifth floor (actually the fourth, unless the mezzanine was counted), from which she handled philanthropic projects.

"Mother would like to see you, and I think I'd better go with you," Collins said.

They walked into Dorothy Bullitt's office and Simmons could easily see that the company owner was breathing fire. "Why do you people always have to pick on us?" she asked. "There are other people in town who are fighting the [height] controls."

After doing the commentary, Simmons learned that Harbor Properties was owned by Stimson Bullitt. The commentary had made it look like Dorothy Bullitt's company was attacking the son who had left King under painful circumstances. "I've got to plead ignorance," he told her. "I didn't know it was related." Then he took a gamble. "But I've got a feeling that if I had known, I would have done it anyway, because since I came here I've been told to ignore these kinds of conflicts."

This was one of those moments where Dorothy Bullitt had a way of killing time when she thought about what to say. Her favorite technique was to reach for her pack of cigarettes and fumble for a lighter. "I suppose that's true," she said finally. "But it seems unfair you have to always pick on us."

Simmons apologized again.

"Now, now, mother," Collins said, patting her arm.

Nothing more came from the incident. To Simmons, it served as a reminder of how rarely Dorothy Bullitt tried to influence news coverage.

Mrs. Bullitt also chose not to interfere with another family entanglement, a romance between McGaffin and her granddaughter, Dorothy C. Bullitt. Stim's daughter was sometimes called Young Dorothy. The girl who had survived Meany Middle School and Garfield High School had blossomed into a poised, dark-haired woman who inherited her father's intensity and her mother's patrician beauty. In the late 1970s, while she was still in law school, Young Dorothy met McGaffin at a holiday party at the home of Bob Block, an old friend of Stim's and a long-time Democratic Party activist. Recently divorced, McGaffin was older than Dorothy by some twenty years, but a romance began. Almost from the first, McGaffin saw her as the keeper of the King Broadcasting flame. More than any of the other Bullitt grandchildren, Young Dorothy seemed to embody the commitment to social responsibility and excellence that had guided King Broadcasting's journalism. They soon became an item around town, riding on McGaffin's motor scooter. During their two-year relationship, McGaffin urged Dorothy to claim the mantle of the company's leadership. She had the brains, the love of Seattle, and the right values to lead the company, he told her. They never got around to discussing how she would begin.

For Young Dorothy, it was intoxicating to hear herself ranked as the successor to her grandmother, to think about the instrument of King Broadcasting and what she could do with it. And it was made all the more heady because her grandmother had encouraged her to consider the possibility. On one occasion, the elder Dorothy took Young Dorothy aside and told her to get training, to prepare herself in case the opportunity arose for her to run the company. But was that a real possibility? As Stim's daughter, she held little if any financial interest in King Broadcasting. One of Patsy's or Harriet's children should have been a more likely choice, but none of them showed an interest in management. By contrast, Young Dorothy was very interested. She believed in the mission. She believed in the ideal that the legacy of the Bullitt family was civic leadership. Many of the Bullitt grandchildren had chosen alternative lifestyles and had developed their own missions. But Young Dorothy wanted a business career. After law school, Young Dorothy planned to get an MBA. She was serious and dutiful. In her, McGaffin saw the true successor to Dorothy Stimson Bullitt. It was no coincidence that Young Dorothy spent hours asking her grandmother about business. Her grandmother's philosophy of management—set the overall goal; hire good people; then step aside and let them get the job done—reflected her own.

Young Dorothy was the dutiful contrast to her carefree brother, Ben Bullitt. While she studiously readied herself for civic leadership, he acquired a reputation as a frivolous local playboy. In the end, he created a crisis for his family and the company.

In November 1981, Ben held a party on his new $360,000 yacht, the *Pegasus*. At twenty-four, Ben was a high school dropout, a party animal, a drug user. He was also very outgoing, handsome, and athletic, which he proved by swimming across Lake Washington and climbing mountains. Some years earlier he and his father had barely survived a snowstorm during a climb of Mt. Rainier.

A lot of booze and cocaine were consumed that night on the *Pegasus*. Ben was driving the sixty-seven-foot boat fast and erratically, and he got angry when a friend insisted on taking control. At about midnight, Ben changed into a business suit and dived into the water in the Leschi area of Lake Washington. His girlfriend, Jo Anne LaBoff, tried to talk him into swimming back to the boat. Instead, he joked about drowning. "Jo, everything I have is yours!" he called. She jumped into the frigid water and persuaded him to swim to the boat. She tried to lift him out of the water, but he slipped back in and was never seen again. Police were called. KING-TV news got wind of the story, sending a reporter and photographer to the scene.

An awkward news event began to unfold. What had happened to Ben? Was he dead? Or had he disappeared to avoid problems with some drug dealer? That scenario was fueled by the fact that Ben was a very strong swimmer and had jumped into the water with a thick envelope, rumored to contain as much as $50,000 in cash, stuffed into his pants. Also, at about the time he entered the water, an unlighted, low-flying seaplane had landed near Leschi. When Stimson Bullitt arrived, news director Paul Steinle briefed him on what the station's reporters had learned.

The story became page one news. Over the next several weeks, details of Ben Bullitt's lifestyle and his friendship with wild, even dangerous people were made public. Ben was close friends with a "financial advisor," Robert King, who traveled with Ben in rented limousines, claimed a background of work for the CIA, and kept a collection of guns and other weapons. Before Ben's last cruise, King had asked of Ben's whereabouts and, ominously, had been seen carrying thumb shackles (one of his playthings) and a large canvas bag, big enough to hold a person. One of the most shocking stories came from McGaffin. Acting on what he had learned from Young Dorothy, McGaffin reported that Ben had borrowed $600,000 from five Seattle banks shortly before his disappearance. On the air, McGaffin said: "Bullitt never had been employed except in menial jobs and operated a small antique shop for a time—at a loss. The business closed recently, and he was evicted for nonpayment of rent." McGaffin reported that Ben had used cocaine and other drugs heavily and often carried large amounts of cash. Most tantalizing, he reported there were rumors that Ben Bullitt was alive.

The Bullitt family, already suffering over the disappearance of a son, saw their grief become a daily news topic. Stim hired a submarine to search for the body in an area where Lake Washington reached depths of 200 feet. The elder Dorothy Bullitt had dinner with a psychic who drew a map of the lake's northern shore where Ben may have gone. McGaffin and Young Dorothy separately inspected the area, but no trace of Ben was ever found, there or anywhere. KING-TV news played the story aggressively—obsessively, in Young Dorothy's view. The other stations seemed to show restraint, but not KING. Yet no Bullitt considered muzzling McGaffin or the rest of the news crew. Paul Steinle, as news director, was given no instructions on how to handle the story. There was no interference.

And there was the irony: At perhaps the most painful public moment in the Bullitt family's history, no attempt was made to compromise the integrity of KING's newsroom. It wasn't the most important story in Seattle, but it was nonetheless a proud moment for the newsroom of King Broadcasting, especially for McGaffin, who was more pleased by the Bullitts' enduring commitment to journalistic values than by the $18 million remodeling of KING's headquarters that year. McGaffin used his personal contacts to the Bullitt family to report what he thought the public should know. And nobody tried to stop him. His inside track to the family put him in the odd situation of getting calls from other reporters. And in talking to them, he told himself to be careful. McGaffin believed Ben had fled to Canada. He promised the elder Dorothy Bullitt that he would find her grandson, but he never did. No one did. The disappearance of Benjamin Bullitt would remain one of Seattle's mysteries.

The family tragedy was soon followed by a corporate embarrassment.

By 1982, King Broadcasting's flagship station had won numerous awards, including all of the top national honors (see Appendix). That year, KING picked up another, the American Press Photographers' highest award, for the third time in four years. KING was a leader of the industry, but there was a major problem. While KING's news department spoke of the great Bullitt tradition of values and high-quality journalism, the station was not holding its audience. KING-TV's principal newscast, the five o'clock show, had slipped to third in the ratings behind two stations led by former KING employees, Jim Harriott at KOMO and John Lippman at KIRO. Safe, dull KOMO was second. And a resurgent KIRO, adopting flashy news graphics and attention-grabbing self-promotion, had pulled into the lead for the first time in years. KING had been the first in the Northwest to launch a full-time bureau in Washington, D.C. But KIRO leased a helicopter and promoted the machine on an equal basis with its anchors. KING's staff sniffed that a helicopter was a dubious use of dollars, but viewers liked the immediacy of the live reports. KING still called itself the best local news in the country, but in truth, its nightly report had become ponderous, and KIRO was winning a good share of local Emmys. The *Weekly*'s David Brewster called KING-TV "the lofty loser" and noted that KING was falling behind its rivals in investments in new equipment, such as video-tape cameras that captured news and put it on the air faster than could the old film cameras. KING had photographers who loved the texture of film, but while they were souping and editing film, trying to get words and pictures just right, KIRO was on the air, scooping KING with the story.

The ratings showed that audiences preferred live, urgent reports over the thoughtful, longer stories produced in the studios. A big fire in Ballard seemed more compelling than a review of legislative issues. What's more, said the *Weekly*, KING's commentary no longer had bite. On a deeper level, it was apparent that KING was so bound by tradition that it had failed to recognize a new era of TV journalism in which flashing police lights rated higher than a debate of civic issues. News director Steinle was convinced that high quality eventually would win out. He commissioned Mike James to do a five-part series on the New Federalism, while KIRO hyped the weight-loss effort of its rotund sportscaster— "Watch Wayne Shrink." Some KING staffers grumbled that maybe the public didn't want quality. The low ratings were beginning to hurt morale. Proud King Broadcasting was in danger of becoming irrelevant.

TV can be a brutal business. Before much longer, news director Paul Steinle was out. In March 1982 the company brought in Don Dunkel, a huge bear of a man who also acted like one. A senior ABC news producer who helped launch *Nightline* during the Iranian hostage crisis, Dunkel loved to hunt and fish and had grown tired of the network grind. Ancil Payne was impressed with him and passed him along to station manager Sturges Dorrance. KING's management saw Dunkel as providing a new opportunity to rein in the unruly news staff. Ancil Payne believed that KING had a talented staff who did good work, but he told Dunkel that he had to take control. In Payne's opinion, too many of the staff were divisively independent.

There was no shortage of outside opinions. The *Weekly* reported that part of the problem was KING's management. Payne, it suggested, undercut Steinle and other managers by involving himself in newsroom affairs. This was denied by Payne, who was nonetheless keenly sensitive to the industry perception that news directors at KING lasted as long as snow in Seattle. In nearly fifteen years, KING had employed seven news directors.

Dunkel wasted no time. Before he even arrived in Seattle, he sent a memo from his room at the Hilton in Milan, Italy, putting everyone at KING on notice. Three chances were all they would get—one, to learn from an error, two to validate the education, three, to find another job.

In Seattle, at his first meeting with McGaffin he offered no pleasantries. "I understand you're going to be my tough nut," Dunkel told McGaffin. "How tough are you, McGaffin?"

"Tough enough for you to find out," McGaffin replied. McGaffin figured that Dunkel was about six feet five and weighed 240 pounds. The thought of punching his new boss went through his mind. He figured Dunkel was big, but soft. He had taken bigger men. But McGaffin wasn't ready to be fired.

Dunkel's plan included reining in McGaffin and Simmons. Independent commentary and analysis had been the hallmark of KING, but Dunkel made it clear that he didn't like it. Nobody had ever asked to read their copy in advance—till now. Dunkel wanted to see what Simmons was going to say. When Simmons resisted, Dunkel asked him: So nobody should have control over you? You are such a good journalist that no one should give you orders? It was a bullying style of argument, and Simmons fought back. Once Simmons just tossed a memo back at Dunkel, "I'm not going to answer this bullshit thing," Simmons said. But Dunkel was wearing him down.

Dunkel wanted to erase KING's image as a liberal establishment. He complained to the *Post-Intelligencer* that the station had been aloof and superior, and it hadn't helped itself by favoring a state income tax and standing against the Vietnam War. McGaffin was appalled. "Hadn't helped itself?" McGaffin thought otherwise. Stimson Bullitt's stand on Vietnam was one of the company's finest hours. Not just because he was right about the war, but because KING had done the editorial regardless of ratings and public attitude. McGaffin didn't know how much backing Dunkel had from KING's top management. But he knew that Payne, who admired journalists, wanted to see their energies focused by someone in charge. As much as McGaffin felt close to both of them, McGaffin never went to Ancil Payne or Dorothy S. Bullitt to complain about Dunkel. McGaffin saw himself as a loyal employee. He would keep his mouth shut.

When Dunkel agreed to fill the station's 6:30 P.M. slot with a new program, Simmons, McGaffin, and others were eager to take the opportunity. KING launched *Top Story,* a thirty-minute program that would examine a single issue each day. It was a significant commitment in an industry that usually restricted stories to two minutes or less. McGaffin saw it as a chance to do in-depth, substantive journalism, which he thought was rare in television. It was not just a huge opportunity but a huge problem too. How to fill 150 minutes a week? McGaffin gave up his column for the new show, and Simmons gave up his commentary. They were too busy to do anything for the 5:00 P.M. show. It was a crushing work load.

But Dunkel, not McGaffin or Simmons, tired first. In August 1983, less than a year after coming to Seattle, Dunkel quit, saying he wanted to work less and play more. After all, he said, he had come to Seattle to hunt ducks and get reacquainted with his wife. The station named managing editor Linda Gist as acting news director.

That same month, McGaffin's mother died. A widow, she had been living with her son for the past three years. Her lung cancer had triggered an outpouring of support from people at KING, including many of the news staff, who came to visit. Even Mrs. Bullitt had paid a visit, a gesture that deeply pleased McGaffin. But the stress of her illness and death, which triggered squabbling with his sisters over his mother's estate, left McGaffin drained. He took August off.

In November 1983, McGaffin went in to tell Gist that he wanted to go with a Seattle group that was visiting Nicaragua. Earlier, McGaffin had done reports from El Salvador that had won several awards. He figured getting approval for Nicaragua would be routine. It wasn't. You're not going, said Gist. Simmons is.

Something came over McGaffin. It was more than getting turned down. It was something that he had felt coming for a long time at KING. The place was changing. He had stayed too long. Fourteen years. A lifetime in television. Several lifetimes. He still had a lot of good journalism in him, he felt. But KING was no longer the right place for him.

"Well then, I quit," he replied.

He phoned a station in San Francisco and said he would accept the job they had repeatedly offered: feature columnist. It was a big spot with KPIX-TV, a CBS-owned station in a market much bigger than Seattle's.

He posted a note on the newsroom bulletin board—one sentence— saying he was quitting. He told people there would be no party. A few friends dropped by to sip from the Wild Turkey McGaffin kept at his desk. Gist was stunned by McGaffin's decision, but she made no effort to keep him. There was no big discussion, no effort by management to talk him out of leaving. One of KING's most ardent believers was out, joining other believers who had gone before: Lee Schulman, Bob Schulman, Otto Brandt, Stimson Bullitt.

McGaffin rented out his house and furniture, put his clothes and a few other possessions into his Honda Accord, and headed south on I-5. It was the beginning of the long rainy season in Seattle. His parents were dead. McGaffin was headed to a bigger city where he would be a star, earning a six-figure salary and speaking to an audience of one million, more than twice KING's viewers. Yet he felt no joy. He was leaving the station that had given him so much freedom and the city that was home to many whom he loved. He felt alone. He wept as he drove.

Don McGaffin left a company that had changed dramatically since his start there in 1970. King Broadcasting had grown from 447 employees to 1,112 employees; from revenues of $16 million a year to $100 million; from three to five TV stations; from five to seven radio stations; and from cable-TV service with 19,000 customers in four cities to 92,000 customers in nine cities. As a diversified communications empire spread over five states, the company had gained prestige in the industry and in the community.

But events surrounding the kidnapping of a ten-year-old girl dealt King Broadcasting a damaging blow. It led to public scrutiny of the very foundation of KING's journalism—whether its reporters told the truth. Proud KING was the only Seattle station ever called on to endure such a controversy, made all the more painful because its own staff publicly wondered if the company had betrayed its values.

It began one afternoon in October 1985, when a reporter tipped KING-TV night assignment editor Bill Baker that something was going on with the FBI, whose radio frequency crackled with coded, urgent conversations among agents. Baker called the FBI's spokesman, who told him that a major incident was under way and the press had to stay away, but he wouldn't specify what areas were to be avoided. That put Baker in a tough spot because KING, like all Seattle stations, was under tremendous pressure to have its cameras and transmitting gear pre-positioned and to be first with live pictures. So KING had to be close, but not too close. As the situation unfolded over the next twenty-four hours,

Baker and other editors discovered that they were covering a kidnapping of a Bellingham girl involving locations on Interstate 5.

As part of the team covering the story, Baker assigned Julie Blacklow, one of the first woman reporters at KING-TV. Blacklow was a character cut from a feminist version of *The Front Page*. She had big hair and a big mouth. She talked as tough as the men, returned sarcastic jokes with profanities that could burn paint off a car, and prided herself on not letting anyone get between her and a story. According to the *Times*, she had been hired in 1972 at age twenty-four with no prior broadcast experience, convincing KING's news director that she had a "longtime" close friend at KING, whom she had actually just met. As a rookie, she had taken a lot of sexist jabbing from McGaffin, Royer, and the other men of the department, but she took their scripts home, studied broadcast writing, and worked to be their journalistic equal.

Four months after her hiring, she made one notable goof-up. "Oh, shit I made a mistake. Oh, shit, let's do it again," she had said on the air, forgetting that her microphone was on. She muscled her way into news stories that often became part of legends at KING. Once, she rushed to the scene of a suicide jumper on the Aurora Bridge and didn't see anyone official to interview. She turned to a man standing next to her and asked, "Has he jumped yet?" "No," he said. "I haven't." She talked with him till police arrived.

Other times, she turned on the charm to coax reluctant sources to give her exclusive interviews. But there was also an abrasiveness that turned some people off. It was quite a coup for KING to get one of the first TV interviews with Microsoft head Bill Gates, and Blacklow got the assignment. In typical style, she went for an attention-getting question to break the ice, asking the software mogul about his sex life. Microsoft's PR department went ballistic and complained to KING management. Blacklow insisted it was a joke.

She felt a kinship with Dorothy S. Bullitt, a mentor to women in the newsroom, whom she visited weekly at the old lady's fifth floor office, not far from Payne's. She and Dorothy Bullitt had many long talks. They also went to the movies or to dinner, and they often split a bottle of wine or two.

But Blacklow didn't feel completely welcome in King Broadcasting's upper ranks. She felt, for instance, that Payne had an antipathy toward her—probably didn't like aggressive, strong women, Blacklow figured.

Blacklow believed she was a close friend of King's controlling shareholder. But Dorothy Bullitt always placed the company and the management system above any individual employee. Mrs. Bullitt let her managers run the company in the way they saw best, and company longevity was no barrier to removing a problem employee, including Blacklow. Blacklow didn't know it, but when Don Varyu was hired to replace Dunkel in 1983, station management gave him a list of troublemakers to be replaced. The list included Blacklow. Varyu, however, kept those people because he found them valuable.

In October 1985, several times during the kidnapping crisis, various KING vehicles came close to or actually entered stakeouts run by the FBI or Bellingham police. The police were monitoring the kidnapper, James V. Miller, as well as the girl's father as he followed complicated instructions to make stops at points along I-5 between Bellingham and Tenino, about 130 miles south near Olympia. What caused an uproar began after Blacklow and photographer Mark Anderson left the freeway at Exit 212, north of Everett. They drove up to a silver van that had the look of a police vehicle: government license plates, two antennae, and tinted windows. Blacklow asked if they were police or FBI. No, they said. "Why is it that I don't believe you?" she asked.

As they drove away, they overheard on their police scanner someone saying that a KING vehicle was in the vicinity. They then got a radio call from Baker, saying the FBI had called him, to request that the KING vehicle leave the area. Blacklow and Anderson left the scene. In Olympia, other KING vehicles also stumbled into stakeouts and were ordered out.

Eventually the child was recovered unharmed; the kidnapper shot himself and died; and the incident was over. But the chief of the Bellingham police department was enraged. He called a press conference to denounce KING-TV for "blatant and repeated interference in the investigation." His message was clear: reckless KING reporters had jeopardized the life of the kidnapped child. Varyu denied that KING had interfered in the case and said KING had honored all requests to stay out of sensitive areas, but the controversy continued. Ancil Payne wanted the issue put to rest. When Varyu and station manager Sturges Dorrance met with the police chief in Bellingham to calm things down, people in KING's newsroom figured it was a diplomatic mission: say nice things but never budge from the position that the newsroom had been doing its job under confusing circumstances. But to their astonishment, Dorrance and Varyu called a press conference and apologized for the stations' unintended actions—an event carried live, painfully, by KING itself. Members of the newsroom watched the press conference and broke into shrieks of disapproval. The reporters and photographers, who firmly believed they had done nothing wrong, felt the company had sold out to police pressure and had made itself look stupid.

When Dorrance got back to Seattle, reporter Jack Hamann stormed up to his office, and, in a rage, demanded an audience. Hamann had been one of those covering the kidnapping that day. He was also a union shop steward. Hamann believed Bellingham police had mishandled the investigation and were trying to blame KING. "How dare you apologize for my behavior without even doing me the courtesy of talking to me about what happened?" Hamann shouted.

Journalists often gripe about the judgments of editors, but, in this instance, they felt that the public apology was something else altogether. By and large, employees of KING-TV news had been proud of their work and the company's reputation. For more than three decades, they had embraced the notion that King Broadcasting was set above the rest. But on this day, many in the newsroom were truly embarrassed. They felt management was deeply, utterly, publicly wrong.

The apology might have put an end to a corrosive public controversy, except that the parents of the kidnapped girl filed a lawsuit accusing King Broadcasting of willfully endangering the life of their daughter. The parents' lawyer took depositions from many in the news department on what they had been told and had done that day. That created a new problem: contradictions in employees' statements. After reviewing Julie Blacklow's statement, management concluded that she had lied about not knowing what she had been covering that day. Blacklow said she was sent out the door without any briefing; that Baker had specifically said he didn't know if her assignment was connected to a kidnapping in Olympia. She insisted that isolated chatter she had picked up later from the FBI frequency hadn't given any clues as to what was going on.

As King Broadcasting headquarters swarmed with lawyers, at least five of whom represented the company, management was deeply concerned and even fearful. It was bad enough to be seen squabbling with a police chief, but to fight with the parents of an imperiled little girl was worse. King wanted the lawsuit to go away, fast. As newspapers pressed with their coverage, the issue became a daily wounding of KING's pride and reputation. It risked harming the station's relationship with viewers and it damaged the news department, which was by then the station's second-largest source of profits. How could they resolve the problem when one of their best-known reporters had given testimony they felt was untenable? Once the parents' lawyer discovered the contradictions among King Broadcasting employees, he'd have another weapon against the company, whose credibility was already damaged. Varyu and Payne both believed Blacklow's testimony was deceptive: No seasoned reporter would go out into the field completely in the dark about the assignment. Yet Blacklow insisted that had been the case in the haste of the day.

Unbeknownst to Blacklow, a debate about her raged within KING's management. Dorrance and others wanted to fire her. Varyu felt Blacklow should be disciplined but not fired. Others that day had committed worse errors; it would hurt morale to fire someone for doing what others felt was just part of her job, he argued. Dorrance felt he had a Hobson's choice. He hated either option. But he didn't want the public to think that KING-TV had been callous about the life of a child.

With Blacklow waiting outside Dorrance's office, Varyu and Dorrance began a heated argument that Varyu described later.

"We've decided to do it," Dorrance said.

"What do you mean, you've decided to do it?" Varyu shouted. "She's *my* employee!"

"We've got to do this. We've got to take a stand," Dorrance insisted.

So they called Blacklow in, gave her a severance check, and told her she was out. Blacklow and Varyu walked downstairs to KING's newsroom.

"I can't believe this is happening," Varyu heard her say. "I think it's wrong, but I'm not concerned because Mrs. Bullitt will fix it."

Eventually Blacklow did see the old lady, but Blacklow realized her friend—by then ninety-four years old and slow-moving, but still alert to more than she let on—could not help. It was not Mrs. Bullitt's way to publicly oppose management. Payne often told people he had never gotten a direct order from Dorothy Bullitt, nor had she ever reversed him on a decision. Blacklow later would not make public what she and Mrs. Bullitt had said to each other.

The problem got bigger. The newspapers, especially the *P-I*'s TV columnist Susan Paynter, aggressively probed the theme of whether Blacklow's firing represented some compromise of the KING tradition. Although night assignment editor Bill Baker, too, was fired, the coverage almost exclusively focused on Blacklow, who was characterized as a fine reporter rudely dumped by a timid corporation—a complete departure from the image nurtured by Dorothy Bullitt and embodied by Bob Schulman, Stimson Bullitt, Charles Royer, Don McGaffin, and others.

Everything seemed to strengthen the perception that KING-TV had soured. One of its newest stars, anchor Aaron Brown, had recently defected to arch-rival KIRO, which crowed about its ascendancy. Brown was widely admired for his writing and reporting skills. His wasn't a pretty face but it was memorable: at certain moments, his eyebrow would arch, his lips would form a sneer or a faint smile of bemusement that looked sophisticated to some viewers, arrogant to others. He was an impassioned and capable journalist who saw himself as carrying the Bullitt ideals. During contract renegotiations, Brown had complained that KING could only handle one star, anchor Jean Enersen. He thought she was given more than her fair share of advertising promotions. KIRO offered him a better deal, and he left in sadness. "KING would allow me to grow no further," he wrote to Payne. KING, for its part, had expected to see its talent go to the network, not to the competition.

After the Blacklow dismissal, the *Times* reported that the KING newsroom "seemed on the verge of mutiny." The *Times* quoted staff members who worried about the direction of the company: "We wanted to know if those dismissals represented some shift in the company's commitment to aggressive journalism," said news anchor Mike James. "Could any of us go out that door again feeling we had the support of management?" Clearly, he remained dubious. The *Times* story also quoted Blacklow: "I love KING. But the place is coming unraveled. This is the last, final proof that what KING once stood for, it stands for no more."

That, of course, was putting the matter too simply. A television station, especially one with KING's lustrous reputation, hardly stood or fell based on the treatment of a single employee. Before and after Blacklow, the station produced outstanding work. In September 1985, for example, a month before the Bellingham kidnapping, the station had pre-empted an entire evening of network programs to air a remarkable three hours on a topic most stations would have avoided—the economy. *Washington 2000* described the region's slow but powerful shift away from timber-cutting and fishing, and its development of modern industries tied to world trade. It featured reporting by Jean Enersen in Japan and by the entire news department throughout the Northwest. The program won a DuPont–Columbia University Silver Baton Award. In December of 1986, Enersen would travel to the Soviet Union to do a profile of life there. This was one of several Soviet programs that later led to Enersen's doing reports for Moscow television, as one of the first U.S. journalists to report to the Soviet people on events in their own country.

So, despite the Blacklow distractions, KING was doing good work and would continue to do more. But none of that was being told now. Only the bad news about KING was getting prominent headlines.

KING, as a news organization, should have known how to handle the press. Instead, for management, the Blacklow case was a nightmare that got worse. When Blacklow filed a union grievance to get her job back, many in KING's newsroom attended her legal fund-raiser, which was co-hosted by Mayor Charles Royer, basketball great Bill Russell, and anchors of all three stations. Dorothy Bullitt's company was isolated. Her station had largely enjoyed good union relations, but now it was in a fight with Blacklow and the American Federation of Television and Radio Artists, representing reporters and photographers. (As a manager, Bill Baker had no recourse through a union.) Twisting the knife, the union requested that an arbitrator's hearing be open to the public and the press. KING refused, putting itself in the unaccustomed position of blocking news coverage rather than seeking it. KING management watched with amazement as Blacklow skillfully played her case in the printed press. Paynter reported in the *P-I* that "Blacklow's firing sent a shudder through the ranks of local TV reporters." Barely mentioned in the coverage was the fact that the Bellingham family had settled out of court for an undisclosed amount. Company management sweated the outcome. Expecting the arbitrator's decision to come down while he was in Hawaii, Ancil Payne directed vice president Eric Bremner to make sure that Mrs. Bullitt and Patsy Collins heard of the arbitrator's ruling from Bremner personally—not from a reporter calling for a reaction. Payne told Bremner to reiterate to Mrs. Bullitt "just why and how Julie was separated." In what would have been unthinkable at any other point in the company's history, KING found it necessary to issue a statement denying that it was willing to sell out its reporters: "Any suggestion that KING has compromised its high journalistic standards or withdrawn its support for reporters in response to public criticism is factually unsupported."

Then another problem erupted in the fall of 1986. Because of a foul-up in negotiations, KING lost the *Phil Donahue Show*, a valuable lead-in to its main newscast. Viewers turned instead to KIRO, which got the talk show. As KIRO's news ratings rose and KING's fell dramatically, the lesson seemed obvious. Many viewers had watched Channel 5 only out of inertia. What KING journalists regarded as their wonderful, distinctive work had failed to draw back an audience lured to Channel 7. KING-TV again sank to third in the ratings. The single most important player in Seattle TV-news ratings was not Jean Enersen, not KING's quality tradition, not the legacy of "First in the Northwest" or the company's fine staff. It was a guy in Chicago who interviewed people with weight problems or marital discord.

Powerful changes were taking place in broadcasting. The rise of interview programs was just one manifestation of a trend that blurred the line between journalism and entertainment. *Donahue* was only the beginning. To grab and hold an audience, KING would have to change significantly. But to what? There was no one at KING offering a successful approach.

It was a bad time to be prisoner of tradition.

Finally, in February 1987, arbitrator Joseph Kane made a ruling that swept aside the company's claims. He said that King Broadcasting Company had wrongfully discharged Julie Blacklow. Kane said there was insufficient proof that Blacklow had made untrue or deceptive statements. He ordered the company to rehire her and pay all back wages. In other words, King Broadcasting had to take back a reporter whom it had publicly labeled as a liar and an unacceptable liability to the entire TV news operation. It was Blacklow, not KING, whom the arbitrator had chosen to believe. Blacklow felt vindicated. In press accounts, King Broadcasting came across as just another big corporation that had tried to squash an individual—the sort of topic Bob Schulman might have covered years earlier in a documentary. No reporter obtained a statement from Dorothy Bullitt. Could decades of public service be tarnished by one disgruntled employee?

A party was held that night at the Virginia Inn, a downtown tavern. Both the *P-I* and the *Times* covered the event, which attracted many of KING's best-known employees. Sitting across from Blacklow, sharing her triumph, was a greatly changed Don McGaffin. The legendary raconteur and carouser wasn't telling many stories or drinking that night. Instead, he was nearly silent, a slightly crooked smile on his face, his body tilted to the left as if he were leaning to hear better.

McGaffin had become a successful TV-columnist and media critic in San Francisco. One morning in 1985, two years after leaving Seattle to join KOIN, he had been reading a newspaper article about some foul-up in a military bureaucracy, when he jumped to his feet and told his producer, "Boy, I've got to do a piece on this . . ." His legs crumbled. He struggled to get up, looking around to see what had tripped him. He took a step, and collapsed—unconscious from a massive stroke brought on by phenomenally high blood pressure. The stroke nearly killed him, paralyzed the right side of his body, and destroyed his capacity for speech. Doctors thought he would die, but at age fifty-two, he kept breathing. In a nearly comatose state, he was shipped to a hospital in Seattle, where he eventually rallied and began months of intensive physical therapy. He was like a two-year-old. He had to be taught how to dress himself, move his limbs, and speak. Each day he practiced speaking aloud and listening to himself on a tape recorder. It was tedious and painful. He hated needing anyone's help.

And now, fourteen months later, there he was sitting across from

Blacklow, his stiff right arm hanging from his shoulder. He had improved enormously, but sometimes his speech had a slurred quality, as if he were drunk. His six-figure income had shrunk to a $777-a-month disability check from the government he had once hounded. One of the odd consequences of the stroke was a weakened grip on his emotions. Tears would come easily to his eyes, for example. A lion of Seattle journalism had become a limping spectator, cheated by a body that had once gotten him through fist fights. The last thing McGaffin ever wanted was pity. He wanted to be back in journalism. But brain damage is a powerful obstacle, and he fought to bring life to his limbs.

McGaffin's first public speech had been at the fund-raiser for Blacklow. He had written everything first. Then he practiced getting his lips to form each word. "Let me tell you, if you'll please excuse my weird voice, what has been done here," he said slowly, almost ending the slur. "What has been done to her has been an ugly, obnoxious battering at journalism." For years, KING had been perhaps the nation's finest television station, in no small part due to Dorothy Bullitt, he said. "She gave us permission to seek the truth. Even when we tweaked her friends—and enraged her—she never withdrew permission."

Clearly, from McGaffin's view, the Bullitt values had been lost. He left unsaid, and unexplained, why the old woman had allowed KING to slip. But the woman was in her nineties. What could be expected? The question had to be directed instead at Ancil Payne, the foreman of what had become a very large ranch spread over several states. McGaffin said Julie Blacklow didn't deserve what had happened to her—nor did KING's viewers. "They were the ones who really lost. Julie was fired, but the viewers, they were punished."

McGaffin sat close to Blacklow on her victory night and he felt good to see the wrong against his friend righted. To put an end to the horrendous publicity, KING management decided to welcome Blacklow's return and not to mention its own legal bills of $50,000. Payne directed that everyone in the company should treat her well. There should be no animosity, no bitterness, and no retribution.

Blacklow had won a tremendous victory, but it was a bitter triumph for anyone who cared about King Broadcasting. Don McGaffin, in particular, was saddened that the case had damaged the reputation of the company he had loved and supported, owned by a woman he loved. King Broadcasting was changing for the worse, he felt. He wanted to help, not as an employee, but in some way that could turn KING back to its moorings. He didn't know that the company at the time was sitting on one of the most explosive stories in the city's history, a sordid tale involving abuse of power inside the city's establishment that KING's newsroom wanted to expose.

For a long time, the Gary Little story said something good about Seattle—about the son of a stenographer and a truck driver whose intellectual talents impressed his peers and teachers at Lincoln High School and won him a place at Harvard College. The young man set out to join the group that ruled Seattle, and he did so brilliantly. As a teacher, he mentored sons of Seattle's elite at the prestigious Lakeside School. As an assistant attorney general, he helped quell riots at the University of Washington. As general counsel to the Seattle School District, he counseled parents struggling to obey a rule that required busing of their children. As a civic activist, he helped elect judges and helped launch CHECC, the group that reformed city government, and joined the campaign that ousted King County Prosecutor Charles O. Carroll. As a judge, he established himself among the brightest jurists who handled the most complex cases. He acted as a liaison to journalist organizations. He seemed to know everybody, and everybody was impressed. Lunching at the Seattle Tennis Club, attending the theater or sitting on the board of the Seattle Symphony, Little established himself as a peer of the powerful in law, politics and the media. He was close friends with the *Post-Intelligencer*'s top libel attorney. He considered himself a friend of the leading families whose sons and daughters attended Lakeside. He always dressed well, kept himself tanned and fit, and spoke with such charm, wit, and energy that people were dazzled. He liked to command attention and be in control. He could walk into a room full of strangers, stretch out his hand, and be introducing everyone by the end of the evening.

And yet there was something else about Gary Little, and the problem for King Broadcasting was whether to tell the public. Was his private life a public issue? Were old stories relevant to today's public officials? Could pimps and prostitutes and thieves be believed? KING-TV, like other news organizations, was being drawn into the private lives of elected officials. The Little case would ensnare KING and both Seattle newspapers and would force editors to make difficult choices. Some at KING would see the Little case as a test, one that the company would fail.

In 1985 the story came to the man who held The Chair in KING's news room—Jim Compton, one of the bright ones hired during Stimson Bullitt's era. Compton had been recruited personally by Ancil Payne right out of Reed College in 1964. He worked for the company in Portland and Seattle, opened the company's first Washington, D.C., bureau in 1977, and then moved on to NBC, where he covered the Middle East. The squabbles between Don Dunkel and Bob Simmons eventually led Payne to hire his former colleague for KING's commentator job. Compton was exceptionally bright. Passionate about news, he was an astute journalist but had a hard time expressing his views directly. He felt more comfortable as an analyst, letting facts suggest a conclusion. His hiring ended a long tradition of bold, controversial commentators at KING. The chair that Simmons had tried to protect soon became peripheral to KING news.

One day a source came to Compton with an extraordinary allegation: that Gary Little was a pedophile who was using his position as a judge to gain power over and molest boys. It was an explosive story, highly complex and sensitive. For the next several months, Compton pored through records in which youths had appeared before Little as defendants in the county's juvenile court. He sought out witnesses or victims, nearly all of whom were reluctant to talk, out of embarrassment for themselves or others, or out of fear of Little's power. Victims feared that Little's connections would protect him from exposure. Compton eventually found what appeared to be a pattern of molestation that dated back to 1968, including the four years Little had taught part time at Lakeside; and during this time, teachers, school board members, judges, and others had wondered about Little's keen interest in boys. From time to time, someone might have asked him about his late-night meetings with Lakeside students or other contacts, but Little always indignantly responded that he was going out of his way to mentor youths. Some who watched Little suspected he was a homosexual, but to ask about his sexual interests would have been an intrusion into his privacy.

By early 1986, Compton was moving forward with a five-part series. He obtained interviews with victims from the Lakeside era, discovered a secret investigation of Little in 1983 by the King County Prosecutor, interviewed judges who were outraged by Little's out-of-court contacts with offenders, and found that the State Commission on Judicial Conduct, which was charged with probing judicial behavior, had essentially ignored the allegations. As a judge, Little would impose a heavy sentence on youths but would then agree to reconsider the punishment if offenders showed good behavior. Frequently, Little would then visit a boy afterward and take him on trips around town, give him money or books, or his credit cards in one case, or even take him to his cabin on remote Sinclair Island in the San Juan Islands. He extended his control over these youths for years by formally taking jurisdiction over their cases. Prosecutors noticed that Little took no such interest in non-white youths; it was almost always slender, fair-haired boys. In 1981, Little promised to stop meeting with boys out of court. In 1985, Presiding Judge Norman Quinn removed Little from handling juvenile cases—but still the contacts continued. Frustrated by the lack of action by the judicial commission, in 1985 and 1986 prosecutors, juvenile case workers, and even judges began to talk to Compton in hopes that media exposure might stop Little's behavior.

Compton wasn't the only journalist who knew about Little's history. In 1980, P-I reporter Dan Coughlin talked to a friend of victims from the Lakeside era and also discovered that Little had been charged with assault in 1964 for an incident at his apartment involving a sixteen-year-old. The 1964 case was dropped. None of the Lakeside victims was willing to go on the record. The P-I's editors decided not to publish anything.

The Seattle Times was the first to make public the concerns about Little. In 1985, reporter Peyton Whitely wrote that Little had been removed from juvenile court cases because of outside contacts with offenders. The story referred to many contacts with a fourteen-year-old boy whom Little took shopping, visited on the street, and saw at the boy's home. Little's contacts with youths had become known around the courthouse, wrote Whitely, after a defendant youth appearing before Judge Jim Bates said he wanted to see "Mr. Little."

In Whitely's story, Little characterized the action as a mere policy debate over how best to help children. "I think I am perhaps a little more aggressive when it comes to dealing with the needs, especially of street children. . . . It appeared I was going overboard on his behalf, but I'm a judge, and appearances are sometimes more important than the reality of the situation. I think what happened was he [Judge Quinn] felt that I had mixed my role of judge with the role of what maybe a guardian should have been doing."

As Compton dug deeper, he faced a thicket of reporting problems. The allegations from Lakeside were old. Witnesses for recent incidents were male prostitutes or other street kids who were hard to track down and unreliable. Was there hard evidence that Little had actually molested anyone while he was a judge? Or did his conduct merely reflect an overzealous concern for youths, as Little described it. If there were no proof that Little had molested anyone as a judge, was it newsworthy to say publicly that he was a homosexual? To say he was gay would be to suggest that his contacts with offenders were sexual. It wasn't a story that could be told halfway. At KING, Ancil Payne was loath to appear to be hounding any one individual simply because he was gay. Compton argued there was a difference between homosexuality and pedophilia. This was a story about a sexual predator, Compton said.

Compton was frustrated by what he saw as resistance to the Little story. He scored a major coup by getting a source to show him a secret prosecutor's report on Little. Only three copies of the report existed, and the source who showed it to Compton insisted that Compton wear gloves as he read it, so no fingerprints would show. The source allowed Compton to read it into a tape recorder, but not to make a photocopy. Later, Compton was told that he had to get a copy of the actual report, which, after considerable work, he did. But still KING wouldn't air the material. Compton had the photocopied report, four affidavits from alleged victims from Little's past, and a story that established a pattern of improper behavior. But KING wouldn't run it. Lawyer Dick Riddell, the King Broadcasting board member brought in by Ancil Payne to review the story, said the sexual allegations were more than ten years old. But if Little were up for reelection, that would alter the equation, Riddell said. Compton pleaded with Payne to run the story. He felt that the bar for airing the report kept getting raised and that Payne's true intent was not to air the story. Station manager Dorrance couldn't understand Payne's hesitation. You don't have the smoking gun, Payne said. So Compton and producer John Wilson looked for a more recent incident. Wilson made an appointment three times with one youth, who would only make the arrangements through intermediaries. All three times the youth failed to show. Another witness was the son of conservative Christians who insisted on sitting in on the interviews. Little had spent two years cultivating the youth, taking him shopping and to his island cabin. But with his parents present, the son wouldn't talk.

Payne considered the story the hardest he had ever faced. First, there was a financial risk. Payne was certain that if KING aired the story, Little would sue, and Little was a skilled adversary. KING's lawyers warned Payne that such a case would be hard to win. Payne had run stories in the face of threats before. But this one was a minefield. Payne was bothered by the murkiness of the allegations and the difficulty of nailing down all the facts. He wanted proof that something had happened and that it was illegal. Payne's instincts told him to be cautious, in part because he was reminded of the 1950s. He had personally seen Joe McCarthy suck down a martini in a single gulp and go out and tell stories to an eager press. He had seen half-truths destroy people, such as John Goldmark. The press was quick to publish, to air charges, convinced that it had the truth. Yet the press was not divine, Payne believed. Once it rang a bell, it could not be unrung. The lesson from McCarthyism was that the media should err on the side of caution when dealing with people's reputations, Payne felt. He was determined that King Broadcasting would expose the private life of an individual only if hard facts and a compelling case existed. This case involved the particularly volatile issue of homosexuality as well as the names and reputations of others. He wanted that smoking gun.

To change Payne's mind, Compton tried something highly unusual. He persuaded two King County Superior Court judges to see Payne and make the case for Compton's story. Judge Terrence Carroll had been waging a private war against Little for months. Carroll, no relation to the former prosecutor, was outraged by Little's out-of-court contact with juvenile defendants. In 1986, he persuaded Presiding Judge Quinn to go with him for a meeting with Payne, which was held under the strictest secrecy.

Quinn saw himself as merely supplying facts. But Carroll was passionate about doing something to stop Little. Carroll was frustrated by the lack of action within the judiciary itself, by other judges, and especially by the judicial commission. For Carroll, it was something out of Kafka. It seemed to him that the courts, the prosecutors, the press, the entire establishment all knew about Little's dark side, yet no one would stop him. Within the judiciary, Carroll himself felt pressure and professional risk just because he wanted Little stopped. It was nightmarish. The Seattle establishment was doing nothing. Carroll wanted King Broadcasting, the Seattle *Times*, somebody to bring the story out and stop Little. Quinn agonized over whether they, as judges, should even be meeting with Payne to discuss Little. It was highly irregular for members of the judiciary to meet with the head of a news organization under such circumstances. It was unusual for any judge to speak ill of a colleague, much less to discuss an explicit wrongdoing that the public should know about. And for Payne, it was the first time in his career he had been lobbied to air something by two sitting judges. The judges themselves did not want anyone to find out about the meeting, which was never reported.

The meeting didn't change Payne's mind. He still wanted proof, he said. It wasn't enough that Little's conduct was common knowledge. What was the evidence? he asked. Why weren't the judges able to use their authority to take care of the problem? The meeting was amicable, but Carroll got the feeling that Payne was concerned about being perceived as attacking a person for being gay. This is pedophilia, Carroll insisted. Payne wouldn't budge.

Compton thought about quitting, but didn't. Payne always had a line for such situations: If you don't like it, buy your own television station. Over at the *Times*, where Whitely's work grew out of a lengthy review of the juvenile justice system, his editors felt they couldn't get him to sort out hard facts from an assortment of rumors and conspiracy theories involving Little. Eventually, they reassigned Whitely. No other reporter was assigned to Little, and the story was dropped.

Little knew what the reporters had been doing. At a dinner to promote good relations between the press and the judiciary, Little invited KING's Wilson to join him at the head table. Wilson listened to Little talk at length about juvenile justice issues. Finally, Little turned the conversation to how much the children appreciated his work. "It's amazing how loyal these kids become to you," he told Wilson. "I could walk from the courthouse up to my home in the Market and those kids would make sure nothing would happen to me."

Wilson was unnerved. Was this a subtle way of conveying a threat? That Little knew exactly what they were doing, and if they got too close he would send someone after them? Or that street kids would protect Little from the press? Later, Wilson went back to his office and wrote a memo about the conversation.

Compton and Wilson argued that the allegations from Little's past and his present contacts with youths as a judge combined to make a case for airing the story. But the journalists thought they sensed a queasiness from Payne and company lawyers, an avoidance of pedophilia as a subject. The lawyers insisted that the proper course was to find a more recent sexual victim, dating from after Little became a judge. Compton and Wilson could never get over that hurdle.

The Little case stayed dormant for two years, during which time Ancil Payne retired. Little's announcement in 1988 that he was seeking reelection triggered another round of efforts to get him off the bench. Sources returned to Whitely and Compton, begging them to tell the public. Finally, some of those sources went to *P-I* reporter Duff Wilson, who spent weeks on the story. Then a lawyer, who said he was concerned about Little's handling of juvenile cases, said he would run against Little. That was enough to spark KING to report one contact Little had with a juvenile offender after he had been ordered by the presiding judge not to have such contacts. The report included an interview with Little, who said he had the right to contact any juvenile he wanted. A second report detailed the inaction by the judicial commission, despite evidence submitted by prosecutors and witnesses. KING, however, did not disclose allegations of sexual misconduct or mention that KING had interviewed sexual victims three years earlier—thus a crucial element establishing Little's true motive for seeing these boys was not told to the public. When two judges—Gerard Shellan and Terrence Carroll—publicly called for the Commission on Judicial Conduct to clear the air on the matter, Little announced he would not seek reelection and would leave the state.

With the *P-I* still pursuing the story, both the *Times* and KING went back to their sources. This time, more people were willing to talk, and some by name on the record. Still KING would not air the story. Payne's policy—you must have the smoking gun—remained in place after his retirement. Moreover, the company's lawyers said there was now a greater risk in airing the allegations. Since Little was not seeking reelection, his status as a public figure was diminished, meaning KING had less protection if Little filed a libel suit.

Then Little himself resolved the case. In August 1988, knowing that the *P-I* was about to print a story about his molestation of boys, Little went to the hallway at the King County Courthouse, placed a gun to his temple, and pulled the trigger. "I have chosen to take my life," a note stated. "It's an appropriate end to the present situation. I had hoped that my decision to withdraw from the election and leave public life would have closed the matter. Apparently, these steps are not satisfactory to those who feel more is required, so be it. I will say one final time that I am proud of my efforts and accomplishments as a Superior Court judge. I am deeply appreciative of those who have wished me well these past few weeks." Compton heard about the suicide when he was in Atlanta covering the Democratic political convention. He rushed back to Seattle and assembled a special report on Little, including the sexual allegations.

The spectacular end to Gary Little's career attracted national news coverage. The Washington *Post* and ABC's *20/20* program gave detailed attention to how the media had handled the case. Ancil Payne defended his decision not to air the story. He had aired controversial stories before, but this one, he insisted, was not ready. His job, he said, was to protect the integrity of the news department. Privately he was horrified at what Little had done, a reminder of suicides provoked by politically motivated hounding during the McCarthy era. He was glad that Little's death was not on his conscience.

Don McGaffin watched the newscasts and read the newspapers. He felt disgusted with the Seattle media, which he saw as having again shown timidity with a big story. The same media that had largely ignored police corruption had kept silent about a cancer in the courthouse, he fumed. He sat down and with his one good hand typed a letter to the *Times*. Reporters had heard rumors on Little for years and had done nothing, he said. How many boys had been molested while the media stayed silent? he asked.

"Two titans of the Seattle media held back from breaking the story," McGaffin wrote in a letter to the *Times*. "The *Times* and KING television got weak in the knees and shelved the story. KING, its journalists stiff with anger, backed off. . . . The *Times* and KING have to lower their eyes in shame because they could have pressed forward and at least begun to pry the top off the Little story. They have to live with the knowledge that they had evidence that Little might inflict himself on boys in county custody. And neither reported the story."

News director Varyu wrote a letter defending KING's coverage as "both crusading and fair," although he was disappointed personally that KING had not aired more about Little earlier. But McGaffin had drawn attention to questions lingering within the company: Why hadn't KING aired the story earlier? Had the Bellingham kidnapping case made the station cautious? Had Little's friendships with powerful people played a role in holding the story? Critics kept looking for answers to what they saw as a journalistic failure. Gary Little's last victim was the King Broadcasting Company.

It was one of the biggest stories in years and proud KING had held back. Payne told people that his decision had been based on the facts before him and he, after all, had a very large corporation to protect. But Payne's critics wondered: to what extent was his caution a reflection of corporate interests rather than journalistic values? Compton deeply admired Ancil Payne and considered him a close friend. But things were changing at KING, and the Little case seemed to coalesce concerns about the company. Compton would always wonder if things might have been different had he gone to the Bullitt women. He held to a belief that the old standard-bearer, Dorothy Bullitt, would have done the right thing, though that would have meant violating her own policy of not interfering in management. From her, the best of KING flowed. But she was so old. A diminished King Broadcasting was about to lose her, and the rupture of her values would seem complete.

Chapter 24   "Those Who Worked for Her, and Loved Her . . ."

The old lady walked slowly toward St. Mark's Cathedral, her arm linked with her namesake, to say good-bye to a departed friend, United States Senator Warren Magnuson. So many were gone, so many dead. She had lived so long—ninety-seven years. She felt tired. On this rainless day in May 1989, Dorothy Bullitt stepped into the vastness of the cathedral, crowded with more than 1,000 mourners, including Magnuson's colleagues from the Senate, a handsome platoon of former aides, friends, and many others. She clung to Stim's daughter and fought off her fatigue. She wasn't eating much these days, at lunch maybe a cookie or chocolate shake. Everyone was telling her to eat more.

She was nearly as old as the State of Washington, which that year was celebrating its centennial. The state had hired historians, artists, and others to commemorate the phenomenal changes that had occurred over 100 years, yet none so singularly symbolized those changes as Dorothy Stimson Bullitt—daughter of a timber baron and land developer, wife of a reform Democrat, friend of FDR, pioneer in broadcasting, a feminist who wore hats and gloves, a brilliant business executive, a leader, a motivator, a figure of dignity, grace, and values. Few in the history of the state saw the future as well as she did. The once-despised industry of broadcasting had matured into a fabulously profitable and powerful business. With television, she wanted to give Seattle a New York *Times* of the air waves—profitable, yes, but highlighting the good, encouraging the civic-minded, and raising the level of discourse in the city she loved. She was doing good and making money to a degree that would have astonished C. D. Stimson, who had arrived in Seattle one hundred years earlier. King Broadcasting in 1989 had sales of $158 million and a before-tax profit margin of a whopping 39 percent. And now she was one of the richest persons in America—a personal fortune of $200 million or more according to *Forbes* magazine. Her flagship station, KING-TV, alone was worth $150 million. The company as a whole was worth more than $400 million.

Dorothy S. Bullitt had watched Seattle turn from mud streets to the Information Highway, from horse carts to personal computers. Her hometown had grown from 86,000 to nearly 500,000. At age twenty-two, she watched construction of Smith Tower, the West Coast's first skyscraper. The city changed from a burly, bawdy frontier town to a would-be Geneva of the Pacific, idealized in the East Coast media as the prosperous home of the urban outdoorsman. It was a city that felt big, worried about traffic and pollution, sprawled to the foothills of the Cascades, and felt a sharpening division between rich and poor. Yet there remained its beauty, spirit, and intelligence. Seattle was a city of significant medical research, a good university, international financial services, and the corporate anchors of Boeing and Microsoft.

Inside the cathedral, she turned to her grandchild. Young Dorothy was thirty-three and already a growing presence in the Seattle business community. An attractive, articulate, determinedly sensible young woman with thick, dark curly hair that ringed her face, she was always tailored and presentable, just as her grandmother had advised in their many sessions on business etiquette ("never come late to a board meeting; never leave to go to the bathroom"). She was now vice president of Harbor Properties, the company formed by her father with the properties he received when King Broadcasting had split. Young Dorothy had joined the downtown business clubs, had volunteered for environmental causes, housing, and social service groups, and had gotten her abilities recognized. Young Dorothy took her volunteerism seriously. It was a duty she happily assumed. Like her grandmother, she loved business and enjoyed motivating people in an organization. To many who knew the Bullitts, she was the perfect successor to her grandmother. McGaffin had been right about her: She had the brains, the values, the toughness, the preparation, and the desire to lead King Broadcasting.

The elder Dorothy Bullitt may have wanted her grandchildren to take over the company, but few of them defined themselves in conventional terms, much less saw themselves as business leaders. Like Patsy, Harriet, and Stim, the grandchildren generally had little interest in business. In *Dorothy Stimson Bullitt: An Uncommon Life,* biographer Delphine Haley offers a somewhat dismissive view of the grandchildren: "Growing up in the 1960s, each was affected to varying degrees by that tumultuous decade, which brought with it the problems of drugs, alcohol, and depression, cults and collectives, free love, and the questioning of authority. For the Bullitt grandchildren, the turbulent times were compounded by a sense of familial prosperity that, for some of them, diminished the need for higher education or ambitious accomplishments in their lives." Patsy, Stim, and Harriet had authorized and supervised the Haley book. The grandchildren felt unfairly labeled and hurt by the description. The harshness and finality of the assessment seemed to echo the one made by Dorothy S. Bullitt of Patsy, Stim, and Harriet.

Yet by any measure, Young Dorothy was no victim of "turbulent times." She had prepared herself for business leadership. If any grandchild deserved a place at King Broadcasting, she did. But her goal became another casualty of the family discord.

In 1988 the old woman had invited Young Dorothy to lunch at the Rusty Pelican restaurant. That day, Dorothy S. Bullitt closed the door on her granddaughter's chosen career. The old woman looked embarrassed as she said that Patsy and Harriet had been to a seminar in California on family-owned companies. The sisters learned that problems sometimes erupted when a third generation took over a family business. They wanted to avoid squabbles, so they wanted to sell. The old woman said that, after her death, it was their right to do what they wanted. You won't be taking over the company, she said. If Patsy and Harriet want to sell, it's their choice. She was not going to interfere with their decision. I'm sorry, she said.

For the elder Bullitt, there was no point in discussing the depth of her disappointment. It had been her fervent desire to see the grandchildren take an interest in business and keep the company in the family. She wouldn't accept the obvious—the two daughters who had resented their mother's interference in their lives would hardly want to be caretakers of their mother's "fourth child." To accept that point would have been to acknowledge a painful truth about her unsatisfying relationship with her children. And Dorothy Bullitt did not care to discuss painful family matters with anyone. When Ancil Payne had come to her in 1985 and urged a sale, because prices for TV stations were at a high, she had refused. (Payne later figured the delay cost about $150 million because values of TV stations dropped.)

"I want to keep it in the family," she had told Payne, insisting that the company would go to her daughters.

"Mrs. Bullitt, you built the company. They don't have the same feeling as you do," said Payne. The sisters cared deeply about the environment and world affairs, he felt, but not King Broadcasting.

"Oh, but when they take charge, they will," she replied.

So Payne dropped the subject. But eventually the sisters told their mother, and now the news had filtered down to Young Dorothy. As she listened to her grandmother, Young Dorothy felt disappointed, but not entirely surprised. She knew it would have been very complicated for her to enter the company. And it was impossible to imagine the elder Bullitt doing anything with her last will and testament to steer control of the company to one grandchild. It was grandmother's way to treat her children equally, Young Dorothy believed. And there probably would have been opposition from some of Patsy's or Harriet's children. But therein lay the tragedy: of all Dorothy S. Bullitt's grandchildren, Young Dorothy was the most interested in running King Broadcasting. Unfortunately, she was the daughter of the ousted prince. Her wing of the company had no say in the future of King Broadcasting or who ran it. It was made very clear that there was no hope of Young Dorothy's coming into the company.

The company had changed. It was so big. In 1986 the company had added its fifth and sixth TV stations: K38AS, a low-power NBC affiliate in Twin Falls, Idaho, and KHNL in Honolulu, which was the company's first station with no network affiliation. Dorothy S. Bullitt kept telling Payne that the company had gotten big enough. Then he'd come around with another acquisition idea, and she couldn't resist taking a peek at the numbers. Even at her advanced age, she loved the game. Next thing you knew, the company had done another deal.

The biggest change in 1986, however, was the change in management.

The foreman of the ranch, as he liked to call himself, was making good on the vow he made when he replaced Stimson Bullitt—he would retire at age sixty-five. Ancil Payne was stepping down from the presidency, though he would remain a board member. And this was no small matter. Payne had a genius for manipulating people in ways that they actually enjoyed. With Dorothy Bullitt's support, he had skillfully kept the sisters from interfering with the operating of the company. Though they held lofty titles—Patsy as chairman of the board and Harriet as chairman of the executive committee—Payne had fiercely protected his turf. Payne said privately that the titles were meaningless. The job of a chairman was to call a board meeting to order. As far as he was concerned, he continued to work for their mother, the chairman emeritus. When the headquarters were remodeled, he told the sisters; "You have everything to say about the outside of the building. I have everything to say about the inside of the building." He said it in a way to make them laugh. And they did. But for all the appreciation and affection they had for Ancil Payne, there was also a degree of resentment of his control of them, a feeling made worse because they knew that they needed him. They felt the same dependency that Stim had felt.

In June 1986, Ancil Payne wrote a memo to Patsy Collins that described "the problem as well as the opportunity" in finding his successor. Payne wanted the Bullitts to pick his replacement, though he wanted to be able to veto anyone he thought was a wrong choice. Board members Dorothy Bullitt, Patsy Collins, Harriet Bullitt, Richard Riddell, and Alexander Fisken formed the search committee to look for the new president. Eventually three leading candidates emerged: George Willoughby, the vice president and head of KING's legal staff; Eric Bremner, the vice president of television broadcasting, and Steve Clifford, the vice president of finance.

Willoughby was considered an excellent lawyer, but he had little management experience; the board got the impression he didn't want the job that much. Bremner was a Tacoma native and University of Washington graduate who had worked his way up from TV floor director, had managed the TV stations in Spokane and Seattle, and was perceived as Payne's protégé. Bremner was a sentimental favorite: King Broadcasting was the only company he had ever worked for, and, with his velvety baritone voice and elegant phrasings, he was a smooth ambassador for the company.

Clifford was a finance guy. A New Jersey native and graduate of the Harvard Business School, he was the son of Paul Clifford, a noted professor of mathematics and a pioneer in the use of statistical equations for industrial quality control. Having inherited his father's brains, Steve Clifford ran numbers better than most and could quickly grasp the essentials of a business issue. As New York City's deputy controller in the mid-1970s, he had helped steer that city through a financial crisis. He was often the smartest person in the room, though because of his slight build and quiet manner, he was easy to overlook. He had Seattle liberal credentials; he was married to the daughter of David Sprague, an old friend of the Bullitts and a stalwart of the Democratic Party. Clifford lacked, however, the warmth and charisma that Payne used so effectively. But then, so did most people. Some saw Clifford as an eccentric. He often had no cash with him—he once borrowed from a receptionist so he could take someone to lunch.

Despite Bremner's long tenure with the company, the board felt it was an easy decision and picked Clifford. But Bremner got a consolation prize, the new title of president of broadcasting. There were two other possible reasons for picking Clifford, both unspoken. The family was keeping private the fact that the company might be sold, but Clifford was perfect for that task. He had had experience dealing with New York investment houses and knew how to cut costs and raise revenue, which would increase the company's selling price. And for the sisters, there was a benefit in selecting someone not as closely tied to Ancil Payne. Picking Steve Clifford was a subtle declaration of independence, and a hint that the company would be run differently, with the two sisters having a greater say.

After Clifford took over in June 1987, King Broadcasting stopped looking to buy TV stations and instead poured its profits into expanding the cable division. Cable was a smarter investment, but the company's shift away from broadcasting had significance. Cable was a business of cash-flow and profits, of little romance or glamour—and it was unencumbered by the pretense of being anything like the New York *Times*. Over the next four years, King Broadcasting bought or built enough cable franchises to more than double its cable-customer base, from 100,000 to 215,000 subscribers. It was a smart business decision. Broadcasting was losing value out of a perception that TV signals would increasingly by-pass stations and reach homes through wires. No longer was television a government-protected oligopoly. Because an advertiser had greater choices, a station could not charge as much for air time. The era of ro-bust growth in revenue, with profits growing annually by 15 percent, was over. And that was a sea change for every TV station in America, KING-TV included.

For news, technology had dramatically altered a station's relationship with viewers. After home-metering systems came to Seattle in 1987, a rating agency could tell a news director the size of a newscast's audience measured in fifteen-minute segments. That meant a news director knew which kinds of news stories and graphics attracted, increased, or lost viewers, a report card that could be read the morning after a newscast. Because viewers could choose from among thirty-five cable channels in Seattle and thousands of videotapes, KING and other stations had to follow national trends and make their broadcasts quicker, punchier, more urgent. Not just for the sake of who had the biggest audience, but which newscast made the most money. Station finances were not pub-lic, but the National Association of Broadcasters estimated that each of the three Seattle stations brought in $45 million of revenue in 1988, about a quarter of that as pre-tax profit. Local news was known to con-tribute significantly to that sum. Local news was just too valuable to be considered "a playpen of the most obstreperous five-year-olds."

King Broadcasting's new focus on cable caused trauma. Longtimers at KING-TV saw spending for the station slow down, watched projects get cut and eliminated, and worried that the company was losing sight of its mission of service.

One of the biggest jolts came at that year's Christmas party.

"They bought the eggnog!" went the cry that swept through the five floors of King headquarters. The party was always an elegant and costly affair highlighted by a high-octane eggnog hand-made in an old-fash-ioned way that took hours. The Bullitt women personally poured for each employee. The warm glow from the eggnog reminded employees of their good fortune to work for a special company.

But that day, six months since Ancil Payne had retired, the punch bowl was still crystal but the eggnog came from a paper carton—store-bought stuff. Among those who took note of the change was news director Don Varyu. To him, nothing more symbolized the changes sweeping the company than that cheap drink being served by the Bullitts.

Some in news saw Steve Clifford as the enemy, a cold-hearted bean counter. He began to personify what people didn't like in broadcasting: increased attention to ratings, more focus on the bottom line, and less willingness to spend big. KING-TV reporter Jack Hamann saw Clifford's promotion as a key element in the decline of King Broadcasting Company. As shop steward for the American Federation of Television and Radio Artists (AFTRA), Hamann thought Clifford's bottom-line approach turned good union relations into bitter fights. Certainly, it didn't help that Clifford lacked Payne's common touch. Clifford was shy, but some saw him as aloof, the old tag hung on Stimson Bullitt. But most of the criticisms were unfair. Clifford was doing exactly what the board, including the Bullitts, wanted him to do. It was true that he asked the news department to do things at less cost. He was trying to preserve quality journalism at KING, but he also was pursuing the other primary goal Dorothy Bullitt had established from her first day at King Broadcasting: to make money.

Dorothy Bullitt now was a diminished force. In her last days, she began telling people, "I shouldn't be here." Stories circulated at KING that the old woman had become senile. She closed her eyes and seemed to drift from the conversation. But in fact, when she didn't want to deal with someone, she occasionally pretended to be senile.

Some still made visits to her office at King, where she arrived each morning and chatted with people about the newscast or sales, or what people were doing in their personal lives. But there was one problem with those talks—her memory was failing, and she knew it. To minimize her embarrassment, she began cutting back on visitors or appearances. But that, in turn, made her feel lonely. She didn't even own the house she lived in anymore. As part of many steps to minimize her estate taxes, her house had been assigned to a charity upon her death. "I have to stay here. I can never leave," she told a friend one night.

So many from her life were gone. And now Warren Magnuson, too.

Dorothy Bullitt continued into St. Mark's Cathedral with her grand-daughter and stopped at the guest book. Her eyes twinkled.

"Let's sign it together," she said.

But Young Dorothy said she had already signed it.

"No, please. Let's sign it together," said the grandmother.

The old woman picked up the pen. "Dorothy S. Bullitt," she wrote. She handed the pen. "Dorothy C. Bullitt," wrote the granddaughter.

The Magnuson family had reserved a seat for them in the front row. The incoming Speaker of the House, Thomas Foley of Spokane, was scheduled to give the eulogy. But the elderly Dorothy S. Bullitt wanted to sit in the back in case she had to go to the bathroom or leave early.

The funeral pleased the old woman: the parade of congressmen who lined up to praise the man who had thrived in politics and had few enemies, a legend in Congress, whose political career had begun with a job given him by her husband, Scott Bullitt. "I'd like my funeral to be like this," she told her granddaughter. Young Dorothy got a powerful feeling from her grandmother that this service was triggering a willingness to die. The old woman leaned to her and commented on the music, the pageantry, the various readings. "I'd like this at my funeral," she kept saying.

Afterwards, when Dorothy S. Bullitt walked out, some who saw her noticed a dramatic change. She looked suddenly much older, more frail, deteriorated. Her back was giving her pain. A few days later, she became ill and never left her bed. Within a few weeks, on June 27, 1989, she died in her Capitol Hill home. When Young Dorothy visited the woman's bedroom, she found an indicator of the feisty spirit that had kept her grandmother's body alive for so long: a bar for chin-ups.

Her death was page one news, followed by lengthy stories on her life. Dorothy Bullitt's funeral at St. Mark's was arranged by her children who believed their mother would not have wanted an elaborate service. No eulogy was given. It was simple, restrained, formal, and was over within forty minutes. Some 500 people were there, enough so people had to stand along the walls of the cathedral.

KING commentator Jim Compton wrote a tribute for that year's annual report:

From a garage on Queen Anne Hill and a little radio station in Smith Tower, she created one of the nation's premier communications companies. A trophy case full of major industry awards is testament to her vision. Dorothy Bullitt capped nearly a century of robust life and good works by leaving behind a company committed to the ideals of public service she cherished. Those who worked for her, and loved her, will miss her.

The annual report also showed company profit of $37 million on sales of $140 million. There was no doubt her 1949 investment of $375,000 to buy KRSC-TV and FM had been a good one.

At a very special memorial service at King Broadcasting headquarters, Patsy and Harriet told employees that they would continue to operate the company as their mother had. They would be dutiful and would continue their mother's tradition in the city. But many in the audience knew this was a promise that could not be kept.

Chapter 25 | "Not Even Close to the Rain Forest"

After more than a half century of living in their mother's shadow, the daughters of Dorothy S. Bullitt were on their own. They controlled one of the West's more powerful communications empires, with a TV, radio, and cable-TV audience in the millions. With King Broadcasting in their hands, Patsy Collins and Harriet Bullitt finally had a chance to step into the forefront of civic life as individuals. The women had long been active in charities and social causes, but their work was often viewed as an offshoot of their mother and her money. Now some friends saw them plagued by doubts and uneasiness to a degree that seemed mirrored by Seattle's own uneasiness. Just as King Broadcasting Company had grown rapidly since the 1970s, so too had Seattle. The downtown, once a friendly scene for the browser, an eclectic place to explore pawnshops and to dodge lawyers and drunken sailors, had changed during the decade into a gleaming canyon of glass and steel, with look-alike towers that seemed to dwarf the pedestrian. In the spring of 1989, voters put the brakes on skyscraper construction with a citizens' initiative. The city, it seemed, wanted to pause and reassess its future.

So too for Patsy and Harriet. With their mother finally gone, what was ahead for them? What sort of company did they have? What could they do with it? Under Steve Clifford, overall profitability was up, but what was the future for broadcasting and cable? With the company less sure of its footing, it was no coincidence that station editorials were halted.

In 1989, the sisters faced critical issues. The company's image had been stained by the Julie Blacklow affair. At KING-TV, the company's flagship station, the main newscast had lost half its audience since the *Phil Donahue Show* had departed in 1986 to KIRO. Morale was down, especially in the newsroom. A company-wide survey painted a devastating portrait of management at KING. Employees still embraced the values established by Dorothy S. Bullitt, but they felt unmotivated to perform and uninvolved in decisions that affected them. They felt that managers settled for substandard work.

Ancil Payne, who remained a board member, urged the sisters to sell. Three months after Dorothy Bullitt's death, he wrote a seven-page memo that analyzed the threats faced by the company. Payne said that King Broadcasting faced continued growth in competition from new cable channels and from new technology that would allow regional telephone companies to transmit video over copper wires. With their huge financial resources, telephone companies would scare away speculators who had driven prices high for the kind of cable-TV systems owned by King Broadcasting; expanding cable channels would cut into advertising revenue by offering ad agencies new outlets for their messages. The company could pursue strategies to face these issues, such as joining with other companies, but Payne said the best approach would be to sell. The time was now, he said. He noted that television license values were diminishing at a rate of 5 to 10 percent a year. That decline could accelerate, he said, pointing out that radio licenses had dropped 75 percent in value in the eight years after television took hold in 1948. Payne distributed his memo to all of King Broadcasting's board members, but it was never placed on the agenda for discussion, even though at least one other board member, Glenn Pascall, wanted it discussed. Payne sensed that the sisters had already decided what to do and didn't want to air the issue outside the family, especially when they were telling employees that the company would not be sold.

Dorothy Bullitt had been forty-three when she took over her family company. Patsy Collins and Harriet Bullitt took control of King Broadcasting at an age when most people were retired.

Patsy was sixty-nine. She lived in a small, $600-a-month apartment on First Hill and worked out of the home where her mother had once lived, now called the Stimson-Green Mansion. She ran a catering business and rented rooms to parties and weddings, sometimes personally delivering breakfast to a new bride and groom. Patsy had bought the mansion in 1986 to keep it from being turned into a lawyer's office. She carefully restored the building to its original glory and it now served as a kind of shrine to the Stimson legacy. A nearly life-size portrait of Dorothy S. Bullitt looked down on people in the main living room, a majestic and dominant image that baffled Bullitt watchers. Why was Patsy, a woman so anxious to show her independence, working out of a shrine to her mother? It was another seeming contradiction among the elder Bullitts, who were faithful to the past but faintly resentful of its burden.

Patsy's health was shaky. In the summer of 1989, she had surgery for lung cancer. The brush with death would make her think about what she was accomplishing in life. Business did not bring her joy. As a board member of King Broadcasting, she asked good questions of management but without enthusiasm. The company didn't bring her the fulfillment she found in other causes.

Harriet, at sixty-four, had even less interest in King Broadcasting. Like Patsy, she was bright, but she was much more willful and unconventional. Harriet lived on Lake Union in a tugboat moored next to her barge. Both vessels were equipped with sprung floors for her latest hobby—flamenco dancing. A sticker on the barge read: "There's no abyssness like show abyssness." While Patsy wore plain, schoolmarm outfits, Harriet wore bold scarves, unusual jewelry, and avant-garde clothing. She came and went as she wished, wherever she wished. Twice divorced, widowed from her third marriage, she traveled frequently and spent much of the year in a cabin on Icicle Creek near Leavenworth in the Cascade Mountains. Her newsletter for the Pacific Science Center in Seattle had evolved into the independent *Pacific Northwest Magazine.* The full-color publication was a glossy blend of Northwest lifestyle features (to attract advertisers) and environmental journalism (to satisfy Harriet's reason for starting the magazine). The readership grew to 80,000. It never made a dime, but it came close in 1987, the year Harriet sold it because, she said, she was turning sixty-three and wouldn't own it forever.

Whatever residual interest Patsy and Harriet may have held in managing King Broadcasting was absent in their children.

Patsy's three sons—Jacques, Charles, and William—were often described as carefree spirits. Jacques, a strict environmentalist, lived at the

Country Club, a community of old Seattle families on Bainbridge Island. Jacques went to Bowdoin and had worked at KING in various low-level jobs. Had people ever asked, he said, they would have heard that he had zero interest in being a manager; but no one asked. Jacques worked as a messenger on the island and around downtown Seattle. According to Jacques, Bill Collins worked as a groundskeeper in a community north of Seattle, and Charles wrote poetry and traveled, often showing up unannounced to see Jacques. Bill and Charles never went to college. Many at King Broadcasting believed it was unrealistic to think of Patsy's children running a communications empire.

Harriet's children, Wenda and Scott Brewster, more conventionally accomplished, were taught to make a contribution in the world and make their own path. Wenda came close to pursuing a career at King Broadcasting. She worked in accounting at the company and in advertising in New York. But she lost interest in management and eventually got a Ph.D. in psychology from Stanford, going on to write and edit for scholarly publications and to run a childbirth clinic in the Bay Area. She became interested in serving on King Broadcasting's board. Harriet discussed the idea with Payne, but after some private discussions in the family, Wenda never got the invitation she wanted. Payne never learned why Wenda was kept off the board. She had no desire to work as a manager at the company. Her brother Scott served in Vietnam, considered and then dropped the idea of working in broadcasting, and wound up working as a fireman and later as a pilot for a regional airline.

In short, there was no pressure on Patsy and Harriet to preserve something for their children—in stark contrast to another Seattle communications family, the Blethens, who carefully encouraged each new generation to take an interest in managing their Seattle *Times*. So why should the Bullitts keep the company? It was all duty, little pleasure. When someone didn't like a disk jockey, or a news anchor, or a policy, the complaints came to them. Friends particularly criticized KING-AM for carrying an abrasive talk-show host. If the company won an award, or if King Broadcasting was cited as an example of a quality business, the credit went to their mother. The sisters got all the blame and little of the fun. At KING, there was an endless complaint: "This wouldn't have happened if Dorothy Bullitt were alive." The daughters were burdened by a ghost who each year kept getting wiser, more generous, and less concerned about profit.

The sisters worried about frivolous spending at the company, but would say nothing for fear of interfering with management. They heard that one crew from KING's program department ran up a big bill in South America for an entertainment segment devoted to beachwear. Patsy mentioned her disgust to her son Jacques. "They went down that far and didn't even go to the rain forest?" asked Jacques Collins. The two environmentalists were stunned. How could anyone not visit the single greatest example of mistreatment on the planet?

"They didn't even get close to the rain forest," said Patsy. For Jacques Collins, that was the first sign that the sisters were beginning to think that there were better ways to use their wealth.

Nothing more symbolized their thankless role than the flap over Sturges Dorrance, a KING station manager who was fired in September 1989. Unlike past executives who left quietly after their stock was bought up, Dorrance hired a lawyer who thought the stock was worth far more than the company was paying. With the threat of another legal row looming, a repeat of Blacklow-style embarrassments, and Patsy as board chairwoman potentially having to face a grilling during a lawsuit— settling with Dorrance became a high priority. The company ended the dispute by promising Dorrance more money for his shares, but the sisters got another reminder of the burden they felt, as well as of the change in relationship between employees and ownership. King Broadcasting had once seemed like a big family to many at the company. Now it was something else. It wasn't yet an unfeeling corporation. King's employees knew the company was still a good place to work. But as if the entire company were traumatized by the loss of Dorothy Bullitt, people now expressed open doubts about the company's direction. The choice as Dorrance's replacement to be day-to-day manager of King Broadcasting's flagship station would be a critical sign of the company style, post–Dorothy Bullitt.

The new man arrived within weeks of Dorrance's departure. Rick Blangiardi, the new general manager of KING, made it clear that he was no custodian of tradition. "I represent change," he said, at his first appearance before his staff. "I like competitive, aggressive people. I like confrontation. I like open conflict. I am not a political animal."

In the past, King Broadcasting had sought out polish, sophistication, warmth. As a former college football coach who grew up in Boston, Blangiardi had charm but all the polish of a street fighter. Plucked from his job as general manager of KHNL-TV, the Honolulu station the company had recently bought, Blangiardi said he would tolerate no mediocrity. "Every day is game day in television," he said. Some in KING's newsroom thought their station had been taken over by a small-market tough guy. Others were pleased to see someone announce that he was going to kick butt; KING-TV needed to get back in the competitive game.

No one doubted that Blangiardi was determined to be in control. During his first two weeks, he fired KING's general sales manager, local sales manager, and business manager. Blangiardi gave news director Dan Varyu a chance to prove himself. Varyu had a staff of ninety-two, the city's largest, but his newscast was running third in the five o'clock ratings. Worse, the TV staff had developed a reputation of being slow to cover breaking news, as if hard news were beneath them. While KOMO and KIRO had redesigned their sets and their on-air packaging to give their presentation a sizzle, KING's seemed stagy, stiff, and sedate. The shock from the *Donahue* switchover had failed to motivate KING's news staff to regain lost viewers. Varyu talked openly of his frustration. It was a constant struggle to get reporters just to show up on time and turn in scripts for timely editing, despite numerous memos and threats. At one point in 1987, Varyu demanded that editors, reporters, and photographers be ready for their assigned slot in the newscast. It was embarrassing. KING was struggling to regain viewers, he complained, "at the exact time when our coverage was coming unglued." With cable splintering the audience, all three network affiliates saw a dominant newscast as key to their future. But KING's newscast lacked that overwhelming presence. There was no hustle, no hunger for the news. Three months after Blangiardi arrived, Varyu was fired.

If Varyu had been too nice, his replacement represented another kind of change. Arriving in April 1990, Bob Jordan seemed to go out of his way to bully, demean, or anger people, his critics said. And to destroy the notion that KING had a tradition to uphold. When Jordan's hiring was made public, the newsroom at KING got a condolence card from a Florida station where Jordan had worked. From KSTP in Minneapolis, another past Jordan employer, came another call: "You're toast," the caller told his friend at KING.

The call had more meaning than either realized, for soon the friend would be gone from KING. More significantly, Jordan represented bigger change than Blangiardi. Jordan was going to haul a screaming, kicking newsstaff into modern broadcast journalism. If that wasn't the way Bob Schulman or Charley Royer or Don McGaffin had done it—well, tough. Jordan knew how to build an audience. Jordan came with a reputation; Clifford and Blangiardi, and presumably the sisters if they were paying attention, knew exactly what King Broadcasting's flagship station was getting.

Balding, baby-faced Jordan came to KING from KCRA-TV, the NBC affiliate in Sacramento where the early-evening newscast drew more viewers than the CBS and ABC affiliates combined. Jordan's techniques were familiar to practically anyone who watched TV news, except in Seattle, one of the last cities in America to be swept by the if-it-bleeds-it-leads style of electronic journalism. In essence, the technique was to look for hot emotional content in the day's events—fear, happiness, whatever, so long as it burned hot on the screen. The formula was heavy on crime, helicopters racing to the scene, and live shots from anywhere, even from another part of KING's newsroom. Features on calluses and bunions were aired to hold older viewers. Animals were featured at 5:26 P.M. The style was relentless and in your face. Day and night, promote an item from the next newscast with snippets that shock or arouse. (KING wasn't alone with hyperkinetic promotions; KOMO's tease to one newscast: "Believe it or not—a family that freeze-dried Fido.")

Jordan wanted changes everywhere. He flooded the staff with memos, sometimes two or three a day, establishing new policies, canceling old ones. Photographers were told to use brighter lights to give events a harsher, more urgent look. Bow ties were out; so were dangling earrings. The order of one night's story line-up reflected his stamp: pregnant woman raped in a park; statistics on local violent crime; how women can protect themselves against attack; police in suburb alerted to the presence of a released sex offender; files released on the rape-charge case of William Kennedy Smith; Seattle woman arraigned on charge of abusing her niece; charges filed in child abuse case. And so it went. News on the city of Seattle was cut back to make room for a broader treatment of western Washington. The remaining emphasis on the city was heavily focused on threats to personal safety. The new KING, like stations elsewhere scrambling for ratings, gave its viewers a different portrait of their city. It was more dangerous, violent, unpredictable.

The credo handed down from Dorothy Bullitt to Stimson Bullitt to Ancil Payne was that ratings weren't the first priority for news. Jordan tossed that First Commandment into the trash. "We're not in the news business; we're in the audience business," he told his staff.

There was horror in the news department. Was he serious? Did the Bullitt sisters know about this guy? Some in the department saw Jordan as talking like that to shock people out of their complacency. Ratings did matter. Without an audience, their work was irrelevant. Jordan noticed that KING's 5:00 P.M. newscast was losing viewers from the *Oprah Winfrey* talk show that preceded the newscast. People were switching the channel when KING's news program came on; KIRO and KOMO gained viewers. Jordan would change that. From his perspective, he was simply taking KING into the modern age of TV journalism, where slow, dull stories were replaced by "hard news," stories happening now. He wanted stories that were faster paced. That's what viewers preferred; it was the reality of the marketplace, said Jordan's defenders.

But some of his comments seemed harsh.

One morning, Jordan looked up at his monitor to watch the morning newscast. To his surprise, a portion of the screen showed a woman doing sign language for the hearing impaired. Jordan yelled: "What's that woman doing on my air?"

That was how he talked. KING's broadcast was his air.

He was told that signing of the morning newscast had been done for years, begun while Dorothy Bullitt was alive. There was a dispute about what he said next.

"That's it. Get that off my air. Dorothy Bullitt is dead!"

He later denied saying the part about Mrs. Bullitt, but both the Seattle *P-I* and the Seattle *Weekly* said their sources confirmed the incident. Even if the incident were untrue, it rang true to traditionalists inside KING.

They saw Jordan as representing a complete reversal of the values that had made the company special. For his part, Jordan thought the news staff was living in the past, coasting on a reputation that was no longer deserved. He insisted that there was no conflict between journalistic integrity and commercial success. The newscast had to be based on hard news, he said. Those who didn't march to his tune were out, or were put on nights or weekends. The message: Get lost.

Four days after starting at KING, Jordan called in senior producer John Wilson, head of KING's special projects. Wilson had worked on some of KING's biggest stories, including political coverage and the Gary Little story. Wilson told what happened:

"I don't have any need for your services," Jordan told Wilson.

"For anything?" asked a startled Wilson.

"No. You're gone. I have a severance check for you."

Wilson was out. He later got a call from the chairman of the King Broadcasting Company. "I feel awful," Patsy Collins said. "I'm very upset. I don't know what's going on."

Wilson told her that he had checked into Jordan's past. More changes were coming. "You're going to see a dismantling of the legacy," he told her. "Many of the things you viewed with pride are going to be attacked."

"I'm hoping that won't happen," she said.

Wilson urged her to talk with Clifford. But Wilson didn't get his job back.

Feature reporter Greg Palmer had barely returned from a trip to the Soviet Union when he got a message to see Jordan. Palmer heard that Jordan was meeting individually with staffers to get to know them and assess their work. Palmer showed up in Jordan's office with a tape of some of his pieces, expecting a good reception. Hired in 1977 as an arts reviewer and reporter, the first in Seattle TV, he had no TV experience, but Palmer went on to establish himself as a popular if unconventional TV presence. He was a trademark KING personality: the opposite of the blown-dry TV newsface. He was bald. A few wisps of hair formed eyebrows. Bags hung from his eyes. And he never, ever smiled. Still, he wrote beautifully, gained a following for his quirky, irreverent reports, and won thirteen Emmys. By the time Jordan took over, Palmer had been promoted to feature columnist and appeared in his own segments, called *The Palmer Method*.

Jordan didn't need to review Palmer's tape. He had already reached a decision. The two met for about forty-five seconds. "I've decided I don't need any feature work," Jordan told him, as Palmer later related. "Thank you very much. We won't be renewing your contract."

Palmer suspected that Jordan was trying to make a point: pick someone believed to be untouchable and get rid of him. It wasn't just that Palmer had won Emmys and a following; he was popular with the Bullitts as well. Not long after he was hired, the old woman herself had come up to him and said: "Quite often, I don't understand what you're talking about, but I always enjoy it." The sisters liked Palmer, too. When Palmer set off to the Soviet Union to shoot scenes for a film that would be shown during the 1990 Goodwill Games Arts Festival, Harriet went along. Although Patsy was the one most often involved in international affairs, Harriet liked the idea of turning an old Russian folk tale into a film that would be shown to Americans and Soviets. (On that trip, Harriet was accompanied by a Russian man, some thirty years younger than she, who became husband number four.)

When they got the news of Palmer's firing, both sisters called him at home to express their shock. Patsy talked with him for an hour. Palmer was touched. He knew neither would interfere with a management decision—that was a rule set by their mother, who believed in delegated authority.

For decades, reporters and photographers had run KING's newsroom. They were good, they figured, so why not? Jordan changed all that. After more than twenty years of effort by KING-TV news directors, Bob Jordan was the first news director who truly took control. Within four months of his arrival, at least a dozen staffers—reporters, a photographer, producers, and editors—had been fired or quit. Among those who remained, some felt Jordan had brought a needed jolt to the newsroom. "We're making progress. There's a lot of energy in the room; most of it positive," reporter John Sandifer, a veteran of KOMO and KING, told the *Times* later. "We've begun to think that Mr. Jordan maybe isn't Hitler; just Napoleon."

Winning Emmys had once been viewed as validation of KING's quality-first philosophy. After KING won a slug of Emmys, Jordan uttered a remark that was copied down and spread by electronic mail to others in the newsroom: "Emmys are nice; Nielsens are better." Referring to the ratings service, Jordan said: "I would rather have no Emmys and win the Nielsens."

Jordan told people he was bringing in his kind of people and that he had the support of King Broadcasting's top management, including Steve Clifford. The *P-I* reported that one of his hires, Jim Forman, stepped into the newsroom and proclaimed: "I'm not a journalist. I'm a ratings machine." One night, Forman spoke live from a rape scene. His words fanned emotions: "I'm just two football fields from where the rape took place, right in the center of where the fear and anger is really running tonight."

During a period when all three newscasts were being measured for their share of the audience, KIRO, KOMO, and KING worked aggressively to hype their newscasts and hold viewers. The airwaves were saturated with reports of terrified residents, strange and shocking tales, bizarre births, even Satanic cults in rural Mason County. The *P-I* concluded that KING sank the lowest by showing a black-and-white photograph of mass murderer Ted Bundy's head after his execution.

How long could this go on? Nasty firings and now on Dorothy Bullitt's airwaves the head of a corpse? The *P-I* reported that staffers wanted Patsy Collins and Harriet Bullitt to break tradition, to get involved in day-to-day operations and boot Jordan. "If they don't, some say, the integrity and dedication to public service that the late Dorothy Bullitt insisted upon when she bought the less-than-year-old station in 1949 could be destroyed. There are those who insist serious deterioration had already begun," wrote the *P-I*'s John Engstrom. But there was an even larger point. All three newscasts had gotten bad, alternatingly shocking, funny, or helpful, but never thoughtful, wry, irreverent, or truly fresh. With Seattle news directors all getting overnight ratings, each could precisely follow the other newscasts and look for bumps or dips in ratings. That may have explained why the three newscasts had become interchangeable, equally bland, seemingly responding to the same ratings consultants who went from city to city, spreading same-ness, killing the quirky, the original, the bold. KING seemed a long way from Dorothy Bullitt's goal of quality and distinction. Sadly, perhaps, the new KING seemed closer to what viewers across the nation wanted. They didn't want Mr. Chips. They wanted short summaries, ninety-second snippets, not eight-minute lectures. As sound bites shrank, hardly anyone got to speak longer than five seconds. Ironically, the volume of local TV news grew as KING and other stations nationwide added weekend, noon, and morning news broadcasts. With helicopters, satellite transmitters mounted on trucks, and other powerful equipment, news crews from the nation's 1,500 broadcast stations could be anywhere, even matching the networks on a given story. But as local television news became more powerful, it became less pertinent to viewers' deeply felt concerns. Expanding across the daily listings, local news became a mile wide, and an inch deep. Rather than cover great issues with its costly hardware, or use its added time to sort through the complex and important, local TV generally stuck to the simple and the obvious. The hallmark of local TV news became the live broadcast from a station's helicopter of a police car chasing a suspect.

Jordan was a symptom of these trends, not the cause. However Patsy and Harriet may have loved the old ways, they were not about to dump him. They couldn't. His style was making things unpleasant, but they weren't about to disrupt management. Not while ratings of the newscast were climbing. Not while they were pursuing a secret plan hatched even before Jordan had arrived.

Dorothy Bullitt had been dead less than a year when her daughters gave the news to Steve Clifford, chief executive of King Broadcasting Company. They were about to cut short his career along with their ties to the company. Their relationship with Clifford had never been anything like the one between Ancil Payne and their mother. Payne had been far more than the foreman at the ranch. Payne had been the great orchestrator of the company and interpreter of the elderly Dorothy Bullitt's utterances. Payne had thrived at the vortex of the Bullitt family. He had survived the schism and left the company with a large chunk of stock and a reputation as the savior of King Broadcasting.

Clifford never had a relationship like that. To the sisters, Clifford was a skilled employee. Although relations were cordial, he had no special status in the family. He was someone hired to run things. He was never completely in their confidence, but perhaps no one in his role could be, for the sisters were not comfortable with the company they owned. Well-meaning but naive, they wanted increased profits, good journalism, and happy employees. They saw no conflicts among these goals. Dorothy Bullitt had understood that an owner, like a parent, can't please everyone all the time. To increase profits, Clifford had to make changes that disrupted people who cherished King Broadcasting's traditions. He, like the sisters, had to deal with the vaunted memory of how Dorothy Bullitt had run things. But much of that was a mythology created by Ancil Payne, who ran things with far more autonomy than many knew.

Clifford did not try to talk them out of selling. He knew it made sense from a purely financial perspective and, given the sisters' lack of affection for the business, it wasn't a complete surprise. So the question was not whether to sell but how. To their credit, the sisters wanted the sale structured to keep the company intact and cause minimal trauma for employees, many of whom they considered friends. They wanted a prestige buyer who would pay a high price and retain King Broadcasting as something they could be proud of—a pair of goals that would be difficult to achieve. The buyers with the biggest money would probably be speculators, whose aim would be to shrink, not maintain, an expensive news staff. Or a buyer might see a quicker return by breaking up King Broadcasting and selling its pieces. Typically, buyers borrowed for purchases, and then cut expenses on what they had bought to help pay down the debt. That almost always meant the purchased company went through painful cutbacks.

The other problem was timing. Recent changes in federal regulations of leveraged transactions, the overall slump in the industry, and tightened credit made it unlikely that the company would fetch a high sale price. But the sisters wanted to sell now and put their proceeds into the Bullitt Foundation, which their mother had established in 1952 as a vehicle for family giving. With an endowment of $5 million, the foundation had given small amounts of money to various Northwest causes: to St. Mark's Cathedral, theaters, the Lakeside School, and other groups. In the 1960s, reflecting a greater presence of the sisters, the foundation began to focus on environmental causes and gave money to such groups as the Oregon Rivers Council, the Nature Conservancy, and the Natural Resources Defense Council. It bought land to create state and city parks. In later years, the foundation provided seed money for the Target Seattle anti-nuclear events and provided support for visiting Russians during the 1990 Goodwill Games in Seattle.

Before she died, Dorothy Bullitt had given away much of her stock in King Broadcasting. By 1987, her stake had shrunk to about 28 percent of the company, with Patsy owning about 26 percent and Harriet owning about 21 percent. Relatives, directors, and employees held the rest. The sisters told their mother they didn't want her stock after her death. Why give millions to millionaires? they asked. Instead, they suggested the stock go to the foundation. After her death, the bulk of her stock did go there, but its cash value was relatively small because King Broadcasting paid only modest dividends. Selling the company would turn that stock into cash, boosting the foundation's giving-power to as much as $8 million a year. An expanded foundation was a chance for them to have something that was completely their own and so make a mark on the region. Since childhood, the sisters had been trying to find their way out of their mother's shadow. Selling King did that.

One last time, they needed Ancil Payne. Clifford recommended Payne because he was available, knew the company, and had extensive contacts in the communications industry. Payne took the job as broker for the deal, but he made it clear to Patsy and Harriet that, for legal and fiduciary reasons, his duty was to represent not just them but all shareholders—a group that included himself. In other words, he wasn't going to see them give away the company.

Payne went hunting for a buyer. A detailed financial statement on the company gave an impressive portrait of King's profitability: since 1985, net revenues had doubled to a projected $206 million for 1991. King Broadcasting by then operated four network TV stations, one low-powered network affiliate, one independent station, three FM and three AM radio stations and thirteen cable systems serving 202,000 subscribers. The company employed 1,279 full-time people and 694 part timers. It had an excellent reputation, held attractive markets, owned first-rate facilities, and employed quality managers. To make the company more attractive, Clifford was shrinking operating expenses—at KING-TV alone, down $1.5 million to a projected total of $24.9 million for 1990.

The sales statement noted that the already-strong profits could be easily improved. "Because of the company's orientation towards maintaining the highest quality facilities and productions and its commitment to winning industry and community awards, its television stations fall below average industry levels for profit margins. A prospective owner would have the opportunity to improve these financial measures," the statement said. Or to put it bluntly, the company could be squeezed for higher profits.

Payne made the rounds, contacting Gannett, the New York *Times* Company, and other potential buyers. The sentimental favorite was the Washington *Post* Company. Payne briefed chairman Katharine Graham, but the *Post* had internal money problems. Other potential buyers were scared off by the downward trend in broadcasting prices.

When secret efforts to sell the company failed, the sisters had to go public with their decision. Before their announcement, Payne quietly contacted a professional public-relations consultant to prepare the sisters for the huge public attention that would focus on the sale. The principal PR goal was to prevent the sale from being characterized as an abandonment of Dorothy Bullitt's legacy. As part of the strategy, the story was leaked to the afternoon Seattle *Times* so close to deadline that reporters would have little time to gather reaction to the news. The Bullitts did not want an emphasis on the anguish of surprised employees who had believed the sisters' promise to keep the company. The Bullitts wanted the first publicity "bounce" to be their own story, not the views of others on their decision.

In late August 1990, the sisters called a press conference at the Stimson-Green mansion to reveal their plans. The event was scripted to tie the sale with their desire to preserve "environmental quality in the Pacific Northwest through the Bullitt Foundation," as a press release stated. The sale would increase the foundation's assets twenty-fold to nearly $100 million, based on Dorothy Bullitt's estate alone. The sisters estimated the company would sell for more than $500 million.

"In part because of our age (we have both passed our 65th birthdays) we prefer to sell at a time of our own choosing rather than wait until a sale would be required by our deaths. It is our objective that the new owner of King will be deeply committed to our values of service to the community and respect for employees. It is our objective that the new owner will be a good employer, a responsible operator and an outstanding corporate citizen," the sisters said in a joint statement. "A sale under these conditions will provide the maximum stability and continuity for the valued employees of King."

The sisters also issued a statement to "our good friends—all the people who work at King Broadcasting." The statement took pains to root their decision to sell in the civic traditions of the family, dating back to C. D. and Harriet Stimson. "Mother continued the family's tradition of giving when she started the Bullitt Foundation. Enhancing this foundation through the sale of the company will fulfill many of her and our dreams."

The sisters said their decision followed many talks with their mother before her death and implied that selling was something their mother had wanted. But had she? It was a critical question, since the company for decades had been run on what people thought she wanted. But that question would never be settled. Many who considered themselves close to Dorothy S. Bullitt insisted that she had wanted the company to stay in the family. There was even talk that she had been interested in selling to the employees. Sallie Baldus, Dorothy Bullitt's longtime hired companion, insisted that before her death the old woman had contacted lawyers to see about preventing a sale of the company. People's views tended to reflect their own desires; if they had wanted the company to remain Bullitt property, that's what they saw in the old woman's last utterances. Patsy insisted that people who thought they knew her mother were often wrong about Dorothy Bullitt's beliefs.

The announcement made headlines in the local press as well as the *Wall Street Journal*, *BusinessWeek*, the New York *Times*, and other national publications. Only *BusinessWeek* looked beyond the sisters' stated rationale and wondered if any of the sisters' children wanted the company to stay in the family. The sisters told the magazine that none of the children had shown an interest in running the company. They wanted to avoid the kind of fight that had erupted in the Bingham family, owners of the Louisville *Courier-Journal*, when a disgruntled family member threatened to sell her shares to an outsider, precipitating a public spat. No reporter bothered to check that scenario by contacting any of Dorothy Bullitt's grandchildren. The sisters didn't volunteer that the grandchildren had not been consulted, only informed. It was the sisters' company, and the decision to sell was their own.

John Wilson, the former KING news producer, wrote a lengthy letter to Patsy, pleading with her to not sell the stations. You can serve the environmental community and preserve the company's journalistic contributions by selling only the cable division, he argued. After the cable sale, you can earmark cash to enhance coverage of the environment by the stations. She wrote back that there was no other way. She didn't add that she was tired of audience complaints about the newscast or the radio disc jockeys.

Patsy wanted to save salmon, not King Broadcasting. There were many reasons why she did not share her mother's feeling for King Broadcasting. It was always her mother's company, not hers; Ancil Payne had made that clear. It had become a large corporation, spread over several states, less intimate for employee or owner, less suitable to showcase her own maverick views. Dorothy Bullitt had failed to convince her children that the company should be preserved. Modern television remained a difficult environment for serious journalism; King's reputation was founded on a kind of reporting that perhaps no longer held audiences. And finally, management and the Bullitts eventually succumbed to corporate interests and allowed ratings to be the newsroom's dominant goal.

King Broadcasting's idealism had hit its high point when Stimson Bullitt became company president. The decline of those values began when he left, and King had drifted from his high-minded goals. From then, the values of the company were sustained not as much by management as by key individuals, such as Charles Royer and Don McGaffin, who saw the company as a civic treasure. Like other staffers dating back to Bob Schulman and Herb Altschull, Royer and McGaffin tended to think their work was better or more effective than it actually was, but that was part of King Broadcasting's passion. Like Stim, they had a vision and agenda for their city that was strongly conveyed to viewers, giving KING-TV an attitude different from any other Seattle newscast. But when Bob Jordan walked into King Broadcasting, what remained unique to those ideals was soon gone and a new sort of company began, one like any other, on any channel.

So King Broadcasting Company was sold.

In March 1991—forty-two years after their mother had bought KRSC-TV—Harriet and Patsy sold the TV and cable divisions to the Providence Journal Company, a family-controlled company that owned newspapers, TV stations, and cable-TV companies. The sisters had made good on their promise to find a reputable buyer—publisher of a daily newspaper in Rhode Island since 1829, the Providence Journal Company was a class act. Its *Providence Journal* newspaper had won three Pulitzer Prizes.

The purchase price was not disclosed, but most assumed it was for $500 million. The radio stations were not part of the sale. The sisters later sold money-losing KING-AM for $1.5 million to Bonneville International Corporation, which renamed the station KINF, then again to KNWX, and moved it to the 770 dial position. The sisters gave classical music station KING-FM to a consortium of Seattle arts groups. Eric Bremner and Steve Clifford bought the company's mobile-television division.

The sale generated cash for more than 275 stockholders, including Bullitt family members and their friends, employees, and various trusts, charities, and universities.

Among the largest shareholders, Dorothy S. Bullitt's stock (held in a trust) went for $87.8 million; Harriet Bullitt's stock for $9.4 million; and Patsy Collins's stock for $9.4 million. Collins and Bullitt trusts held stock worth $165.8 million. Stock held by Stimson Bullitt's Harbor Properties partnership went for $10.2 million. Of employees, Ancil Payne led the list with stock sold at $8 million.

The Bullitt family was out of the communications business.

The Providence Journal Company promised that it would make no sudden moves with its new property, but within a few months the inevitable took place: the new owners eliminated virtually all of the corporate-level administrative jobs in Seattle. Those tasks would be performed by managers in Providence. There were countless other cutbacks. Technicians, publicists and others would quit and not be replaced, leaving remaining staff with more work. The King Broadcasting building lost some of its energy. No longer the hub of an expanding empire, but instead a piece of one, the building became another asset for a company across a continent with no agenda for the city, no editorials to move minds, no owners deeply rooted in the life of the community. It remained a competitive presence, however. At the start of 1996, Providence Journal launched a twenty-four-hour cable-news service linking the staffs at former King Broadcasting stations in Seattle, Portland, Boise, and Spokane. At a cost of $5 million, Northwest Cable News featured headlines, weather updates, and a sprinkling of business and health stories and longer stories called "Extra." In the low-cost operation, each reporter did his or her own photography.

Inside KING's newsroom, the turnover was almost complete. Nearly all of the long-timers were gone, replaced by a group of young faces.

The notable holdover was Jean Enersen, the last icon of KING-TV's tradition of quality journalism. And that was a supreme irony: the woman whose promotion to anchor was once viewed as a capitulation to the corrupting values of entertainment in TV journalism had become KING's emissary of intelligence and integrity. Enersen remained the city's most visible, indeed only symbol of news judgment with a perspective from the past. She remained KING-TV's franchise player and Seattle's most admired news anchor. But increasingly, her role seemed more the facade of an empty house. For her, the days of reporting trips to Asia and Russia were gone. She introduced reports by reporters who clearly didn't know the city. It was difficult to imagine any of the new reporters taking on Charles O. Carroll, trying to explain a complicated legislative payoff system, or having time to cultivate sources. Like Seattle's other stations, KING maintained no full-time reporter in Olympia or Seattle City Hall. In recent years, Seattle debated its schools, regional transit, the fate of the Seattle Mariners baseball team, and a Commons park proposed for a site south of Lake Union, but KING-TV made no effort to lead that debate, only to reflect it. Commentary—once the hallmark of King Broadcasting—left KING-TV's newscast. KING's one-time commentator Jim Compton moved to a Sunday issues program, one of few still aired in Seattle. Children's programming, once Dorothy Bullitt's passion for television, was sharply cut back. KING's public affairs programs, which had involved lengthy treatment of electric shortages and other sober issues, were eliminated. King Broadcasting's noble spirit was gone. Whatever Jean Enersen thought of these changes was her secret. If she felt disappointment, she kept it private.

I n 1985 Stimson Bullitt brought his daughter into Harbor Properties, the company formed from the assets he received when he left King Broadcasting. The moment was as poignant as the day Dorothy S. Bullitt took over her deceased husband's business at the height of the Depression. Finally, a new generation of Bullitts was taking a senior position in a family company.

Dorothy C. Bullitt, age thirty, was prepared to spend the rest of her life at Harbor Properties and to use it as a vehicle for her liberal politics, her community activism, and her determination to see a profitable company run ethically. She had decided not to have children so that she could devote herself fully to civic and business affairs.

Since leaving King Broadcasting, Stim had spent twenty years in a fitful effort to build his most ambitious project: a large complex overlooking Seattle's waterfront and the Alaskan Way Viaduct which included a hotel, apartment towers, office buildings, and shops, bisected by a grand staircase designed by famed Canadian architect Arthur Erickson. The site was a short walk from the spot where C. D. Stimson had come ashore nearly a hundred years earlier.

Harbor Steps was intended to be a series of beautiful platforms that would provide places to sit and view the waterfront, or the people coming and going. It would be a wonderful gathering place, something like Rome's Spanish Steps, a public place of dignity, reflection, and inspiration. Stim had not given up on the uplifting of Seattle. But the project, estimated at $50 million or more depending on the design, was stalled, and some naysayers in the downtown business community snickered that Stim Bullitt was still a lousy businessman.

As the new vice president and chief operating officer, Young Dorothy was determined to treat each employee with dignity and respect. She would be accessible, would listen, and would motivate rather than command. While her father remained isolated from public life, she threw herself into civic issues, joining the Seattle Human Rights Commission, the Downtown Seattle Association, the Rotary Club, the Pike Place Market Foundation. She joined groups promoting racial unity and affordable housing. She lived the life of her dreams. As a manager, she was the popular opposite of her father, who appeared occasionally at the company. Harbor Properties was largely hers to run.

But daughter and father clashed over Stim's dream. Stim wanted to see the Harbor Steps project built, and he was willing to borrow against all of the company's assets. Dorothy believed that the project was too risky and should be scaled back. She was thinking of the risk to her siblings and others who received income from the company. Maybe her business acumen reminded Stim too much of his mother. If the sisters were feeling liberated by the sale of King, then maybe Stim was, too. He was going to do what he wanted to do. Convinced that his daughter was trying to undercut him, he ended the debate by firing her in 1992.

Within two years, Stim completed a scaled-back Harbor Steps project. Dorothy took an office a short walk from her old office and opened a business as a management consultant. All around her office were pictures of her grandmother, her siblings, her mother, and even her father—a miniature Bullitt museum. Dorothy never said a harsh word about her father, even though their relationship remained strained for more than two years. They would hardly speak. She tried to repair their relationship by sending him notes with positive messages. She felt that her entire future had been obliterated and that she had been forced to discover a new identity for herself. Ever the practical Bullitt, she worked through her anxiety by writing a book on how to cope with loss—business and personal. Eventually, she and her father did resume regular contact but, entering the second century of Dorothy Bullitt's family in Seattle, they never discussed the company.

King Broadcasting Company Awards: 1953–1989 (Partial Listing)

1953 Award for *Televenture Tales* and *March On*

1957 Peabody Award for *Wunda Wunda*
Thomas Alva Edison Award for youth programming

1961 Award of Institute for Education by Radio and Television
(Ohio State University) for *Bitter Harvest*
DuPont Award for overall excellence in broadcasting

1966 Radio and Television News Directors Association Distinguished
Achievement Award for Stimson Bullitt's editorial on Vietnam

1968 Motion Picture Academy Award (Oscar) to King Screen for the short
documentary, *The Redwoods*

1970 National Sigma Delta Chi Distinguished Service Award for
public service
Saturday Review Award for Distinguished TV Programming in
the Public Interest

1973 Gavel Award, American Bar Association, for *Are Prisons Safe for People?*

1974 Peabody Award for *How Come?*

1981 Champion Media Award for *Electrical Storm*

1983 DuPont Award for *Epidemic: Why Your Kid Is on Drugs*

1986 Peabody Award to Dorothy S. Bullitt

Champion-Tuck Award for *Washington 2000*

1988 Edward R. Murrow Award for best local news operation in the
United States

1989 Peabody Award for *Project Home Team*

Source: King Broadcasting Company

The story of King Broadcasting has been pieced together from a variety of sources: printed material, video and film, and interviews.

Several sets of papers found in the archives of the University of Washington were helpful, especially the *Seattle* magazine collection, which gave a sense of tension among management over the magazine's financial losses. Useful in providing a glimpse of Seattle politics and the Bullitt family's involvement were the papers of Henry Jackson, Irving Clark, Jr., Warren Magnuson (although many files dealing with King Broadcasting Company remain closed to the public at this time), John Goldmark, John L. O'Brien, and the Washington State Federation of Labor.

The Bullitt family possesses many of Dorothy Bullitt's personal and business papers, but Patsy Bullitt Collins declined to make them available to the author, though the family has said that the papers may someday be donated to the University of Washington Library.

Many company memos, press releases, newspaper clippings, annual reports, and other materials were made available by Ancil Payne, Del Loder, Jack Hamann, Jim Compton, Bob Schulman, and Herb Altschull.

The archives of the Federal Communications Commission should have been invaluable. Instead, to save storage costs, the agency threw out much of its old files, including files of letters from listeners and viewers commenting on political coverage by stations. Nonetheless, the FCC archives do contain some material on KRSC's founding and the early years of Dorothy Bullitt's ownership of what became King Broadcasting Company.

Among the books that proved helpful in understanding broadcasting were Erik Barnouw's *Tube of Plenty: The Evolution of American Television* (New York: Oxford University Press, 2nd revised edition, 1990); Les Brown's *Encyclopedia of Television* (Detroit: Visible Ink Press, 3rd edition, 1992); and Edward Bliss, Jr.'s

Now the News: The Story of Broadcast Journalism (New York: Columbia University Press, 1991). For local broadcast history, David Blair Richardson's *Puget Sounds: A Nostalgic Review of Radio and TV in the Great Northwest* (Seattle: Superior Publishing, 1980) gives an affectionate portrait of the early radio and TV personalities. For Seattle history, the best book written about Seattle remains *Skid Road* by Murray Morgan (Seattle: University of Washington Press, first illustrated edition, 1982). Roger Sale's *Seattle: Past to Present* (Seattle: University of Washington Press, 1982) focuses on Seattle's history since World War II and offers some fascinating theories about Seattle's growth. Norman Clark's *Mill Town* (Seattle: University of Washington Press, 1970) gives a vivid portrait of the Everett Massacre and union radicalism. An unpublished master's thesis, "*Seattle:* Failure of a City Magazine," by Ruby Mae Apsler (University of Washington, 1977) provides a good postmortem on *Seattle* magazine's publication and useful figures on its circulation and revenue. *Washington: The First Hundred Years,* by Don Duncan (Seattle: The Seattle *Times,* 1989) is exceptionally helpful for tracking events of the Northwest.

Books about the Bullitt family were useful. Delphine Haley's *Dorothy Stimson Bullitt: An Uncommon Life* (Seattle: Sasquatch Books, 1995) is an entertaining, intimate, and well-written account of Dorothy Bullitt's life which provided many details that are used here. Haley is the daughter of Andrew Haley, Dorothy Bullitt's lawyer; her book was commissioned by the family. For insight into Stimson Bullitt's personality, his *To Be a Politician* (New Haven: Yale University Press, 1977), *River Dark and Bright* (Seattle: Willows Press, 1995), and *Ancestral Histories of Scott Bullitt and Dorothy Stimson* (Seattle: Willows Press, 1995) give helpful information and dates, but are hardly forthcoming about pivotal moments in family history. An updated *To Be a Politician* was published in 1994 by Willows Press of Seattle. Stimson history comes from *The Stimson Legacy: Architecture in the Urban West* (Seattle: Willows Press, 1992) by Lawrence Kreisman. (Willows Press is the Bullitt family publishing arm.) Thomas Stimson Bayley, a cousin of the Bullitts, gives a useful background on the Stimson clan in *The Stimson Family* (Taipei, Taiwan: L-C. Publishing Co., 1976).

Newspapers were essential, particularly those of 1970 and after, when coverage by the Seattle *Post-Intelligencer* and the Seattle *Times* devoted much attention to station programming and the coming and going of station personnel. At the two papers, Susan Paynter, John Voorhees, John Engstrom, and Kit Boss wrote insightful articles. Very little, however, was written about the business side of television which, of course, interested Dorothy Bullitt and drove many of the headlined changes. Theresa Morrow's portrait of Patsy Bullitt Collins and Harriet Bullitt in the Seattle *Times* in 1990 gave a candid account of tensions between Dorothy Bullitt and her children. David Brewster's portrait of King Broadcasting Company for the now-defunct *Argus* weekly in 1973 established many of the themes followed in this book. Brewster went on to found the Seattle *Weekly*, with its ongoing and insightful coverage of KING. John S. Robinson gives a perceptive portrait of Dorothy S. Bullitt in *Washingtonians: A Biographical Portrait of the State* (Seattle: Sasquatch Publishing, 1988; pp. 217–42), edited by David Brewster and David M. Buerge.

Unfortunately, very few local programs broadcast by KRSC-TV and KING-TV before the 1960s can be viewed today. As was typical of the industry in its early years, newscasts and other programs that were broadcast live were not preserved; films and kinescopes (film of live broadcasts) were typically thrown away, lost, or cut up. Scripts were not kept or catalogued.

KING did retain some documentaries, such as *Lost Cargo* and *Suspect*. Other reports were kept by the people who made them: Herb Altschull and Don McGaffin. McGaffin, who is working on his memoirs, has spent years tracking down lost KING-TV footage. He possesses a copy of *The Buck Stops Here*, the report he created with Charles Royer. Charles Herring kept some videotape made from film of his newscasts. Much of the material produced by KING-TV news before 1965 was destroyed. After 1965 the material produced by TV news and the program department was gathered into one library, but viewing the old material is a challenge. Much of it is physically delicate or can be shown only on special projection equipment; as a result, King Broadcasting typically declines requests to view the material. The company is much more willing to show whatever film has been copied to the VHS format.

By far, however, the bulk of the material in this book came from interviews with more than 130 people, some of whom gave dozens of hours of their time. Most were former employees of King Broadcasting, though sources at the *P-I*, *Times*, KOMO, and KIRO were also interviewed. The complete group is listed in the acknowledgments, but among those who were particularly helpful and patient were: Ancil Payne, the retired company president; Dorothy C. Bullitt, granddaughter of Dorothy S. Bullitt and daughter of Stimson Bullitt; Bagley Wright, friend of Stimson Bullitt and former board member of King Broadcasting; Don McGaffin, former KING commentator; Kay Bullitt, former wife of Stimson Bullitt; Ruth Prins, who played "Wunda Wunda" on KING; the late Jack Shawcroft, former chief engineer at KING; and Jim Neidigh, former national sales manager at KING. The children of Dorothy S. Bullitt—Stimson Bullitt, Harriet Bullitt, and Patsy Collins—were not cooperative. Patsy Collins gave one interview on her father and declined any more, saying she was too busy. Harriet Bullitt did not respond to repeated requests, and Stimson Bullitt declined, despite several phone calls and letters. By contrast, Dorothy S. Bullitt's grandchildren were very cooperative, including Margaret Bullitt, whose several hours of taped interviews with Dorothy S. Bullitt were the basis for descriptions of King Broadcasting's early strategic moves. The grandchildren and various Bullitt friends helped provide understanding of the complex relationship between Dorothy S. Bullitt and her children.

(For full bibliographic information on books cited below by title or author, see preceding Notes on Sources.)

1. Prologue

The account of KING-TV's 25th anniversary celebration is based on a videotape copy kept by King Broadcasting.

2. C. D. Stimson

Seattle in the late 1880s is based on information found in chapter 2 of Murray Morgan's *Skid Road;* in *The Stimson Family;* and in contemporary accounts in the Seattle *Times* (Feb. 4–7, 1889). Other material comes from Margaret Bullitt's interview with Dorothy S. Bullitt. Bayley's book says C. D. Stimson lost his arm at age nine.

3. A City Like Heaven

Dorothy S. Bullitt's girlhood account is based on Margaret Bullitt's interview with Dorothy S. Bullitt; John S. Robinson's profile of Dorothy S. Bullitt in *Washingtonians;* a speech by Dorothy C. Bullitt in March 1992, "Four Generations of Leadership" (supplied by Dorothy C. Bullitt); an interview with Patsy Bullitt Collins; and *The Stimson Legacy.* The turkey story comes from Del Loder, who got the story from Dorothy S. Bullitt. Seattle's economic development comes from *Seattle: Past and Present;* and *A Century of Seattle's Business* (Bellevue: Vernon Publications, 1989) by James R. Warren and the staff of *Seattle Business* magazine.

4. Brave Words

The account of the romance between Scott Bullitt and Dorothy Stimson comes from Margaret Bullitt's interview with Dorothy S. Bullitt. Details of Bullitt's background come from a biography for his 1926 campaign found in the Seattle *Times* library; and from *Ancestral Histories of Scott Bullitt and Dorothy Stimson*. Patsy Collins supplied the anecdote about Scott Bullitt's attitudes on serving liquor during Prohibition. Other material is based on *Skid Road* and *Mill Town*. Details of Scott Bullitt's campaign derive from contemporary articles in the Seattle *Times* (Oct. 20, 1926; Sept. 1, 1928; and Nov. 8, 1928), and the Seattle *P-I* (Dec. 29, 1926). The account of Thomas Stimson's death comes from Margaret Bullitt's interview with Dorothy S. Bullitt; the funeral data comes from *The Stimson Family*.

5. The Depression Hits Dorothy

Seattle during the Depression comes from *Skid Road* and an interview with Kathleen Corr (the author's mother). Scott Bullitt details come from *Ancestral Histories*, the Margaret Bullitt interview with Dorothy Bullitt, and *To Be a Politician*. Dorothy Bullitt's struggle as a Depression landlady comes from *Four Generations* and the Margaret Bullitt interview with Dorothy Bullitt. Details of the Bullitt household after Scott's death comes from Theresa Morrow's Seattle *Times* article (Nov. 11, 1990). Harriet in braces comes from an interview with Mrs. Alexander Fisken. Delphine Haley described the children-mother relationship as "glazed-over bitterness." Other Dorothy details come from *Ancestral Histories*. Seattle during and after World War II comes from *Seattle: Past to Present* and Kathleen Corr. The "here's your money back" quotation comes from page 230 of the John S. Robinson article in *Washingtonians: A Biographical Portrait of the State*. The portrait of Fred Stimson comes from Ancil Payne and Dorothy S. Bullitt in the Margaret Bullitt interview. King Broadcasting's early years comes from a brief history of the company written in 1948 by Dorothy S. Bullitt, and from interviews with Philip Padelford, Frances Owen, and Ancil Payne. The number of radios in Washington state is listed in the *Radio Annual, 1947*, found in the Broadcast Pioneers Library in Washington, D.C. The 1948 King promotional brochure is from the collection of Del Loder.

6. The First Broadcast

The portrait of Seattle comes from *Seattle Story* by Hector Escobosa (Seattle: F. McCaffrey, 1948) and the U.S. Bureau of Labor Statistics Bulletin #951, July 1948. The Malcom Cowley quotation comes from *Seattle: Past to Present*, page 196. Leberman's dream of sending a newspaper over the airwaves comes from Lee Schulman. Leberman's cash needs are noted in the archives of the FCC, KING-TV boxes. *Puget Sounds* describes Leberman's background. Jack Shawcroft described how KRSC and later KING employees viewed Schulman. Details of the first broadcast comes from the Seattle *Times* (Nov. 24, 1948), Shawcroft, and Lee Schulman. Jerry Hoeck described the conversation with Loren Stone. Dan Starr gave the estimate of KRSC-TV's losses.

7. In Her Hands

The description of Dorothy Bullitt's purchase of KRSC comes from the Dorothy S. Bullitt interview with Margaret Bullitt, Jim Neidigh, and Robert Priebe. Early KING details are from Lee Schulman, Kit Spier, *Puget Sounds,* and Del Loder. KING's early programming is described by Henry Owen in a letter to the FCC, Jan. 5, 1950. Dan Starr and Jim Neidigh discussed the commissions earned by KING's salesmen. Roger Rice described the departure of Hugh Feltis. The description of Otto Brandt telling Dorothy Bullitt she could get back to buying hats comes from Dorothy C. Bullitt, who heard the story from her grandmother. Thelma Brandt described her feelings about moving to Seattle. Jim Neidigh and Jerry Hoeck described the early promotion of KING. Coverage of the hydro races comes from *Washington: The First One Hundred Years,* pages 79–80; a retrospective in the Seattle *Times* (Aug. 8, 1990); and Jim Neidigh and Lee Schulman. Charles Herring described early newscasts. The account of the Rosellini crime hearings comes from Albert Rosellini and coverage in the Tacoma *News Tribune* (Nov. 25–Dec. 3, 1951).

8. The Good Fight

Characterization of Stimson Bullitt comes from Dorothy C. Bullitt. The letters to Henry Jackson are among the Jackson papers at the University of Washington Library archives. Speculation on why Stimson Bullitt ran for office came from David Sprague. Carolyn Kizer, who declined to be interviewed, was described by Ancil Payne, Jerry and Rosemary Hoeck, and Jonathan Whetzel. Stimson Bullitt's letter to potential supporters is among the John L. O'Brien papers in the University of Washington Library archives. The campaign brochure was found in the Washington State Federation of Labor papers in the University of Washington Library archives. Irv Hoff, Patsy Collins, Bruce Mitchell, and Hugh B. Mitchell described the campaigns. The "Bullitt Asserts . . ." headline comes from the Seattle *Times* (Oct. 6, 1952), and Stimson Bullitt's declaration that he was not a Communist comes from the *Times* (Oct. 12, 1952). The killing of the anti-Pelly ad comes from Jerry Hoeck and Del Loder. The visit by Senator McCarthy to KING comes from news accounts in the Seattle *Times* (Oct. 24, 1952), Richard Riddell, and memos written by unnamed KING managers for company files made available to the author by Ancil Payne. Irv Hoff described Magnuson's "wrong foot" comment about McCarthy.

9. Strategic Moves

The Dorothy S. Bullitt interview with Margaret Bullitt describes in detail the hearings for the Portland license and the dealings with Hearst. King's early profitability and negotiations with Hearst come from a tax protest prepared by Dorothy Bullitt and Stimson Bullitt from the late 1950s; the date on the copy kept by Philip Padelford is illegible. The speculation that Dorothy Bullitt had used political pressure to keep the Fishers out of TV comes from Bagley Wright, who says he was told this by Ken Fisher. (Fisher did not return calls, and W. W. "Bill" Warren, KOMO's longtime manager, declined to be interviewed.) The annual *International Television Almanac* (New York: Quigley Publishing) for 1956 and 1963 supplied statistics on TV ownership. Concerns about the company's financial losses came from Frances Owen. The comment on Sol Haas was retold by Dan Starr, who heard it directly from Henry Broderick. Royal Brougham's TV program was described by Kit Spier. Ancil Payne described the attitudes of the Portland-based rivals of Dorothy Bullitt. The reaction of Bill Warren to NBC's defection comes from the Seattle *Times* (Oct. 17, 1958). Dorothy Bullitt's comment was part of a 1987 historical program on the company's history, kept at the archives of King Broadcasting. Jim Harriott described Bill Warren's attitude towards King employees. Jim Neidigh described Logan Bullitt's firing.

10. "Cue the Sun"

Early programming by KING-TV comes from interviews with Charles Herring, Stan Boreson, Ruth Prins, Herb Robinson, Kit Spier, Del Loder, and Jerry Hoeck. In a retrospective article (April 17, 1985), the *P-I* quoted the boy about getting sick. Details on the Treasure Hunt came from press releases, dated Jan. 27 and Feb. 12, 1958, kept by Del Loder, and an interview with Thelma Brandt. Kit Spier told the story of the wobbly Warren Magnuson. Middlebrook was quoted in the *Times* (April 27, 1956). Additional material on Dave Beck comes from the Seattle *Times* (May 9, 1957).

11. "We Can Open Eyes"

The early KING-TV documentaries were described by Robert Schulman, Kit Spier, Earl Thoms, and Richard Larsen, and in company press releases, including those of Dec. 23, 1958, and June 30, 1959, and in news clippings kept by Robert Schulman. The *Times* described *Lost Cargo* in articles from June 20 through June 26, 1959. Chet Skreen's review ran June 26, 1959, and the *Marine Digest*'s review ran July 11, 1959. Videotape copies of *Lost Cargo, A Volcano Named White,* and *Bitter Harvest* are in the King Broadcasting archives. *Newsweek* quoted Dorothy S. Bullitt, April 9, 1962. Schulman gave his speech May 11, 1961, and *Broadcasting* magazine (May 11, 1961) carried the Otto Brandt quotation. Ken MacDonald discussed attitudes toward the documentaries. Robert Block described Stimson Bullitt's reaction to being named company president. Bagley Wright spoke of Stimson Bullitt's desire to make KING a model company; Bullitt's view of Jews is contained in his *To Be a Politician,* on page 225 of the Yale University Press edition.

12. Stim Takes Charge

Comments on the early period of Stimson Bullitt's presidency come from Bagley Wright, Peter Bunzel, James Halpin, Jim Neidigh, Charles Herring, Ancil Payne, and J. Herbert Altschull. Ancil Payne described the airport scene. Robert Schulman and Kit Spier described *Suspect,* which is in the archives of King Broadcasting. The remark about Reed College comes from page 222 of Timothy Egan's *The Good Rain* (New York: Alfred A. Knopf, 1990). Copies of *The Vigilante* are in the John Goldmark papers at the University of Washington Library archives. KING's newsroom was described by Ted Bryant, Charles Herring, and Kit Spier.

13. "Discard Axioms"

Descriptions of *Seattle* magazine are based on copies of the magazine, various letters, and memos found in the magazine archives at the University of Washington Library, and interviews with Peter Bunzel, Ancil Payne, James Halpin, Roger Hagan, Edward Hewson, David Brewster, and Frank Chin. Peter Bunzel described the magazine's birth and death in *Seattle* (December 1970). The letter to Bunzel from Bullitt is dated July 19, 1963, and is in the KING archives at the University of Washington Library. The magazine's purpose was declared in the first issue (April 1964). The "musty" city council article ran in May 1965, and the "hick city" column ran in August 1965. Bunzel's persecution remark was found in a letter of Feb. 18, 1965; his letter to William Allen, Sept. 22, 1965; and his letter to a friend in New York, July 25, 1967; all are in the King archives at the University of Washington Library. The article about Dan Starr ran June 1965. The Bethell memo was dated May 24, 1966.

14. "More People Than Mr. Chips"

Stimson Bullitt's preparations for his Vietnam editorial were described by Ancil Payne and Fred Nemo. Other details of the speech come from Roger Hagan and Janet Ruthford Dunsire. The text was reprinted in the Seattle *Times.* Henry Jackson's displeasure was recalled by Ancil Payne. The Vietnam situation and Seattle's economy come from the Seattle *Times,* (Dec. 26, 1966), which printed the Vietnam editorial on Dec. 23, 1966. Company finance comes from a confidential source with access to annual reports as well as from memos in the *Seattle* archives. Warren Guykema described Stimson Bullitt bypassing Otto Brandt. Robert Block contrasted Stimson Bullitt's approach to improving a community with Dorothy Bullitt's. Ancil Payne supplied the copy of the 1965 "King Broadcasting Company Manual," which declares the company's goals. Mike James recalled the "Mr. Chips" comment. The sarcastic long-timer is Kit Spier, writing to Irving Clark, Jr. His letter is dated Jan. 19, 1967. Robert Schulman described his departure from King. Barbara Stenson described employees' concerns over the pension fund. James Halpin described the screen division's long lunches. Roger Hagan described Stimson Bullitt confronting his managers in a Nov. 4, 1965, entry in a journal kept by Hagan. Stimson Bullitt wrote of his treatment by King executives (*River Dark and Bright,* pp. 308–09). A confidential source described Stimson Bullitt leaving the Blair meeting. Peter Bunzel described Stimson Bullitt mocking Otto Brandt. Dorothy Bullitt's parting words to Otto Brandt were described by a confidential source who spoke with Brandt immediately after the incident.

15. "Hyprocrisy Is Rampant"

The portrait of Seattle in 1968 is largely derived from *Seattle* magazine of June 1968; from *Seattle: Past to Present;* and from articles that summer in the Seattle *Times* and Seattle *Post-Intelligencer.* Articles dated July 2, 1968, contained the Buzz Cook quotation. A retrospective in the *Times* (June 14, 1992) provided other details. The "fighting us all" quotation comes from *Seattle* (October 1967). Dorothy C. Bullitt described white classmates being pulled by parents from public schools, a situation given little attention in the news media until later retrospectives on the 1978 citywide busing program (Seattle *Times,* Sept. 10, 1989). Dorothy C. Bullitt estimates that, from the time she was in middle school to high school, the white population in her classes dropped from roughly 40 percent to 4 percent. Middle-class blacks and Asians also withdrew their children, she said. Other details on Seattle in 1968 came from interviews with Bob Faw, Bill Dorsey, Dorothy C. Bullitt, Ancil Payne, J. Herbert Altschull, Ted Bryant, Mike James, Warren Guykema, Bill Baker, Janet Ruthford Dunsire, and Barbara Stenson. Pratt's comment on hypocrisy comes from a *Times* article

(Jan. 28, 1969). The *Times* carried two other articles on Pratt that year (Jan. 27, and Jan. 30). A more recent (Jan. 19, 1978) article on the Pratt killing by Erik Lacitis of the Seattle *Times* provided additional details. The statistics on KING-TV's employment of African Americans are found in a May 22, 1969, letter from Stimson Bullitt, provided by Ancil Payne.

16. Darkness at the Center

The Charles O. Carroll description comes from *Seattle* (Sept. 1968), as well as from clippings on Carroll's career, found in the Seattle *Times* library. A *Times* article (Jan. 19, 1967) describes patrol officers harassing bar operators. Carroll describes King County as "clean" in a *Times* article (Sept. 12, 1952). Other useful articles are from the *P-I* (Aug. 21 and 22, 1968, and June 30, 1970), and the *Times* (Aug. 23, 1968). Details of the summer of 1968 are in part from Walt Crowley's article in *Eastsideweek* (Sept. 1, 1993). The Humphrey anecdote comes from *A Certain Democrat: Senator Henry M. Jackson,* by William W. Prochnau and Richard W. Larsen (Englewood Cliffs, N.J.: Prentice Hall, 1972). Other details came from David Jessup, Herb Robinson, Don McGaffin, Larry Brown, Dee Norton, James Halpin, David Brewster, Peter Bunzel, Dan Starr, and Louis Guzzo. The Oct. 15, 1968, Oles letter to Dargan, and Bunzel's letter, are in the *Seattle* archives at the University of Washington Library, as is the "secret sits in the center" letter by Bunzel, dated Oct. 30, 1968. The Berger arrest is described in the *P-I* and *Times* (Oct. 9, 1969). The 1971 grand jury was described that year in the *Times* in various articles (especially July 28 and Sept. 9). Mifflin's "rats" remark ran in the *Times* in a retrospective (Nov. 22, 1984); his comment on the indictments ran in the *Times* (May 17, 1973). *On the Take: From Petty Crooks to Presidents,* by William J. Chambliss (Bloomington: Indiana University Press, 1978), supplies a comprehensive portrait of Seattle's payoff system but contains many errors. Eugene Corr is the author's father.

17. In the Palace

The robbery of Stimson Bullitt is described in a Seattle *Times* article (May 1, 1971), and in *The Washington Teamster* (May 14, 1971). Ancil Payne described the merger of the Bullitt Company into King Broadcasting and the aborted merger with the Reade Theater company. Barbara Stenson described the staff reaction to Bullitt's robbery. *Les Brown's Encyclopedia of Television* described network news programs. Data on Seattle's economy comes from *Seattle: Past to Present* (p. 232 for the "turn out the lights" billboard) and KING's finances are detailed in the company's 1971 annual report. Ancil Payne described the conversation between Warren Magnuson and Dorothy S. Bullitt; he also described the sisters' desire for bigger dividends; Jonathan Whetzel described the reluctance of bankers to make loans to the sisters secured by King Broadcasting stock. Other details are from Marvin Durning and Roger Hagan.

18. Ousting the Prince

The portrait of Ancil Payne is based on my interview with Ancil Payne and an article quoting him in *Broadcasting* (April 24, 1972). Stimson Bullitt's note on the closing of *Seattle* is from the collection of Ancil Payne, Sept. 18, 1970. Comments on the deteriorating relationship of Ancil Payne and Stimson Bullitt came from Roger Hagan as well as Payne, who also described the maneuvers leading up to Stimson Bullitt's departure. Margaret Bullitt compared King Broadcasting to another child of Dorothy S. Bullitt; she also described how family members reacted to Stimson Bullitt's resignation. Bagley Wright offered his reaction to Stimson Bullitt's resignation. The description of the board member who lobbied the sisters to scrutinize their brother came from the board member himself, who insisted on anonymity. Details of Stimson Bullitt's relationship with his mother are found throughout Delphine Haley's book. On pages 280–87, Haley gives the Bullitt family's version of Stim's departure from King Broadcasting.

19. The Foreman Takes Charge

Ancil Payne described the period following his becoming president, including the debate over a 60-minute network newscast. King Broadcasting's annual reports detail the company assets before and after the creation of Harbor Properties. Wenda Brewster O'Reilly described her mother, Harriet Bullitt, in a 1994 documentary on Harriet for KCTS-TV in Seattle. Much of the detail of Harriet's and Patsy's childhood comes from the Theresa Morrow article, Nov. 11, 1990. Alec Fisken and Philip Padelford described board meetings. Fred Nemo explained why he changed his name from Scott Bullitt. David Brewster's *Argus* ran Nov. 23, 1973. Regarding families giving up control of businesses, the Seattle *Times* (June 20, 1995), described research by the Bork Institute of Family Business of Aspen, Colorado.

20. The Playpen

KING's newsroom was described by Don McGaffin, Bob Faw, and Norm Heffron. Charles Royers' childhood was told in an article in the Seattle *Post Intelligencer* by Michael Sweeney and William Prochnau (Dec. 25, 1977). Jim Harriott described Bill Warren's attitude toward commentary. KOMO's commentary, the size of the three stations' newscasts, and the views of Lloyd Cooney and

Charles Royer were described by *Seattle Business* magazine (Dec. 9, 1974). Ray McMackin described his desire to get attention and the booing incident. Jean Enersen described how lucky she felt. McGaffin and Bob George described the "burned child" incident; McGaffin has kept a copy of the documentary of the report, which aired April 17, 1972. The Dysart episode was described by Royer, Payne, Heffron, and McGaffin, and was covered in the Seattle *Times* (especially Oct. 28 and Oct. 31, 1972). Albert Rosellini supplied the copy of Royer's commentary on Dysart, which aired in early Nov. 1972 (exact date unknown). The description of *The Buck Stops Here,* which aired Sept. 14, 1975, is based on copy kept by McGaffin. Mardesich's criticism of KING was quoted by the Seattle *Times* (Dec. 4, 1975). Royer complained of the print-press's inattention in an interview with *The Weekly* (later the *Seattle Weekly*) (Sept. 15, 1976). Bob Royer and Don McGaffin described the burning golf bag incident. Royer, McGaffin, and Carol Lewis described the circumstances and aftermath of Royer's decision to run for mayor.

21. Fissures

The scene of Charles Royer declaring his candidacy and the campaign for mayor are based on interviews with Royer, Don McGaffin, Carol Lewis, Norm Heffron, Richard Larsen, and John Wilson, as well as coverage by the Seattle *Post-Intelligencer* and the Seattle *Times.* Royer's speech was quoted in *Changing of the Guard: Power and Leadership in America* (New York: Simon and Schuster, 1980) by David S. Broder, p. 393. Lewis's "argumentative questions" is quoted from the *Times* (Oct. 5, 1977). The litany of national publications describing Seattle as "livable" is described by Tim Egan in *The Good Rain,* page 101. Royer's "never been awed" comment is from the *P-I* (Dec. 25, 1976). Carol Lewis and Linda Brill described KING crashing a no-cameras press gathering. Bob Royer and Don McGaffin described the Edwardian party. Watson's column ran in the *P-I* (Aug. 9, 1978). Bob Simmons and William Prochnau described the effort to find a replacement for Royer as KING's commentator. Simmons described the Bullitts' response to his commentary. Dorothy C. Bullitt told how McGaffin and her grandmother encouraged her to see a future in King Broadcasting. McGaffin, Dorothy C. Bullitt, Paul Steinle, and news accounts from the *Times* described the disappearance of Ben Bullitt, and the family's reaction. Payne described his instructions to Don Dunkel. *The Weekly* described the turmoil in KING's newsroom (April 7, Sept. 22, and Oct. 6, 1982). Dunkel complained about KING's image in the *P-I* (May 10, 1983). McGaffin and Payne described conversations with Dunkel. Linda Gist and McGaffin described his decision to quit.

22. Public Lies

The status of King Broadcasting in 1970 comes from a memo by Ancil Payne, written June 19, 1986. The description of Julie Blacklow's personality and her firing is from interviews with Blacklow, Sturges Dorrance, Bill Baker, Ancil Payne, Don Varyu, Don McGaffin, and Jack Hamann, and from documents submitted to the arbitrator, kept by Ancil Payne, who also provided internal memos on the subject. Blacklow says she does not recall saying "Mrs. Bullitt will fix it." Reporting by Susan Paynter in the Seattle *Post-Intelligencer,* and by Linda Keene and Ross Anderson in the Seattle *Times* was valuable. The following *Times* stories dealt with Blacklow: March 3, 1986; May 9, 1986; June 22, 1986; Jan. 20, 1987; Feb. 2, 1987; and Feb. 5, 1987. Paynter's column (Nov. 11, 1986) described the "shudder through the ranks." Payne supplied the memo by Aaron Brown, dated Jan. 16, 1985. It should be noted that many from King Broadcasting stations went on to the networks, such as Lou Dobbs, Robin Lloyd, Bob Faw, Jim Compton, Don Porter, Ann Curry, Dennis Murphy, Joe Witte, James Hattori, and Hattie Kaufman. Aaron Brown later left KIRO for a job with ABC. The Payne instruction to Bremner is from a Feb. 17, 1987, memo. The description of McGaffin's stroke comes from McGaffin and Frederick Case's article in the *Times* (Aug. 17, 1986).

23. Private Lies

The Gary Little description is based on interviews with Jim Compton, Sturges Dorrance, Don Varyu, Ancil Payne, Terrence Carroll, John Wilson, Don McGaffin, Peyton Whitely, Kathy Triesch, and Norman Quinn. It uses reporting by Duff Wilson in the *Post-Intelligencer* and Eric Nalder, Peter Lewis, Peyton Whitely, Richard Seven, and Carol M. Ostrom in the Seattle *Times.* Especially helpful were articles in the *Times:* May 25, 1985; Aug. 19, 1988; Sept. 2, 1988; Oct. 14, 1988; and Nov. 11, 1988. Payne's views on the Little case also come from his speech to the Monday Club on November 25, 1991.

24. "Those Who Worked For Her, and Loved Her . . ."

Dorothy S. Bullitt's last days were described by Ellen Neel and Dorothy C. Bullitt. The funeral was written up in the Seattle *Post-Intelligencer* (July 1, 1989). The estimate of King Broadcasting's value comes from a June 28, 1989, article in the *Times.* Ancil Payne described his conversation with Dorothy S. Bullitt about keeping the company in the family, and he supplied a June 1986 memo on the selection of his successor. The estimate of the profitability of Seattle TV stations comes from the Seattle *Times* (Sept. 9, 1988). Don Varyu described the egg nog party, Seattle *Times* (Aug. 23, 1990). Steve Clifford and Jack Hamann commented on Clifford's time as chief executive. Ruth Prins described Dorothy Bullitt's feeling trapped in her home. Compton's tribute to Dorothy S. Bullitt, and also the company's financial results, were carried in King Broadcasting's annual report, 1988–1989. Ellen Neel described skepticism toward the sisters' promise not to sell the company.

25. "Not Even Close to the Rain Forest"

Seattle Weekly reported on King's morale problems (Dec. 13, 1989). A memo by Ancil Payne, Sept. 13, 1989, detailed the argument for selling the station. Glenn Pascall commented on the board's not addressing the memo; Ancil Payne speculated on the sisters not wanting to air the issue. Theresa Morrow's Seattle *Times* article (Nov. 11, 1990) described Patsy Collins's cancer surgery and Harriet Bullitt's flamboyant lifestyle. Details on Patsy's children came from Jacques Collins, who also described the rain forest conversation with his mother; details on Harriet's children came from Wenda Brewster O'Reilly. Rick Blangiardi's arrival at KING was described in *Seattle Weekly* (Dec. 13, 1989), and in the Seattle *Times* (Oct. 5, 1989). Jack Hamann provided copies of management memos to newsroom staff, including one dated April 18, 1971, and another Aug. 11, 1987. John Wilson and Greg Palmer described their departures from KING. *Seattle Weekly* (May 2, 1990), the *Times* (Nov. 30, 1990), and the *P-I* (May 30, 1990) covered Bob Jordan's tenure at KING. Bob Jordan described his attitude toward the newsstaff. Hamann kept a copy of the "Nielsens are better." The *P-I* described Jim Forman (May 30, 1991). Delphine Haley's description of the grandchildren comes from her book, page 390.

26. "Nothing Is Forever"

A confidential source described the sisters' goals as naive. Steve Clifford described his reaction to the sisters' decision to sell. The Seattle *Times* (Nov. 11, 1990) described the Bullitt Foundation's gifts. Ancil Payne supplied the detailed financial statement, dated June 1990. A confidential source described the PR strategy. A King Broadcasting press release, Aug. 21, 1990, quoted the sisters and their letter to employees. Sallie Baldus, Dorothy S. Bullitt's companion, says Mrs. Bullitt did not want the company sold. *BusinessWeek* covered the sale (Sept. 10, 1990). Jacques Collins said the grandchildren were not consulted about the sale. John Wilson described his letter to Patsy Collins and her reply. Figures on the stock held by family members and employees come from a document dated April 29, 1991, filed with the Federal Communications Commission.

27. Epilogue

Dorothy C. Bullitt described her departure from Harbor Properties and her relationship with her father.

Acknowledgments

Numerous people helped me to get this book launched, researched, and written.

For getting the project started, my thanks to Tim Egan and to Kris Dahl of International Creative Management.

This book could not have been completed without the generosity of the Seattle *Times,* which granted me a leave to research the book. At the *Times,* my thanks to Paul Andrews, Carole Carmichael, Steve Dunphy, Alex MacLeod, Cyndi Nash, Carol Pucci, Chuck Taylor, Debbie Van Tassel, and the dedicated staff of the Seattle *Times* library. The staffs of the Federal Communications Commission and the Seattle Public Library were always gracious about helping me track down old files or obscure facts.

Evelyn Iritani, Roger Ainsley, John McCoy, Dan Butterworth, Sally Tonkin, Susan Bonner, Bill Prochnau, and Laura Parker provided writing advice and emotional support, while Cora and John Picken provided a refuge. Patsy Smith of PS Consulting, formerly of the University of Washington Press, supported the concept of the book and skillfully worked the manuscript into its final form. Gerald Baldasty, Don Balmer, and Brewster Denny provided helpful comments.

More than 100 persons took time to answer questions. Some gave dozens of hours and searched through many files to verify names, dates, and other details. Some wish to remain anonymous, but my gratitude goes to them as well as to the following individuals:

David Adams, Herb Altschull, Rick Anderson, Nancy Antonelli, Bill Baker, Gil Baker, Sallie Baldus, Christopher Bayley, Thomas S. Bayley,

Andy Beers, Knute "Skip" Berger, Julie Blacklow, Bob Block, Stan Boreson, Kit Boss, Thelma Brandt, Eric Bremner, David Brewster, Linda Brill, Larry Brown, Bill Brubaker, Ted Bryant, Dorothy C. Bullitt, Kay Bullitt, Margaret Bullitt, Emory Bundy, Peter Bunzel, Virginia Burnside, Ritajean Butterworth, Terrence Carroll, Bruce Chapman, Frank Chin, Steve Clifford, Jacques Collins, Patsy Collins, Jim Compton, Eugene Corr, Kathleen Corr, Lou Corsaletti, Sturges Dorrance, Bill Dorsey, Don Duncan, Janet Ruthford Dunsire, Marvin Durning, Jean Enersen, Bob Faw, Richard Fishbein, Alec Fisken, Bob George, Linda Gist, Warren Guykema, Louis Guzzo, Roger Hagan, Delphine Haley, James Halpin, Jack Hamann, Don Hannula, Jim Harriott, Norm Heffron, Charles Herring, Ed Hewson, Jerry Hoeck, Rosemary Hoeck, Irv Hoff, Jarlath Hume, Mike James, David Jessup, Bob Jordan, Scott Klug, Richard Labunski, Richard Larsen, Carol Lewis, Del Loder, Ken MacDonald, Don McGaffin, Floyd McKay, Ray McMackin, Anne Marshall, Hugh B. Mitchell, Ellen Neel, Jim Neidigh, Fred Nemo, Dee Norton, Wenda Brewster O'Reilly, Charles Odegaard, Frances Owen, Philip Padelford, Greg Palmer, Glenn Pascall, Ancil Payne, Peter Potterfield, Robert Priebe, Ruth Prins, Bill Prochnau, Norman Quinn, Roger Rice, Richard Riddell, Herb Robinson, John S. Robinson, Albert Rosellini, Mary Rothschild, Bob Royer, Charles Royer, Bob Schulman, Lee Schulman, George Scott, Jack Shawcroft, Bob Simmons, Kit Spier, David Sprague, Dan Starr, Paul Steinle, Barbara Stenson, Earl Thoms, Sue Tupper, Kathy Triesch, Don Varyu, Jonathan Whetzel, Peyton Whitely, John A. Wilson, Marshall Wilson, Steve Wilson, and Bagley Wright.

For reasons that they know well, my deepest gratitude and love go towards: Eugene, Kathleen, Kelly, Kerry, Pat, and Chris; and my wife Sally Tonkin, and our children, Evan and Michaela Corr.